Dreams in Early Modern England

This book is an insightful and much-needed account of the nature, variety and use of dreams in early modern culture. By tracing how dreams were interweaved with religious, scientific and philosophical debates and with the landscapes of everyday life in seventeenth and eighteenth-century England, Rivière makes a persuasive case for the active agency of dreams in shaping personal identities and broader cultural processes. This book is a "must-read" for anyone who wants to delve deeper into the relationship between dreams, selfhood and nocturnal culture in the early modern world.

Sasha Handley, *University of Manchester, UK*

Dreams in Early Modern England offers an in-depth exploration of the variety of different ways in which early modern people understood and interpreted dreams, from medical explanations to political, religious or supernatural associations.

Through examining how dreams were discussed and presented in a range of different texts, including both published works and private notes and diaries, this book highlights the many co-existing strands of thought that surrounded dreams in early modern England. Most significantly, it places early modern perceptions of dreams within the social context of the period through an evaluation of how they were shaped by key events of the time, such as the Reformation and the English Civil Wars. The chapters also explore contemporary experiences and ideas of dreams in relation to dream divination, religious visions, sleep, nightmares and sleep disorders.

This book will be of great value to students and academics with an interest in dreams and the understanding of dreams, sleep and nightmares in early modern English society.

Janine Rivière received her PhD in History from the University of Toronto, Canada, in 2013, where she has also been teaching since 2004. She has published widely on the topic of dreams and nightmares in early modern England.

Routledge Research in Early Modern History

For a full list of titles in this series, please visit www.routledge.com.

Honourable Intentions? Violence and Virtue in Australian and Cape Colonies, c. 1750 to 1850
Edited by Penny Russell and Nigel Worden

Social Thought in England, 1480–1730
From Body Social to Worldly Wealth
A. L. Beier

Dynastic Colonialism
Gender, Materiality and the early modern House of Orange-Nassau
Susan Broomhall and Jacqueline van Gent

The Business of the Roman Inquisition in the Early Modern Era
Germano Maifreda

Cities and Solidarities
Urban Communities in Pre-Modern Europe
Edited by Justin Colson and Arie van Steensel

James VI and Noble Power in Scotland 1578–1603
Edited by Miles Kerr-Peterson and Steven J. Reid

Conversion and Islam in the Early Modern Mediterranean
The Lure of the Other
Edited by Claire Norton

Plural Pasts
Power, Identity and the Ottoman Sieges of Nagykanizsa Castle
Claire Norton

Dreams in Early Modern England
"Visions of the Night"
Janine Rivière

Dreams in Early Modern England

"Visions of the Night"

Janine Rivière

LONDON AND NEW YORK

First published 2017
by Routledge
2 Park Square, Milton Park, Abingdon, Oxon OX14 4RN

and by Routledge
711 Third Avenue, New York, NY 10017

Routledge is an imprint of the Taylor & Francis Group, an informa business

© 2017 Janine Rivière

The right of Janine Rivière to be identified as author of this work has been asserted by her in accordance with sections 77 and 78 of the Copyright, Designs and Patents Act 1988.

All rights reserved. No part of this book may be reprinted or reproduced or utilised in any form or by any electronic, mechanical, or other means, now known or hereafter invented, including photocopying and recording, or in any information storage or retrieval system, without permission in writing from the publishers.

Trademark notice: Product or corporate names may be trademarks or registered trademarks, and are used only for identification and explanation without intent to infringe.

British Library Cataloguing-in-Publication Data
A catalogue record for this book is available from the British Library

Library of Congress Cataloging-in-Publication Data
Names: Rivière, Janine, author.
Title: Dreams in early modern England: visions of the night / Janine Rivière.
Description: New York: Routledge, 2017. |
Series: Routledge research in early modern history |
Includes bibliographical references and index.
Identifiers: LCCN 2016055546 |
Subjects: LCSH: Dreams—England—History.
Classification: LCC BF1078 .R53 2017 | DDC 154.6/30942—dc23
LC record available at https://lccn.loc.gov/2016055546

ISBN: 978-1-138-85399-7 (hbk)
ISBN: 978-1-315-18877-5 (ebk)

Typeset in Times New Roman MT Std
by codeMantra

Contents

List of figures	vii
Acknowledgements	ix
A note on transcriptions	xi
Introduction	1
1 "Seasons of sleep:" Natural dreams, health and the physiology of sleep	17
2 Decoding dreams: Dreambooks and dream divination	50
3 "Nocturnal whispers of the Allmighty:" Spiritual dreams and the discernment of spirits	89
4 "The terrors of the night:" Nightmares and sleep disorders	133
Conclusion	165
Bibliography	171
Index	189

List of figures

1.1 "The Sleepy Congregation." By: William Hogarth, Bowles & Carver London. Wellcome Library, London. 23

1.2 "Richard III." Engraving by Thomas Stothard after: James Neagle and William Shakespeare, Geo. Kearsley, London: 2 June 1804. Wellcome Library, London. 31

2.1 "The power of counsel." Engraving by Adrian Collaert after Jan van der Straet, Antwerp, 1567/1605. Wellcome Library, London. 57

3.1 "The three kings are told in a dream not to return to the land of Herod." Engraving. Wellcome Library, London. 96

3.2 "Songe de St. Joseph." Engraved By: Anton Raphaël Mengs after Jean-Baptiste Joseph Wicar and Francois Morel. Wellcome Library, London. 98

4.1 "Stripes of Conscience or the Midnight Hour." Etching by: H. Brocas. Wellcome Library, London. 134

4.2 Drug Jar. Unknown maker. England, United Kingdom, 1670–1740. Science Museum, London, Wellcome Images. 141

4.3 "The Nightmare." By: Henry Fuseli after Thomas Holloway. Appearing in *The poetical works of Erasmus Darwin. ...* By: Erasmus Darwin. Wellcome Library, London. 148

Acknowledgements

The dream is an elusive, amorphous quarry. Its history is hidden in an infinite landscape of published and unpublished works through which I have meandered for the last decade or more. This journey has been made easier by a number of patrons, colleagues, family members and friends. No monograph emerges into the light of day without a vast number of proofreaders and I wish to note here the many readers who helped shape and refine this work in its current and past forms. In particular, I would like to thank Shealah Stratton, Serge Rivière, Rasa Mazeika, Katherine Anderson and Dorothy Rivière. For their in-depth reading of my doctoral dissertation, from which this book is born, I also owe my sincere thanks to Jane Abray, Barbara Todd, Natalie Zemon Davis, Nicholas Terpstra, Jennifer Mori, Ann Marie Plane and Alexandra Walsham. In addition, I would also like to recognize the intellectual and financial support I received during my doctorate from the History Department at the University of Toronto, as well as the National Humanities Center, Collegium Budapest and the Center for Advanced Studies in Behavioral Sciences at Stanford University.

Most especially, I have profoundly benefitted from the interdisciplinary workshops I was privileged to be part of, "The Vision Thing: Studying Divine Intervention," funded by the National Humanities Center and organized by the scholars William A. Christian Jr. and Gábor Klaniczay. These workshops were invaluable in the early brainstorming of the work and exposed me to the research of other young scholars also working on dreams and visions. Here, I would like to extend my sincere thanks to the "Visioneers" for all their astute comments, vibrant conversations and collegiality. Many of the chapters and major findings of this work were also presented at numerous international conferences and workshops. Here, I would like to offer my heartfelt thanks for the comments, suggestions and support of these audiences. For her unfailing interest in my research and her tireless efforts in facilitating international academic conferences and publications, I would also like to thank Éva Pócs. This book naturally would not have been possible without the patronage of a publisher and the careful ministrations of an editorial team. I am grateful to the team at Routledge and my editors for their advice and patience.

x *Acknowledgements*

For keeping me in good humour and providing emotional scaffolding whenever needed, I wish to acknowledge my colleagues and friends, most especially: Heidi Diepstra, Shealah Stratton, Alexandra Guerson, Julie Gilmour, Alan Bell, Kathleen Gibbons, John Christopoulos and Vanessa McCarthy. Finally, for their enduring love and support I wish to thank my parents Dorothy and Serge Rivière and my sister Natalie Rivière, to whom this work is dedicated.

Janine Rivière

A note on transcriptions

For the greater ease of comprehension, I have opted to modernize certain letters. Transcriptions of titles and excerpts have been altered so that "vv" has been changed to "w," the "long s" to "s," "i" to "j" and "j" to "i," "u" to "v" and "v" to "u," where appropriate. Superscripts and abbreviations have been expanded and the thorn has been transcribed as "th" in all excerpts. The titles of printed works taken from online databases have been replicated as they appear in the EEBO (Early English Books Online), ECCO (Eighteenth Century Collections Online), ESTC (English Short Title Catalogue) and Worldcat databases (including all punctuation and capitalization). My citation policy for particularly long titles in early works has been, where necessary, to shorten them to no more than three lines. Omissions in these titles have been indicated by ellipses. All dates of publication and other events are written in the new style, with the year beginning at January 1.

Introduction

At the end of his life, Thomas Tryon (1634–1703), a self-educated English hatter and writer, reflected on two remarkable dreams from his childhood that "made so firm an impression on my Mind, as neither Time, nor the cares and business of this World, could obliterate."[1]

> Being about Six Years of Age, I had a Dream, wherein it pleased God to shew me the Kingdom of Love and the Kingdom of Darkness. I thought that God appeared to me and talked with me Face to Face, in a very friendly and loving manner. Not long after I had another Dream, wherein methought the Devil stood before me and scourged me.[2]

Even after a successful career writing handbooks on husbandry, health and education, Tryon still recalled these early dreams. Inspired by these experiences, he published his own handbook, *A treatise of dreams & visions* (1689), in which he provided readers with a comprehensive understanding of contemporary theories of dreams.[3] However, Tryon was not unique in seriously contemplating his dreams. Numerous other early modern English men and women also recorded and discussed dreams in private writings, leaving us invaluable artefacts of their nocturnal lived experience and echoes of their daily lives.

Historians have long known that dreaming was important to early modern society in a way that has been thought to be fundamentally different from post-enlightenment cultures. But the nuances, the varied strands of dream-use and dream discourse, have been overlooked and misrepresented. This book will show the variety and complexity of early modern English discourses on dreams – from the role of dreams and dream theory in framing religious, scientific and philosophical debates in the period, to the way that dreams continued to offer important spiritual and supernatural guidance and access for ordinary people – through interpreting and using dreams, people exercised agency over their lives in some important and fundamental ways. This book outlines and explores the three broad cultural lens – health, prediction and spirituality – used to understand the dream. Overall, the following chapters seek to demonstrate the complexity and variety of

2 Introduction

co-existing understandings of dreams. While today we tend to conceptualize dreams and dreaming as largely psychological, this study shows how early modern people understood dreams and dreaming as many different things, most significantly as personal, political, religious, medical, philosophical and psychological.

Discussions of dreams appear in numerous discourses and printed works, spanning fields from medicine to demonology and astrology to religion. Likewise, considerations of dreams appear in writings of the most prominent thinkers from the period: Francis Bacon, Robert Burton, Thomas Hobbes, Thomas Browne, John Locke and David Hume all discussed dreams in their major works as part of their larger intellectual concerns.[4] However, less-studied English authors Thomas Hill (1528–1572/6), John Beale (*bap.* 1608, *d.* 1683) and Philip Goodwin (*d.* 1667) published substantive treatises devoted entirely to understanding the origin, meaning and interpretation of dreams.[5] These works endeavoured to provide comprehensive handbooks of dreams drawing from classical and contemporary medical, philosophical, theological and oneirocritical theories. In spite of the abundance of early modern writings on dreams, historians have only begun to explore these works and harness them as rich sources of intellectual and cultural history.

While scholarly treatises on dreams were available for those with higher levels of literacy and the means to afford them, short dream interpretation manuals or "dreambooks" also circulated throughout the early modern period, being more accessible to a broader readership. Most dreambooks were debased and abridged English editions of Artemidorus of Daldis' *Oneirocritica* and popular medieval dreambooks, such as the *Somnia Danielis*.[6] English dreambooks offered readers a brief interpretation of dreams according to specific dream-symbols that were organized thematically for easy reference. Within these works, dream-symbols were interpreted as clues to the dreamer's future health, wealth and relationships: dreams of the loss of teeth, for example, predicted the death of friends. Examples of English dreambooks include Thomas Hill's *A little treatise of the interpretation of dreams, fathered on Joseph* (1567) and the perpetually popular vernacular editions of Artemidorus' work the *Oneirocritica,* issued 24 times from 1606 to 1786.[7]

The success of the early modern print industry was largely due to a lucrative market in the mass production of almanacs, chapbooks and fortune-telling works. In addition to dreambooks, popular fortune-telling tracts and almanacs also featured sections of oneiromancy alongside palmistry, moleoscopy (divination by the moles on the face) and astrology. These ephemeral works filled the packs of itinerant chapmen, peddling their miscellaneous wares across the countryside and they also featured on the crowded shelves of city booksellers, offering even those with modest incomes quick reference guides to their dreams. Examples include the *Oniropolus* (1680) and J.S., *The true fortune-teller* (1698), as well as fortune-telling books ascribed to the best-selling authors of astrological almanacs and prophecies, William Lilly and John Booker.[8] Within these texts, oneiromancy was incorporated as one of the many techniques of divination, presenting readers with the means to decode their dreams and reveal significant insight into individual health, relationships and wealth. Excerpts of dream divination were also a recurring feature of popular "books of knowledge," courtship manuals and courtesy books.[9]

For readers seeking insight into personal health, discussions of the physiological and psychological properties of "natural dreams" appeared in learned and lay medical manuals throughout the period.[10] According to medical authors, natural dreams were caused by a range of internal and external stimuli, including the imbalances of the four humours, indigestion and environmental stimuli or alternatively, the anxieties, desires and preoccupations of the dreamer.[11] Terrifying dreams and sleep disorders were understood as the punitive result of the dangers of excess, including the excessive consumption of alcohol, "hard meats" such as venison and hare and legumes, among other possible causes.[12] A longstanding medical view of dreams based on the writings of Galen suggested that the content of dreams revealed the delicate balance of the dominant humours in the body. Audiences interested in preserving health were therefore able to learn more about the use of dreams as prognostic medical tools from a large echelon of learned and popular medical handbooks, catering for all audiences.[13]

Simultaneously, supernatural and preternatural explanations of dreams also co-existed, providing alternatives to natural theories of dreams. In demonological works and accounts of witchcraft, the "nightmare" was understood as an assault whereby witches and their familiars crept into the bedrooms of sleeping men, women and children in the midnight hours to "oppress" and suffocate their victims. In addition to beliefs in the supernatural origins of certain genres of dreams, preternatural ideas also circulated. Authors of several dream treatises and demonological works suggested that some prophetic dreams masqueraded as divine but were in fact demonic sleights of hand. Alongside demonic dreams, belief in supernaturally inspired divine dreams was also prominent throughout the early modern period. According to Phillip Goodwin's *The mystery of dreames, historically discoursed* (1658), God sent a variety of dreams to sleeping humans including those which were deemed instructive, spiritually edifying or, on more rare occasions, revelations. Discussions about dreams therefore appear in a vast array of early modern writings that reveal a significant variety of different understandings and categories of the dream. In the wake of the cultural turn and historical interest in the lives of ordinary men and women, the dream has surfaced as a potentially rewarding new avenue into understanding past cultures and nocturnal modes of experience.

Dream narratives and history

Two approaches have dominated histories of dreams. First, historians have typically examined the history of dreams working backwards from Freud and the foundation of psychoanalysis. Secondly, scholars have tended to

4   *Introduction*

use psychoanalytical tools to analyze past dream narratives. Since dreams today are understood as the products of conscious and unconscious forces within the individual psyche, the use of psychoanalysis naturally lends itself to understanding the elusive mental worlds of past people. Earlier work by Charles Carlton, Patricia Crawford and Peter Burke applied a fusion of psychoanalysis and anthropology to early modern dream narratives, riding the wave of the cultural turn.[14] In their edited volume, *Dreams and history,* Lyndal Roper and Daniel Pick proposed a more subtle marriage between psychoanalysis and histories of dreams. However, as they themselves acknowledged, one of the lingering problems of this approach is the inherent anachronism, since psychoanalysis is based on Cartesian notions of the self and was a product of nineteenth-century Viennese culture.[15]

By imposing modern psychological theories of dreams onto past people without attention to existing cultural paradigms we not only risk imposing anachronistic models of the self and psyche onto past cultures but also neglect understanding how and why certain dreams were recorded and understood. As Ann Marie Plane reminds us in her study of the dream in postcolonial New England, psychoanalytical studies of past people's dreams are made more problematic by the lack of a dialogic relationship between the analyst and the analysand.[16] Historians using psychoanalytical tools lack access to the subject and therefore the process is a one-sided, superimposed analysis in which the subject has no voice; thus no true psychoanalytical dialogue can ever exist. Moreover, if one follows a psychoanalytic theory of dreams, as Peter Burke and others note, the remnants of dream itself – the dream record – is "doubly censored" and thus leaves historians a text laden with a complex process of production.[17]

One possible solution is to understand the dream as a complex product of both culture and psyche. Before we can understand or analyze historical records of dreams, we must first comprehend the cultural paradigms from which these dreams arose. This premise is based on the significant work of Janette Mageo, Ann Marie Plane and Katherine Hodgkin.[18] As Mageo noted in her study of dreams and subjectivity, culture shapes psyche and vice versa: the content, meaning and interpretation of dreams are therefore shaped by the specific culture of the dreamer.[19] Not to take into account premodern theories of dreams is to neglect this complex relationship. One contribution of this book is therefore to offer an overview of the major frameworks or cultural lens through which dreams were understood in early modern English culture. While I am not suggesting that these frameworks are all encompassing, static or uncontested, they are designed to offer some useful umbrella terms that future studies might further nuance.

Another aim of this book is to deepen our understanding of ideas of more commonplace dreams that occurred in sleep rather than the more rare, contested and ambiguous category of visions. Much work has already been undertaken on understanding dreams as forms of spiritual revelations in medieval and early modern culture. Here I am referring to the work of

William A. Christian Jr., Richard Kagan and Phyllis Mack, amongst numerous others.[20] This book endeavours to be in dialogue with historical studies that focus on the dream as occurring in sleep, such as the essay collections edited by Lyndal Roper and Daniel Pick, Peter Brown and Katherine Hodgkin.[21] Yet, although these collected works have offered significant new insight into historical studies of dreams, with the exception of Carole Levin's study of dreams in Elizabethan England and Ann Marie Plane's exploration of the dream in postcolonial New England, few works have provided an in-depth study of the dream in early modern culture.[22] Nor have any of the previous studies examined in detail the multiplicity of printed works on dreams, including the numerous dreambooks, treatises and private writings, within the specific context of early modern England. Even less work has been devoted to the intellectual history of dreams. One of the few early modern studies to consider this history was Stuart Clark's chapter on dreams in his history of vision.[23] Finally, with the exception of Sasha Handley's recent studies of sleep disorders, historians have fundamentally neglected early modern understandings and experiences of nightmares and sleep disorders, despite their commonality.[24]

Early modern writings on dreams have also been typically subsumed into broad studies of print culture. Dreambooks, almanacs and fortune-telling works to featuring oneiromancy have been largely relegated to footnotes in studies of early modern popular print culture. Although these texts were certainly part of the flourishing genre of cheap print in the period, this book seeks to untangle this specific genre and to contextualize it within discourses on dreams and those reflecting more widespread understandings of oneiromancy. Also, English dreambooks were not created in a vacuum and were companions to the plethora of Continental oneirocritic handbooks circulating in Europe. As Chapter 2 demonstrates, dreambooks were also the direct descendants of classical and medieval oneirocritic handbooks, which changed little over time. In addition to dreambooks, more sophisticated semi-learned writings on dreams, such as the treatises of Philip Goodwin, John Beale and Thomas Hill, have received only cursory mentions in historical studies of dreams. This monograph therefore seeks to restore the variety of writings on dreams to their discursive origins and provide a more in-depth reading of understudied works on dreams.

Dreams, sleep and the night in early modern culture

Since dreams typically occur in a state of sleep, their history is inextricably bound to histories of sleep. While a growing literature on the history of dreams has emerged, less work has been undertaken on the history of sleep. As the sociologist Simon J. Williams noted, "if sleep constitutes a third of our lives, then, one might say, a third of the past is missing from the history books."[25] Historians are beginning to focus more on this fundamentally neglected yet essential facet of early modern daily experience. Initial studies

6 *Introduction*

have revealed important insight into past collective experiences of sleep and have suggested that the eighteenth century was marked by radical changes to human sleep architecture. A. Roger Ekirch, one of the first historians to pioneer the history of sleep and night, proposed that early modern people experienced a segmented sleep pattern of "two sleeps." Ekirch also posited that the establishment of public lighting led to a significant shift in human sleep cycles so that the common practice of biphasic sleep morphed into a longer unbroken pattern of sleep.[26] Recent work by Sasha Handley on the sleeping habits of the social elite in the eighteenth century has done much to deepen our understanding of changes to cultural perceptions and social experiences of the sleep on the cusp of modernity.[27] However, a great deal more remains to be understood about this central facet of past culture and experience. Most studies have thus far focused on the period of the long eighteenth century, neglecting earlier periods. Moreover, to date no early modern studies have considered the dream in relation to sleep, opting to study either one or the other in isolation.

A history of the dream is also intertwined with the history of the night, a subject recently advanced through the formative work of Craig Koslofsky, who suggested that the early modern period underwent a significant process of "nocturnalization."[28] According to Koslofsky, the religious reformations of the sixteenth and seventeenth centuries overturned cultural taboos of the night as inherently evil and closely associated with the Devil. Released from millennia of negative cultural associations, Koslofsky suggests that the social elite harnessed the symbolic night as a representation of political and social power.[29] Overall, Koslofsky's work has done much to reveal the significance of night in early modern culture. However, as Sasha Handley astutely reminds us, although intertwined, the history of the night and sleep are not synonymous and sleep has its own "distinct history."[30] Since dreams typically occur in the state of sleep yet are a unique facet of human psychological and physiological experience, I would suggest that the same could be said of the history of the dream in relation to sleep and the night, which must be viewed as an inherently linked yet discrete category of past experience with its own rich yet unique history. As is demonstrated by historical and anthropological studies of shamanism, experiences commonly referred to as "dreams" also manifest in a range of alternate modes of consciousness.[31] Certain kinds of dreams often also referred to as "visions" appear in transcendental states of consciousness and must be considered separately from histories of sleep. These manifestations of dreams are rather a part of the more complex range of human cultural, perceptual and cognitive experiences. The dream thus has a close relationship to the history of sleep and the night yet, as a discrete category of past cognitive experience, deserves its own history.

Two overarching questions focus the chapters that follow: How did early modern English people understand their dreams and did these understandings change in response to significant events and developments in English history and culture? To answer these questions, I explore early modern English understandings of dreams by studying medical, philosophical, demonological, spiritual, popular and oneirocritic writings as well as records of dream narratives in private letters, diaries and memoirs. I suggest that in the early modern period there were three principal frameworks used to understand dreams: (1) health of the body and mind, (2) prediction/oneiromancy and (3) religion/spirituality. These three frameworks co-existed, often reinforcing or overlapping one another throughout the period. The framework of health saw dreams as naturally occurring products of the body and mind that, at best, revealed insight into the overall health of the dreamer. In the model of prediction or oneiromancy, dreams were deemed significant, yet encoded, clues about the future that required careful interpretation. Finally, in religious or spiritual frameworks, dreams were conceived of as sent by God, angels or the Devil. As important subsets of this category, divine dreams or visions were the most powerful and problematic dreams for early modern people since, as potential divine messages, they conferred direct access to God. Spiritual understandings of dreams were often based upon and bolstered by the Christian tradition of visions as forms of revealed religion, a belief repeatedly endorsed in the Bible. However, this was not the only approach towards spiritual dreams: the Calvinist minister Philip Goodwin presented spiritual dreams as instructive tools for the pastoral care of the soul.

Another point I wish to argue is that early modern writings on dreams reveal the perceived vulnerability of the dreamer to a wide range of internal and external forces. Dreams were a locus where the boundaries between the human and divine, supernatural and natural met and merged, making the individual vulnerable to a host of external and internal forces. A study of early modern writings on dreams shows that dreaming was conceived as a liminal state in which a diverse range of physiological, psychological, environmental and supernatural forces permeated and influenced the body, mind and soul. Dreams were potential gateways to the otherworld, to the realms of the divine, demonic and the dead and a crossroads between the supernatural and natural worlds. This inherent sense of anxiety links to Phyllis Mack's recent work highlighting the way English Calvinist, Quaker and Methodist writings on dreams show the inherent flaws of eighteenth-century teleological assumptions about a shift from an unbounded self to a "fully interiorized self." She suggests that, rather, eighteenth-century writings on dreams reveal the self as a site of "unbounded" mystery and anxiety.[32]

As Chapter 4 discusses, akin to death and inextricably linked to dreaming, sleep itself was conceived as a primal vulnerable state from which men, women and children often sought protection from God and angels against both supernatural and natural night-time assaults through the practice of bedtime prayers and spiritual meditation. Dreams were largely understood as the products of natural and supernatural forces over which the individual had little control. Similarly, the individual was subject to terrifying

8 *Introduction*

dreams and sleep disorders that served to instill the nocturnal hours with a deep-seated sense of fear and anxiety. Since the dream was a potential source of social and religious power as a conduit to the divine, above all, early modern English writings on dreams show that they were frequently an uncomfortable source of intellectual and cultural tension. The ambiguity of the dream, its pervasiveness as a common human experience and its significant place in the religious and intellectual tradition meant that dreams were difficult to both ignore and contain.

Since early modern English writings reveal a diversity of understandings of dreams that never really "declined," a study of them also helps to complicate ideas about the Weberian "disenchantment of the world," a historical debate revitalized by Alexandra Walsham in her significant historiographical article. Walsham's nuanced discussion of the problem of histories that endorse the rise of rational religion and decline of magical worldviews reminds us of the complexity of early modern religious culture and the ambiguous legacy of the Reformations. Her conclusions about the "limits" of disenchantment and the need to reappraise linear models of progress are further supported by the work of historians of witchcraft, Willem de Blécourt and Owen Davies, Alex Owen's study of nineteenth-century occult practices and Jane Shaw in her study of miracles during the enlightenment, amongst others.[33] This historical debate is also inherently tied to revisionist histories of the enlightenment itself, which view the movement, not as Peter Gay described it, as inherently secular and irreligious, but rather reminiscent of a far more complex and dynamic process in which religion and faith were often at the centre of enlightenment thought and principles.[34]

A history of dreams further adds to a more complex understanding of post-enlightenment culture. For, despite the influence of the "new science" and rise of "rational religion," the persistence of longstanding supernatural and natural conceptualizations of dreams and nightmares throughout the period strongly points towards a slow process of change and a diverse oscillating spectrum of beliefs. Galenic ideas about natural dreams as reflective of humoral imbalance persisted from the sixteenth to the eighteenth century, only beginning to evolve in the late eighteenth century as the emphasis on natural dreams shifted towards models that endorsed the significance of the brain and nervous system in producing and affecting dreams. Similarly, ideas about the *incubus* or nightmare, an experience today known more commonly as sleep paralysis, also reflect the continuity of both natural and supernatural understandings. Contemporary ideas about the influence of the four humours and Aristotelian vapours and spirits in causing bouts of the nightmare were slow to erode. These ideas only began to shift in the mid-eighteenth century when John Bond posited a purely physiological theory, which suggested the *incubus* was the result of irregularities in the circulation system. However, Bond's novel theory was largely ignored and remained at the fringe of accepted medical views.

Continental influences and the Reformation

European works unquestionably influenced English ideas about dreams. Several of the printed texts discussed throughout this study were English translations of Continental publications. European medical tracts and philosophical works to discuss dreams circulated in England in both Latin and the vernacular.[35] Amongst the thousands of volumes owned by John Dee was a copy of Cardinal Ferdinand Ponzetti's (1444–1527) *Naturalis philosophia parse tertia* (1515) published in Rome, as well as a copy of the Latin translation of Artemidorus's *Oneirocritica* by the Saxon Humanist scholar Janus Cornarius (1500–1558), printed by Hieronymus Froben in 1539.[36] Thomas Hill (1528–1572/6), the writer of the first original English dreambook, was particularly influenced by these two works in his own dream treatise and he possibly viewed them both at John Dee's library at Mortlake.[37]

Other English writers, such as Philip Goodwin, were well read in the classics and familiar with scholarly Continental works. Goodwin's *The mystery of dreames, historically discoursed* (1658) is littered with an impressive and diverse range of references to both well-known and obscure works of antiquity, the Church Fathers, Continental Protestant theologians and English sermons, amongst others. English scholars and intelligentsia actively hunted for copies of significant works and rare manuscripts in their travels to Europe. John Beale, a prolific correspondent of the Hartlib circle and writer of an unpublished treatise on dreams, sought rare manuscripts in Geneva and Paris whilst employed as a tutor. Likewise, resourceful non-university educated writers gained access to Continental editions of Latin, Greek and Italian texts, perhaps through the generosity of patrons, as Hill's notable English translations of European works demonstrate.[38]

As Chapter 3 explores, English understandings of supernatural dreams or visions, as they were simultaneously termed, were profoundly influenced by the writings of European reformers. Before the age of reformation, discussions of dreams in England and Europe had been firmly enmeshed in a dialogue with the classics that were fundamentally the purview of the learned. The Renaissance had revitalized interest in classical works of oneiromancy, including the *Oneirocritica* of Artemidorus and the oneirocritical verses of Astrampsychus. The writings of Cicero and Aristotle, as well as of Plato and Galen, dominated discussions of dreams within the realms of philosophy and medicine, while Artemidorus and Macrobius informed the discourse on prognostic dreams. However, the authority of classical writings was soon to be supplanted as a consequence of the Protestant Reformation. The problem of dream discernment − distinguishing natural from supernatural dreams − was reignited as sectarian visionaries appeared across the Continent and in England in the wake of the radical reformations and religious wars of the sixteenth and seventeenth centuries. These visionaries and self-proclaimed prophets, including Anabaptists, Quakers and Fifth Monarchists, amongst others, were seen to threaten the secular and religious order. Under pressure

10   *Introduction*

to consolidate belief in dreams within a Protestant ethos and in response to the disturbing events of the Anabaptist Siege of Münster in 1536, reformers such as Martin Luther grappled with the slippery problem of dream discernment. Luther's writings on dreams in his *Commentaries on Genesis* marked a new era in the history of dreams and one that would reinscribe the dream firmly into the language of Protestantism.

Martin Luther's reliance on the Bible as the sole source of all true knowledge about dreams and his rejection of the classics was highly influential on both Continental and English learned understandings of dreams. Philip Goodwin, in particular, quoted extensively from Luther's writings while John Beale followed Luther's lead in overtly rejecting Macrobius' dream classification system in favour of a simplified version of Augustine's tripartite codification of dreams (divine, diabolic and physical). The Reformation fundamentally influenced early modern ideas and beliefs in dreams by shifting accepted notions away from classical ideas and reinscribing them more firmly within a discourse that was fundamentally Christian, Protestant and Scripture-based. Consequently, this led divine dreams to have an even more problematic status that would divide Protestant writers into two camps – those who believed divine dreams had ceased and those who believed they continued. This was primarily the result of the ambiguous legacy of the Bible: it endorsed dream interpretation, most notably in stories of Daniel and Joseph, yet the Scriptures also warned against false prophets and dreams, particularly in *Deuteronomy* and *Leviticus*. This conflicting message about dreams remained at the centre of early modern debates concerning their origins and messages. Finally, dreams also became incorporated into the language of Providentialism: prognostic dreams were seen by Protestant writers not simply as divine revelations but also, as the English cleric John Beale described them, as "visible acts of His Glorious Providence" and "nocturnal whispers of the Almighty."[39]

Although discussions of dreams appear in early modern writings dealing with a diversity of topics and concerns, a closer reading of these texts shows that authors typically sought to understand dreams within the frameworks of health, prediction or spirituality. It is also apparent that these categories often overlapped and were complementary rather than contradictory. Writers of dream treatises often comfortably drew on both natural and supernatural etiologies of dreams. For example, in *The moste pleasaunte arte of the interpretacion of dreames* (1576) Thomas Hill discussed classical and contemporary ideas of the medical uses and causes of natural dreams, whilst also advising readers how to correctly interpret supernatural dreams based on the dreambooks of Artemidorus and medieval vulgar dreambooks. For authors such as Hill, to subscribe to ideas of natural and supernatural dreams, both erudite and popular, was unproblematic and was rather an exercise in distilling the best available knowledge about dreams.

The chapters that follow chart the three broad frameworks early modern English people used to understand dreams: (1) health of the body and mind,

(2) prediction and (3) spirituality. Chapter 1 explores early modern English ideas of natural dreams in relation to discussions of sleep. Through a survey of a wide range of printed texts (medical, philosophical, literary and religious) and unpublished writings, such as medical notes, autobiographies and letters, this chapter elucidates the complexity and persistence of ideas of natural dreams. It also aims to show how sleep was believed to be a particularly vulnerable state for early modern men and women. Ideas of natural dreams and their inextricable relationship to sleep changed little throughout the period, further illustrating that continuity rather than change characterizes the history of dreams.

Chapter 2 discusses the second broad cultural lens through which dreams were understood – prediction. Ideas of dreams as inspired oracles to the future of the dreamer and their immediate families and communities were a legacy of the classical world that continued to dominate understandings of dreams in early modern England. Growing out of the revived interest in divination in the sixteenth century, the practice of oneiromancy was popularized in the sixteenth and seventeenth centuries through the publication of dreambooks. Dream interpretation manuals, such as those written by Artemidorus and Thomas Hill, were simplified manuals that interpreted dreams according to their symbols. Although controversial amongst writers concerned with irreligion and superstition, oneiromancy was a longstanding practice that proved enduringly popular.

Contemporary ideas of prognostic dreams were closely linked to spiritual frameworks. Chapter 3 discusses the third cultural lens used to understand the dream – spirituality. Like the framework of predicative dreams, spiritual understandings of dreams as inspired by God, the Devil and other supernatural beings were equally ancient and continued to thrive in the early modern period. The idea that God and his angels sent divine dreams to warn, inspire and instruct was a powerful and pervasive view of the dream that derived from the Bible. Yet, whilst Scripture asserted that God would continue to send divine dreams, it also warned of false dreams and visions, which were sent by the Devil to mislead the faithful into sin and delusion. For this reason, the idea of supernatural dreams was controversial and fraught with tension, particularly in the wake of the Radical Reformation and English Civil Wars when numerous men and women appeared claiming to be gifted with divine dreams. The spectrum of confessional views also impacted understandings of dreams, further complicating contemporary understandings; yet, the basic idea of dreams as divine continued as a potent belief throughout the period.

Like us, early modern people experienced nightmares and disrupted sleep. The final chapter aims to elucidate the darker side of dreaming and to reveal the dream as a source of terror and anxiety for men and women. Linked to the growth of nocturnalization and as part of the nocturnal experience, sleep disorders and nightmares are an understudied facet of early modern history that reveals the night, sleep and dreams as sources of inherent

12 Introduction

anxiety. Through a study of a wide range of texts and discourses, this chapter brings the study of dreams into the eighteenth century and also discusses the historiographical issue of the "disenchantment of the world," believed to occur in the seventeenth and eighteenth centuries. Since natural and supernatural understandings of the *incubus* or nightmare continued into the eighteenth century, this chapter helps to complicate our understanding of post-enlightenment culture.

Overall, this study is designed to add to the intellectual and cultural history of dreams in early modern England. By exploring a diversity of writings on dreams in religious, medical, demonological, oneirocritic and philosophical texts, as well as private memoirs, diaries and the notes of physicians, I aim to make sense of the seemingly disparate frameworks through which dreams were understood. By studying the broader categories of dreams, rather than focusing solely on the more rare and controversial facet of visions, this book seeks to highlight the cultural significance and history of more commonplace dreams. What is especially clear from my study is that in early modern England the dream was a source of interest and speculation, an ambiguous yet pervasive common human experience that ultimately deserved contemplation and held meaning. But first, as Thomas Tryon noted in his treatise on dreams, "to Discourse Effectually of Dreams, it will be requisit to premise some brief Considerations touching Sleep."[40]

Notes

1 Thomas Tryon, *Some memoirs of the life of Mr. Tho. Tryon ...* (London, 1705), 8–9.
2 *Ibid.*
3 Thomas Tryon, *A treatise of dreams & visions ...* (London, 1689), 8.
4 Francis Bacon, *Of the advancement and proficience of learning* (London, 1640), 434; Robert Burton, *The anatomy of melancholy* (Oxford, 1621), 99–101, 160; Thomas Hobbes, *Leviathan* (London: Penguin, 1985), 344, 429; Thomas Browne, *The Religio Medici and Other Writings* (London: J.M. Dent, 1962), 83–86; John Locke, *An Essay on Human Understanding* (Oxford: Oxford University Press, 1964), 10, 133; David Hume, *Enquiries Concerning the Human Understanding* (Oxford: Clarendon Press, 1957), 49.
5 Thomas Hill, *The moste pleasuante arte of the interpretacion of dreames* (London, 1576); Tryon, *Treatise of dreams & visions*; Philip Goodwin, *The mystery of dreames, historically discoursed* (London, 1658).
6 Artemidorus, *The Interpretation of Dreams: Oneirocritica*, trans. Robert J. White (Park Ridge, NJ: Noyes Classical Studies, 1975); S.R.F. Price, "The Future of Dreams: From Freud to Artemidorus," *Past and Present* 113 (1986): 3–37; Artemidorus, *The interpretation of dreams digested into five books by that ancient and excellent philosopher, Artemidorus* (London: 1690); Lawrence T. Martin, "The Earliest Versions of the Latin 'Somniale Danielis'," *Manuscripta* XXIII (1979): 131–141; *Interpretatiiones seu somnia Danielis prophete revelata ab angelo missus [sic] a deo primo de diebus Lune* (Rome, 1479); *Somnia Salomonis David regis fili una cum Danielis prophete somniorum interpretatione: novissime ex amussim recognita oîbus mendis expurgata* (Venetiis, 1516).
7 Thomas Hill, *A little treatise of the interpretation of dreams, fathered on Joseph* (London, 1567). The first English edition of Artemidorus was *The judgement,*

or exposition of dreames, written by Artimodorus, an auntient and famous author, first in Greeke, then translated into Latin, after into French and now into English (London, 1606). While the printers of the 1786 edition claimed it was the 24th edition of Artemidorus in English, I have found only 13 editions extant from the period. Please see the bibliography for a full list.

8 Anon., *Oniropolus, or dreams interpreter* (London, 1680). While Frederick Hendrick van Hove (1628?-1698), a Dutch engraver and portrait artist who moved to England around 1692, has been ascribed as the author, it seems most likely that he was only responsible for producing the engraving of the title-page, where his signature can be clearly seen underneath the image. On the title page itself no author is given. See also, J.S., *The true fortune-teller, or, guide to knowledge discovering the whole art of chiromancy, physiognomy, metoposcopy and astrology* (London, 1698); William Lilly, *A groatsworth of wit for a penny, or, The interpretation of dreams* (London, 1670); *A groatsworth of wit for a penny, or the Interpretation of Dreams* (London, 1750); John Booker, *Six penny-worth of wit for a penny. Or, dreams interpreted* (London, 1690); John Booker, *The History of Dreams. Or, Dreams Interpreted ...* (Edinburgh, 1800). As some editions of these works were printed posthumously it is unlikely that Booker and Lilly were the authors and that these tracts were ascribed to them for the purpose of marketing.

9 Examples include: Samuel Strangehopes, *A book of knowledge. In four parts* (London, 1679); Marc de Vulson, *The court of curiosity wherein the most intricate questions are resolved by a most curious fortune-book and dreams and visions explained and interpreted* (London, 1681); Anon., *The art of courtship, or, The School of delight* (London, 1686); *Wits cabinet or, A companion for young men and ladies* (London, 1698); Anon. *Dreams and moles, with their interpretation and signification* (London, 1780).

10 See, for example, Anon., *The problemes of Aristotle with other philosophers and phisitions* (London, 1597), F7v-G1r; Thomas Walkington, *The optick glasse of humors* (London, 1607), 76–77; Wilhelm Scribonius, *Naturall philosophy: or A description of the world ...* translated by Daniel Widdowes (London, 1621), 51.

11 Philip Barrough, *The methode of phisicke conteyning the causes, signes and cures of inward diseases in mans body from the head to the foote* (London, 1583), 34; Walkington, *Optick glasse of humors*, 30; Owen Felltham, *Resolves divine, moral, political* (London, 1677), 82; Philip Woodman, *Medicus novissimus; or, the modern physician, 2nd edition* (London, 1722), 191.

12 Walkington, *Opticke glasse of humors*, 30; Gualtherus Bruele, *Praxis medicinae, or, the physicians practice wherein are contained inward diseases from the head to the foote* (London, 1632), 50–55; Thomas Hobbes, *Philosophicall rudiments concerning government and society* (London, 1651), 184; John Bond, *An essay on the incubus, or night-mare* (London, 1753), Preface.

13 Scribonius, *Naturall philosophy*, 51; Felltham, *Resolves*, 83; Tryon, *Treatise of dreams & visions*, 53–54.

14 Peter Burke, *Varieties of Cultural History* (Cambridge: Polity Press, 1997); Patricia Crawford, "Women's Dreams in Early Modern England," *History Workshop Journal* 49 (2000): 129–41; Charles Carlton, "The Dream Life of Archbishop Laud," *History Today* (December 1986): 9–14.

15 Lyndal Roper and Daniel Pick, eds., *Dreams and History: The Interpretation of Dreams from Ancient Greece to Modern Psychoanalysis* (London: Routledge, 2004), Introduction.

16 Ann Marie Plane, *Dreams and the Invisible World in Colonial New England: Indians, Colonists and the Seventeenth Century* (Philadelphia, PA: University of Pennsylvania Press, 2014), 12.

17 Burke, *Varieties of Cultural History*, 24.

14 Introduction

18 Jeanette Marie Mageo, *Dreaming and the Self: New Perspectives on Subjectivity, Identity and Emotion* (New York: State University of New York Press, 2003); Plane, *Dreams and the Invisible World in Colonial New England*; Ann Marie Plane and Leslie Tuttle, eds., *Dreams, Dreamers and Visions: The Early Modern Atlantic World* (University of Pennsylvania Press, 2013); Katharine Hodgkin, "Dreaming Meanings: Some Early Modern Dream Thoughts," in *Reading the Early Modern Dream: The Terrors of the Night*, edited by Katharine Hodgkin (New York, London: Routledge, 2008), 109–24.

19 Mageo, *Dreaming and the Self*, Introduction.

20 Richard L. Kagan, *Lucretia's Dreams: Politics and Prophecy in Sixteenth-Century Spain* (London: University of California Press, 1990); William Christian, *Apparitions in Late and Medieval Spain* (Princeton: Princeton University Press, 1981); William Christian, "Six Hundred Years of Visionaries in Spain: Those Believed and Those Ignored," in *Challenging Authority: The Historical Study of Contentious Politics*, edited by Michael Hanagan (Minneapolis: University of Minnesota Press, 1998), 107–119; Nigel Smith, *Perfection Proclaimed: Language and Literature in English Radical Religion 1640–1660* (Oxford: Clarendon Press, 1989), 73–101; Diane Watt, *Secretaries of God: Women Prophets in Late Medieval and Early Modern England* (Woodbridge: D.S. Brewer, 1997); Phyllis Mack, *Visionary Women: Ecstatic Prophecy in Seventeenth-Century England* (Berkeley: University of California Press, 1992).

21 Roper and Pick, eds., *Dreams and History*; Katharine Hodgkin, Michelle O'Callaghan and S.J. Wiseman eds., *Reading the Early Modern Dream: The Terrors of the Night* (London: Routledge, 2008); Peter Brown, ed., *Reading Dreams: The Interpretation of Dreams from Chaucer to Shakespeare* (Oxford: Oxford University Press, 1999).

22 Carole Levin, *Dreaming in the English Renaissance: Politics and Desire in Court and Culture* (New York: Palgrave Macmillan, 2008); Plane, *Invisible Worlds*.

23 Stuart Clark, *Vanities of the Eye: Vision in Early Modern European Culture* (Oxford University Press, USA, 2009).

24 Sasha Handley, "Sleepwalking, Subjectivity and the Nervous Body in Eighteenth-Century Britain: The Nervous Body in Eighteenth-Century Britain," *Journal for Eighteenth-Century Studies* 35, no. 3 (September 2012): 305–23.

25 Simon J. Williams, *Sleep and Society: Sociological Ventures into the (Un)known* (London; New York: Routledge, 2005), 37.

26 A. Roger Ekirch, *At Day's Close: Night in Times Past* (New York, London: W.W. Norton & Co., 2005), 332–33; "Sleep We Have Lost: Pre-Industrial Slumber in the British Isles," *The American Historical Review* 106, no. 2 (2001): 343–86.

27 Sasha Handley, "From the Sacral to the Moral: Sleeping Practices, Household Worship and Confessional Cultures in Late Seventeenth-Century England," *Cultural and Social History* 9, no. 1 (2012): 27–46; "Sleepwalking, Subjectivity and the Nervous Body in Eighteenth-Century Britain: The Nervous Body in Eighteenth-Century Britain," *Journal for Eighteenth-Century Studies* 35, no. 3 (September 2012): 305–23; "Sociable Sleeping in Early Modern England, 1660–1760," *History* 98, no. 329 (January 2013): 79–104; *Sleep in early modern England* (London; New Haven: Yale University Press, 2016).

28 Craig Koslofsky, *Evening's Empire: A History of the Night in Early Modern Europe* (Cambridge: Cambridge University Press, 2011).

29 Ibid., 1–18, 91–127.

30 Handley, *Sleep in early modern England*, 9.

31 See for example Carlo Ginzburg's important work on witchcraft agrarian cults in early modern Italy and the work of Éva Pócs on witchcraft and folk traditions in premodern Europe as well as Gábor Klaniczay's study of shamanism

Introduction 15

and its connections to witchcraft in the early modern period: Carlo Ginzburg, *The Night Battles: Witchcraft & Agrarian Cults in the Sixteenth & Seventeenth Centuries* (London: Routledge, 1983); Carlo Ginzburg, *Ecstasies: Deciphering the Witches' Sabbath* (New York: Pantheon Books, 1991); Gábor Klaniczay, "Shamanism and Witchcraft," *Magic, Ritual and Witchcraft* 1, no. 2 (2006): 214–21; Éva Pócs, *Between the Living and the Dead* (Budapest: CEU Press, 1999). Classic anthropological studies of shamanism include: Mircea Eliade, *Le chamanisme et les techniques archaïques de l'extase* (Paris: PUF, 1951); translated as *Shamanism: Archaic Techniques of Ecstasy*, trans. Williard E. Trask (London: Routledge, 1964); M. Lewis, *Ecstatic Religion: An Anthropological Study of Spirit Possession and Shamanism* (Harmondsworth: Penguin, 1971); Vilmos Diószegi and Mihály Hoppál, eds., *Shamanism in Siberia* (Budapest: Akadémiai, 1978); Lauri Honko, "Role-taking of the Shaman," *Temenos* 4 (1969): 26–55; Åke Hultkrantz, "A Definition of Shamanism," *Temenos* 9 (1973): 25–37; *The Religion of the American Indians*, trans. Monica Setterwell (Berkeley and Los Angeles: University of California Press, 1979); Anna-Lena Siikala, *The Rite Technique of the Siberian Shaman*, FF Communications 220 (Helsinki: Academia Scientiarum Fennica, 1978).
32 Plane and Tuttle, *Dreams, Dreamers and Visions*, 29.
33 Alexandra Walsham, "The Reformation and 'the Disenchantment of the World' Reassessed," *The Historical Journal* 51, no. 2 (2008): 497–528; Owen Davies, *Witchcraft, Magic and Culture 1736–1951* (Manchester: Manchester University Press, 1999); Willem de Blécourt and Owen Davies, eds., *Witchcraft Continued: Popular Magic in Modern Europe* (Manchester; New York: Manchester University Press, 2004); Alex Owen, *The Place of Enchantment: British Occultism and the Culture of the Modern* (Chicago: Chicago University Press, 2004); Jane Shaw, *Miracles in Enlightenment England* (Cambridge: Cambridge University Press, 2008).
34 Peter Gay, *The Enlightenment: An Interpretation*, Vol. 1, *The Rise of Modern Paganism* (New York: Alfred E. Knopf, 1966); Jonathan Sheehan, *The Enlightenment Bible: translation, scholarship, culture* (Princeton, NJ: Princeton University Press, 2005); David Sorkin, *The Religious Enlightenment: Protestants, Jews and Catholics from London to Vienna* (Princeton: Princeton University Press, 2011); Jeffrey D. Burson, *The Rise and Fall of Theological Enlightenment: Jean-Martin de Prades and Ideology in Eighteenth-Century France* (Notre Dame, IN: University of Notre Dame Press, 2010); Ulrich L. Lehner, *Enlightened Monks: The German Benedictines, 1740–1803* (Oxford: Oxford University Press, 2011); Ulrich L. Lehner, *The Catholic Enlightenment: The Forgotten History of a Global Movement* (New York, NY: Oxford University Press, 2016); William J. Bulman and Robert G. Ingram, eds., *God in the Enlightenment* (New York, NY: Oxford University Press, 2016).
35 See for example: Scribonius, *Naturall philosophy*; Bruele, *Praxis medicinae*; Levine Lemnie, *The touchstone of complexions expedient and profitable for all such as bee desirous and carefull of their bodily health* (London, 1633); Isbrand van Diemerbroeck, *The anatomy of human bodies comprehending the most modern discoveries and curiosities in that art ... translated from the last and most correct and full edition of the same by William Salmon* (London, 1694).
36 Julian Roberts and Andrew G. Watson, eds., *John Dee's Library Catalogue* (London: The Bibliographic Society, 1990), 319, B168, 1103, 1198, B237, B240; *Artemidori Daldiani ... De somniorum interpretatione, libri quinq[ue]*, translated by Janus Cornarius (Basileae, 1539).
37 I will discuss this possibility in more detail in Chapter 2.
38 Thomas Hill, *The contemplation of mankinde* (London, 1571); Thomas Hill, *A contemplation of mysteries* (London, 1574); Thomas Hill, *The newe jewell of*

16 *Introduction*

health wherein is contayned the most excellent secretes of phisicke and philoso-phie, devided into fower bookes (London, 1576); Thomas Hill, *A joyfull jewell containing aswell such excellent orders, preservatives and precious practises for the plague* (London, 1579); Thomas Hill, *A brief and most pleasau[n]t epitomye of the whole art of phisiognomie, gathered out of Aristotle, Rasis, Formica, Loxius, Phylemo[n], Palemo[n], Consiliator ...* (London, 1556).

39 John Beale, "Treatise on the Art of Interpreting Dreams," Undated, 25/19/3B, in *The Hartlib Papers: A Complete Text and Image Database of the Papers of Samuel Hartlib (C.1600–1660)*, 2nd edition, edited by Mark Greengrass, Michael Leslie and Michael Hannon (Sheffield: Sheffield University Library, 2002.

40 Tryon, *Treatise of dreams & visions,* 11.

1 "Seasons of sleep"

Natural dreams, health and the physiology of sleep

Introduction

On the 2nd October 1702 Lady Sarah Cowper, a deeply religious woman and prolific English diarist, recorded the following dream in the first volume of her diary, which was a collection of her spiritual meditations with excerpts of her daily life recorded between 1700 and 1702.

> This night I Dreamt that I was married to the old and Battered Ld Oxford. There was nothing Amourous in the imagination it is plain, nor do I remember any other conceit but that it pleased my fancy to think I shoud Dy Countess of Oxford without Considering at all how I shoud live with him. Sure I am that our Dreams do not alwaies suit the Constitution of our Body, nor Correspond with our Thoughts in the Day. ffor nothing wou'd be more averse to my wakeing Thoughts than Committing Matrimony a second time.[1]

Apart from demonstrating a deep aversion to remarrying and perhaps her unconscious desire to rise above her station as the Countess of Oxford, Cowper's reflections reveal to us how early modern men and women might ascribe meaning to their dreams. Similarly, Cowper's excerpt also illustrates a complex range of ideas circulating about dreams that individuals might consider, accept or reject in the early modern period. Dreams might be natural or supernatural in origin and sometimes even derive from the more ambiguous category of the preternatural. While supernatural or divine dreams were often vehemently contested, due to the spiritual power they often conferred to the dreamer within the community, ideas of natural dreams were longstanding and largely uncontested. Several core understandings of the causes and meanings of natural dreams circulated in printed medical, oneirocritic, religious and philosophical works and also appear in private writings. Early modern writings on dreams and sleep also reveal the inherent sense of vulnerability of both the body and soul to involuntary internal and external forces. Since sleep was understood as a liminal state that left sleepers vulnerable to nocturnal physical and supernatural assaults, early

18 *"Seasons of sleep"*

modern writings frequently portrayed sleep as imbued with a deep sense of fear and anxiety.

As Lady Cowper's dream narrative indicates, dreams were understood largely as part of the natural physiology of sleep and within the framework of health. Drawing on the legacy of classical medicine and philosophy, throughout the period a diversity of authors, including natural philosophers, physicians and writers of dream treatises, argued that certain dreams were "natural" and occurred as a result of normative processes of the body and soul in sleep. Three main ideas underlay the natural theory of dreams and will constitute the focus of this chapter. First, based on the Hippocratic-Galenic system, "natural" dreams were understood as the natural by-products of the complex workings of the humoral system of the body in sleep. Second, the idea that certain dreams were caused by autonomous psychological processes was also common and derived from the ideas of Plato and Aristotle. Finally, writers argued that "natural" dreams were alternately caused by a range of external environmental stimuli, such as noises, the planets, the air and the direct environment of the sleeper. These core ideas about the causes of natural dreams changed little from the sixteenth to the mid-eighteenth century.

Historical studies of sleep by Sasha Handley, A. Roger Ekirch and Roger Schmidt have posited that the eighteenth century marked a significant transitional period in the history of sleep. A. Roger Ekirch suggested in his pioneering study that before the invention of artificial lighting early modern people experienced a pattern of segmented sleep. Ekirch argued that, according to evidence from literature and contemporary writings, most people experienced a fundamentally interrupted sleep cycle with two periods of sleep. Men and women would rise between their "first" and "second sleep" to work, visit neighbours, pray, read, make love or urinate. This common practice began disappearing in the period of industrialization when public lighting became widespread.[2] In response to Ekirch's assertions, Roger Schmidt proposed that patterns of disruptive sleep were a "symptom of modernity" that became "increasingly problematic" for men and women in the eighteenth century as a result of the rise of caffeine consumption, the novel and the use of clocks. According to Schmidt, the period of the enlightenment was heralded by a seismic shift and disruption to "the ancient architecture of human sleep."[3] Drawing from and problematizing the earlier work of Ekirch, Schmidt suggests that the advent of public lighting was merely a product of changes to eighteenth-century sleep habits rather than a catalyst for change.

Like Schmidt and Ekirch, Sasha Handley argues that the long eighteenth century was a transitional period that witnessed significant changes to contemporary sleeping habits, most notably of the social elite. She suggests that the period was one of an increasing practice of "sociable sleeping" whereby persons of the "fashionable" sort deliberately cultivated disrupted sleep patterns and late hours as part of the newly modish "code of civility." This, Handley suggests, was the result of socio-economic changes and physical shifts in the urban and household landscape.[4] These recent studies have done much to reveal unique insight into early modern nocturnal lived experiences and the history of sleep; however, I would argue that before historians can make generalizations about significant transitions and changes in the eighteenth century, we must first understand in more depth cultural understandings and experiences of both dreams and sleep in the earlier period of the sixteenth and seventeenth centuries. Similarly, as Chapter 4 will demonstrate, according to the evidence of medical casebooks and recipe books, early modern people frequently experienced sleep disruptions and disorders much earlier in the period of the late sixteenth and seventeenth centuries.

Intertwined in medical theories of natural dreams was the relationship between dreams and the physiology of sleep. Natural dreams were understood as expressions of the good or poor health of the body and mind that manifested only in the state of sleep. Since natural dreams revealed the constitution of the body and its fragile economy of humours, in addition to the disposition of the mind, dreams were considered useful in the prognosis of diseases of both body and mind. That is to say, according to medical authors and natural philosophers, dreams were fundamental prognostic tools that revealed humoral imbalances in the body as well as providing insight into the unconscious mind or self with all its many base desires and anxieties. These ideas were neither new to the early modern period nor particular to English writers and were rather a legacy of the ancient Greeks, particularly Plato, Galen and Aristotle.

The idea that dreams offered physicians insight into the health of the body and the humours of the dreamer had a long history reaching back to Galen. His short tract "On diagnosis in dreams" (*De dignotione ex insomniis*) advanced a purely physiological understanding of dreams and suggested that dreams might assist in part of the diagnosis of disease.[5] According to Galen,

> The vision-in-sleep [*enhypnion*], in my opinion, indicates a disposition of the body. Someone dreaming a conflagration is troubled by yellow bile, but if he dreams of smoke, or mist, or deep darkness, by black bile. Rainstorm indicates that cold moisture abounds; snow, ice and hail, cold phlegm.[6]

Drawing inspiration from the writings of Galen, Plato and Aristotle, early modern English concepts of the causes of natural dreams tended to revolve around two main theories in the period – the influence of the humours and the "affections of the mind." Owen Felltham explained in his work, *Resolves: divine, moral, political* (1677), "The aptness of the *humours* to the like *effects*, might suggest something to the *mind* ... so that I doubt not but either to *preserve health* or amend the *life, dreams*, may, to a *wise observer*, be of *special benefit*."[7] Since the humours affected the body and mind, while both were vulnerable to external environmental forces such as the air and planets, the dreamer was inherently vulnerable to uncontrollable forces within and

20 *"Seasons of sleep"*

without. Writings on natural dreams therefore suggest a porous model, not only of the body but also of the mind.

The importance of health in early modern England is clearly indicated by the ongoing popularity of both lay and learned tracts on understanding and procuring health. Popular tracts proliferated and some of the bestsellers include Thomas Elyot's *The castle of health,* which was first published in 1539 and went through 14 editions in the sixteenth century alone.[8] Elyot's tract was designed to be an easy reference guide and layman's manual for understanding health and disease. This work offered a comprehensive manual of health in the vernacular so that, as the title page touted, "every manne may knowe the state of his owne body, the preservation of helthe and how to instruct well his phisition in sicknes that he be not deceyved."[9] Elyot's medical manual created an important market for publishers in the late sixteenth century who went on to print numerous health manuals for the laity and non-professionals.

Capitalizing on Elyot's success, other medical handbooks soon followed advertising comprehensive medical knowledge and practical remedies. Multiple editions of these manuals ensued and examples include Thomas Cogan's *The haven of health* (1584) and Nicholas Culpeper's *The English physitian* (1652), which, at three pence, went through over 15 editions by 1700.[10] Within these works discussions of sleep and dreams appear as important features of individual health. "Natural dreams" were explained as being products of the character and imbalances in the four humours. These authors also helped popularize the idea that the contents of dreams – their dominant emotions and symbols – could assist in the diagnosis of disease and identify both the humoral imbalance and overall temperament of the dreamer. Since the inner workings and complex balances of the body were hard to discern, dreams were construed as a useful means of finding clues to the physiological and psychological imbalances of the body and mind.

The bulk of the following discussion on dreams and the physiology of sleep will be based on these popular medical tracts as well as on the lengthier dream treatises by writers such as Thomas Hill (d. 1572/6) and Thomas Tryon (1634–1703), amongst others. These latter works were designed as comprehensive handbooks of dreams and several titles circulated in the period. Thomas Hill's *The moste pleasaunte arte of the interpretation of dreames* (1571 and reprinted 1576) is one of the first known English dream handbooks that offered readers an extensive repertoire of knowledge on dreams and the means for interpreting them.[11] Richard Haydock (1570–c.1642), a physician and infamous "sleeping preacher" who was exposed as a fraud by James I in 1605, wrote a brief handbook of dreams, the *Oneirologia,* as an apology to the Stuart monarch in the same year. Natural theories of dreams predominate in this manuscript and Haydock espoused a largely medical theory of dreaming.[12]

Thomas Tryon published another notable dream treatise later in the seventeenth century. Like Hill, Tryon was a self-educated writer of

"Seasons of sleep" 21

handbooks on a variety of topics. Tryon's *A treatise of dreams & visions* first published in 1689 was printed again in 1695 and 1700 and was perhaps the most popular manual of dreams in the period.[13] In 1706 it was retitled *Nocturnal revels* and extended into two volumes, the second volume being a handbook of oneiromancy published by Andrew Bell. This edition was then reprinted by other publishers in 1749, 1750, 1767 and finally in 1789.[14] In this work Tryon discussed the diverse kinds of dreams, their causes and overall meaning. Although Tryon supported the existence of supernatural dreams, he also argued that certain dreams were "natural" and caused by the humours, thoughts of the day or the planets. Ideas of natural dreams were thus also promoted in early modern English dream treatises and were endorsed alongside supernatural dreams as an important subcategory of dreams in private writings and literary works.

Humours and digestion: Porous bodies, moist brains

Before discussing the relationship among dreams, sleep and the humours, it is first necessary to outline briefly early modern humoral models of the body. Galen's model of the humoral system, adopted from Hippocrates, was the most flexible and prevailing model of health and disease in the early modern period, only declining in the late eighteenth century as new developments in anatomy and medicine slowly eroded the significance of the humours.[15] In this system, the body, mind and soul were understood as an organic, symbiotic unit that was particularly vulnerable to both internal and external stimuli. The body itself was also a kind of nebulous entity, its boundaries porous and sensitive to "noxious" vapours in the air and surrounding environment. Within the fragile bounds of the body, the four humours, black bile, yellow bile, blood and phlegm affected every aspect of the individual's health, including everything from personality, digestion, sleep, complexion, moods and, as I will discuss, dreams. The body was a veritable cauldron for the "concoction" of fluids, vapours and spirits. Elyot's *The castle of health* had helped to popularize the Galenic model of health amongst a broader audience in early modern England by offering a comprehensive summary of Galen's theories in the vernacular. In Elyot's manual sleep, as one of the six "non-naturals" (air; movement and rest; food and drink; sleep and vigil; excretion and retention; and the passions and emotions), was fundamental to the overall health of the individual.[16]

Showing the flexibility of the humoral system, medical writers Christianized Galen's pagan system to show how the events recounted in Genesis had resulted in the imbalance of the perfect humoral complexion of mankind. Christian readings of Galen saw bodies after the Fall as subject to inevitable imbalances and sensitive to outside stimuli, noxious vapours and intangible forces. In his work *The breviarie of health* (1st edition 1547), the physician Andrew Boorde (1490?-1549) explained the cause of the humours as follows, "God made them in man, when he made man, & he did make man perfect

22 *"Seasons of sleep"*

of foure humours, in true porcion, but after that thorow sensualitie man did alter his humours or complexion, setting them out of order and frame."[17]

In the Christianized Galenic system, sleep was understood as a merciful balm to labour and God's benign gift to help to alleviate the punishment of sin. Some English writers intimated that the first sleep followed the Fall. These writers also speculated that the first dream was that of Adam, who slept as God removed his rib to create Eve. Richard Haydock explained in his manuscript on dreams,

> For were it possible for the exact equipage of humours to bee founde which noe doubt with Adams fall transgressed theire appointed limitts: this naturall dreame (discouveringe only the distemperature and disease) should there cease. For sicknes followed sinne. Yet whether Adam in his intigritie should have binne subject to the other kinde of dreames, is hard to judge: except wee may probably callest that hee should have had noe use of sleepe and soe consequently not of dreames. Insomuch as sleepe was graunted as a remedye against defatigation by laboure and laboure and sweat of browes was part of the reward for sinne. As for that sleep which Adam was in when God tooke the woman out of his side, it seemeth to bee extraordinary and compulsive.[18]

According to Haydock, Adam was the first human to experience sleep and while he may have had no need of dreams before the Fall, Haydock implies that with the introduction of sleep, dreams soon followed. John Beale, (*bap.* 1608, *d.* 1683), a Church of England clergyman who was actively involved in the intellectual circle of Samuel Hartlib, also discussed the first "great sleep" in his unpublished seventeenth-century manuscript, *A Treatise on the Art of Interpreting Dreams*.[19] Based on an exegesis of Genesis 2: 21, Beale believed that Adam most likely experienced the first divine dream or vision in the original "great sleep."[20] Both Beale and Haydock situated ideas of the origins of sleep and dreams within a Christian cosmology and based on an exegesis of Genesis. Sleep and, by extension, dreams were ostensibly gifts from God, a balm to ease the punishment of labour, which was itself the "reward for sinne." Whilst sleep was born after the Fall so too was humoral imbalance.

In the humoral system, the early modern body was conceptualized not as a neat model of organs and ordered processes; rather it was a vessel filled with a commingling of fluids, flesh, temperatures and spirits.[21] The body was dynamic, in constant flux and its fragile economy was bursting at the seams so that the fluids seeped out through the skin with excessive sanguine dispositions causing ruddy cheeks and red hair.[22] The interior regions of the body were also porous and contained a primordial soup of fluids, which permeated through to the major organs, moving upwards from the stomach to the brain in sleep and through the heart to the exterior members in waking life. According to the principles of Aristotelian natural philosophy, "animal" and "vital spirits" were also part of the

"Seasons of sleep" 23

Figure 1.1 "The Sleepy Congregation." By: William Hogarth, Bowles & Carver London. Wellcome Library, London.

fungible body and moved through its members to bring animation to the limbs in waking life. Sleep ensued when vapours or "spirits" produced by digestion ascended from the stomach to the brain during the process of "concoction." The healthy person only wakened, it was believed, once this process had been completed. The German physician Wilhelm Scribonius (1550–1600) explained in his treatise of natural philosophy (translated into English in 1621),

> Sleepe is the resting of the feeling facultie: his cause is a cooling of the braine by a pleasant abounding vapour, breathing forth of the stomacke and ascending to the braine. When that vapour is concoct and turned

24 *"Seasons of sleep"*

into spirits, the heate returneth and the sences recovering their former function, cause waking.[23]

Not only was the interior region of the body in flux and fundamentally porous, but the boundaries of the body itself were also permeable and vulnerable to the fumes, fluids and temperature of the external environment. Benign and noxious fluids and vapours seeped through the fragile and porous boundaries of the skin to merge with the interior fluids causing further imbalances, diseases and maladies. Air and temperature were additional catalysts in heating or cooling the fluids and organs of the body, resulting in excessive dryness or moistness: heat or cold further added to the commingling of vapours, spirits and fluids of the body.[24] In this system, women's bodies were believed to be excessively cold and moist while men's bodies were fundamentally hot and dry; the sex of the individual further adding to the complex system of the humours. Digestion or "concoction" was one of the major functions of the body and one that was understood to provide nourishment for the entire body, often at the expense of the discomfort of individuals, depending on their diet and regimen of exercise and sleep.[25]

As Karl H. Dannenfeldt explained in his article on theories and practices of sleep in the Renaissance, as one of the "six non-naturals" described by Galen in his *Tegni* or *Ars parva*, sleep was viewed as essential for the overall health of the individual body and mind.[26] Moderation of all the "six non-naturals" was the ultimate key to good health. In *The castle of health* Elyot argued that "moderate sleep" allowed digestion to occur and that a perfect sleep made "the body fatter, the minde more quiet and cleere, the humors temperate."[27] Since the ideal body was fat and moist, sleep was an important procurer of perfect health. In the manual *Approved directions for health* (1612), Sir William Vaughan (1575–1641) explained that sleep "strengtheneth all the spirits, comforteth the body, quieteth the humours and pulses, qualifieth heat of the liver, taketh away sorrow and asswageth furie of the minde."[28] Excessive "waking" or "vigilance," on the other hand, caused the body to become "dull, oblivious, lazy, faint, heavy, blockish."[29] Levine Lemnie (1505–1568), a Dutch medical writer popular in England, wrote in his treatise on the complexions:

> So againe, watching being not within mediocrity and measure used, dryeth the braine, affecteth the sences, empayreth memory, dimmeth eyesight, marreth the spirits, wasteth naturall humour, hindereth concoction and finally consumeth all the grace, beauty, comlinesse and state of the whole body.[30]

Sleep therefore acted as a kind of equalizer for the body, helping to restore the proper balance of humours, temperature and moistness and fundamentally assisting in the overall health of the individual.

Following the ideas of Aristotle, the most important function of sleep, according to medical writers throughout the period, was to allow for digestion or "concoction" to occur. According to Thomas Hill in *The moste pleasaunte arte of the interpretacion of dreames,* sleep "much helpeth digestion" since it allowed heat to turn inward to "suffuseth" the inner organs involved in "concoction."[31] Richard Haydock explained that sleep was:

> Performed in the time of concoction, by meanes of certaine hott and moist vapours, ascendinge upp by ye jugular veines and arteries, wch meetinge with the cold temper of the braine, are there condensate and converted into a cold deawie substance: and soe fallinge againe uppon the originall of ye sinews, hold them still fast bound, from all outward functions, untill the naturall heat hath consumed the matter of stoppage: wch causeth an interchangable returne unto the former habit of Wakinge, ordeined for Civill affaires.[32]

These ideas of the importance of sleep in the process of "concoction" persisted throughout the period. Even as late as 1768, Francis de Valangin (1725–1805), a physician and Fellow of the Royal College of London, argued that in sleep "the Coction [sic] of the Aliments, the Assimilation of all the Humours all over the Body, the Functions of the Stomach and of all the Viscera are performed happily and without Interruption; all the Parts are gently and agreeably moistened and relaxed."[33] During this process vapours were believed to arise from the stomach to ascend to the brain. The brain as a cold and moist organ was overwhelmed by the heat and quality of these fumes, which also served to block the external senses causing sleep.[34]

The relationship between sleep and dreams becomes clearer by studying humoral theories of digestion and the body since the excess fumes from digestion not only procured sleep but also mysteriously caused natural dreams. In his discussion of sleep and dreams Scribonius elaborated, espousing the ideas of Aristotle:

> [The] Affections of sleepe are Dreames, Nightmare and Extasie, & c. A dreame is an inward act of the minde, the bodie sleeping: and the quieter that sleepe is the easier bee dreames: but if sleepe be unquiet then the minde is troubled. Varietie of dreames is according to the divers constitution of the bodie. The cleare and pleasaunt dreams are when the spirits of the braine, which the soule useth to imagine with, are most pure and thin, as towardes morning when concoction is perfected.[35]

Dreams, understood in this sense, were intertwined with the physiology of sleep and were conceived as the natural by-products of the sleeping body and mind and their natural functions. In this way, dreams and sleep were perceived to have a kind of symbiotic relationship, each affecting the other. Consequently, a close inspection of one's dreams allowed the individual or

26 *"Seasons of sleep"*

physician to gain a better sense of the overall health of the body and mind of the individual. If one's sleep and dreams were disturbed and "frightful" then this was a clear sign of ill health. Haydock explained succinctly, "the Naturall dreame discovereth first ye Complexion then the disease."[36]

Within the humoral system, the vast varieties of dreams were understood to be the result of the individual constitution or "complexion" and the shifting imbalances of the humours. In his tract on *The terrors of the night* (1598), Thomas Nashe (1567–1601) wrote, "What heed then is there to be had of dreames, that are no more but the confused giddie action of our braines, made drunke with the innundation of humors?"[37] While critics of popular beliefs in dreams such as Nashe attacked contemporary beliefs in supernatural dreams as facets of superstition and ignorance, they fully endorsed ideas of natural dreams as products of humoral imbalances.

In a consensus throughout the early modern period, English medical writers and writers of dream treatises understood sleep as the state in which "natural" dreams occurred. In sleep the body lay dormant, the external "senses" hindered or "oppressed," enabling the body's internal operations (respiration and concoction) to function more "perfectly" whilst the body's members were at rest.[38] According to Thomas Hill, "sleepe is the reste of the spyrites and the wakinge, the vehemente motion of theym and the vayne [natural] dreame is a certayne tremblinge and unperfit motione of theym."[39] In his *Treatise of dreams & visions* Tryon further explained,

> *Sleep* is the *natural Rest of a living Creature, or a partial temporary Cessation of animal Actions and the functions of the external Senses, caused (immediately) by the weakness of the Animal Faculty, proceeding from a sweet and stupifying Vapour, arising from the Concoction and Digestion of the Alimentary Food Exhaled from the Stomach and thence ascending to the Brain and watering and bedewing it with unctious Fumes whereby the operations of the Senses are for a time obstructed, to the end the powers both of the Mind and Body may be recruited, refreshed and strengthened.* But besides the Exhalations from the Concoction of the Food received and the native frigidity (or coolness) of the Brain, congealing those exhaled Vapours, there are many accidental Causes, which by consuming the Spirits, occasion Sleep.[40]

Sleep therefore was ultimately viewed as a restful, restorative state in which digestion was the primary catalyst. The vapours that rose from the stomach in sleep permeated the flimsy boundaries of the brain, obstructing the external senses. In this respect, sleep was a passive state in which the body's natural functions operated autonomously and unhindered whilst the external senses and body's members were inactive.

Within the humoral system, the four humours not only affected the quality of sleep, but also via the faculties of the memory and imagination directly produced the images and emotions of dreams themselves. For this reason, medical ideas about the production of natural dreams can help historians to understand early modern concepts of emotions and emotionality. The manifest emotion of a dream, whether anger, joy, terror, sadness, or anxiety, was believed to directly reflect the dominant humour and "complexion" of the dreamer. Natural theories of dreams that espoused a predominantly humoral theory are therefore an important part of understanding early modern theories of emotions. Similarly, as Ann Plane explained in her work on dreams in colonial New England, records of dream narratives themselves also help us to understand the embodied experience of early modern emotionality and affect.[41] Plane suggests that,

> Emotions do not exist *a priori*, outside of their shaping cultural contexts and their experience and expression is, in all ways, part of culturally constructed learned behavior. ... From this vantage point, we should view dreaming itself, along with the beliefs and practices surrounding it, as a deeply contextualized cultural experience, that may, at times, also contain richly embodied "emotional practice."[42]

For this reason, I would suggest that before we can fully understand the emotions expressed through dream narratives it is first imperative to understand the theories of natural dreams that shaped the cultural experience of dreams themselves. This particular cultural lens is key to understanding early modern theories of natural dreams.

In the Galenic schema of dreams, different humoral temperaments or "complexions" determined the nature, quality and length of sleep as well as the kinds of dreams. Drawing from Galen, Elyot asserted that a sanguine person was believed to "sleepe much" and have "dreames of bloudy things, or thinges pleasant."[43] Individuals with a phlegmatic complexion, on the other hand, sleep little and dreamt of "things watery or fish," whilst choleric persons also slept little and dreamt of "fire, fighting, or anger." Melancholic persons suffered from "much watch," that is periods of waking or insomnia and were terrified with "dreames fearfull."[44] This description changed little over the period and we find these humoral schemas of dreams in other medical works and dream treatises, only disappearing in the mid- to late eighteenth century.[45] Writing towards the end of the seventeenth century, Thomas Tryon presented a more extensive explanation of how the complexions affected dreams:

> As for *Complectional Dreams*, they proceed from vapours flying up from that Humour which is most predominant in the Body, unto the Brain and thence Imagination with Representations sutable to such humour; As persons of a *Sanguine Complection*, or in whose mass of humours the Blood bears sway, have generally pleasant chearful and delightfull *Dreams, That they are in Merry Company, Entertain'd with Musick,*

28 *"Seasons of sleep"*

> *Conversing with Persons, fine, beautiful and obliging, drest in splended Robes* and the like divertive objects. Persons of *Cholerick* Complections dream of Anger, Wrath, Brawling; of Quarrelling or Fighting; that they use some violent motion or strugling; that they meet with Bears, Lyons, Dogs, or the like and are in danger to be hurt by them. Such in whome *Melancholy* abounds, are continually disturbed with frightfull Phantasies and Ideas full of Horror, of being surrounded with Darkness, or confined to some close Dungeon, left alone in a Wilderness, oppressed with Poverty, Want and Despair, ready to be torn to pieces, with evil Spirits. Lastly, The *Phegmatick* person is less apt to remember his *Dream*, but they are generally about water, fear of falling from on high down into some great River and being drown'd, or the like. As these several *Humours* are more or less mixed or prevailing in any persons Constitution, so his or her common ordinary *Dreams* will be diversified accordingly.[46]

The knowledge that individual complexions affected dreams was known amongst the wider populace. The prolific dreamer and cleric Ralph Josselin (1617–1683) mused preceding a dream narrative in his journal, "they say dreams declare a mans Temperament."[47] Katherine Austen (1629–1683), also interested in dreams, wrote in her private memoirs, "Dreames are without rule and without reason. They proceed very much from the temper of the body and trouble of the minde."[48] As was shown at the beginning of this chapter, Lady Cowper also demonstrated a clear awareness of natural theories of dreams. In her private journal she mentioned that dreams might reflect the "constitution of the body" or "thoughts of the day."[49]

It was this understanding that the humours directly influenced dreams themselves that made dreams a most useful source of prognosis for physicians. Thomas Wright explained in *The passions of the minde in generall* (1604), "And in effect we proove in dreames and Physitians prognosticate by them, what humor aboundeth, for Choler causeth fighting, blood and wounds; Melancholy, disgrace, feares, affrightments, ill sucesse and such like."[50] While Thomas Nashe argued that dreams were neither predictive nor meaningful, he did acknowledge, "Phisitions by dreames may better discerne the distemperature of their pale clients."[51] The physician Richard Haydock explained that dreams were "forerunners of a subsequent disease as smoake is of fier."[52] The dream was therefore a useful sign of illness and one that, if correctly interpreted, allowed for proper diagnosis and treatment. Although the credibility of dreams as predictive oracles or as divine revelations was debated during the period, the idea that dreams might provide essential insight into health and disease was both uncontested and longstanding. However, as mentioned earlier, the humours were also linked to the inner faculties of the mind that in sleep mysteriously stimulated the imagination to produce dreams from incoherent fragments of memory and fantasy.

The imagination and inner senses: Dreaming as a "litigation of the senses"

Whilst the humoral model of the body dominated writings on sleep and dreams, throughout the period the mind and its inner senses and functions were understood as "intimately connected" to the workings of the body and its overall health. Francis de Valangin noted in his 1768 work on diet, "The Body and the Mind are so intimately connected, that whatsoever affects the one, constantly influences the other."[53] Medical writers and natural philosophers followed an Aristotelian model of the production of natural dreams during sleep in the mind; they argued that the external senses – taste, touch, smell, sight and hearing – were inhibited or "bound" so that only the inner sense of the imagination or "fancy" was freed, producing dreams. Robert Burton described sleep as a "litigation of the senses" that was caused by an "inhibition of spirits, the way being stopped by which they should come."[54] Thomas Cogan (1545–1607), a Manchester physician, suggested that sleep makes us senseless even to the point of imbecility:

> In sleep the senses be unable to execute their office, as the eye to see, the eare to heare, the nose to smell, the mouth to tast and all sinowy parts to feele. So that the senses for a time may seeme to be tyed or bound and therefore Sleepe is called of some *ligamentum sensuum*. And for this imbecility, for that Sleepe after a sort maketh a man senselesse and as it were livelesse, it is called in Latine *Mortis imago*.[55]

Since the senses were bound and the body lay in an immobile state, early modern people often compared sleep to death. The cultural metaphor of death as sleep was a popular theme of funeral sermons and Thomas Cheesman, the minister of East-Ilsey, Berkshire, published his sermon *Death compared to a sleep in a sermon* to commemorate the death of Mary Allen, who died February 18, 1695.[56] Similarly, across the Atlantic the prolific clergyman, Cotton Mather (1663–1728), published his funeral sermon *Awakening thoughts on the sleep of death* (1712) in which he wrote, "that to Dy is to go to Sleep. *Sleep* is the *Rest* of certain Spirits in us; which Retire to be recruited. We shall find a *Rest* in *Death*; and because it will bring us *Rest* with it, therefore it will be a *Sleep* unto us."[57] Here we might also consider the famous soliloquy of Hamlet by Shakespeare:

> To be, or not to be: that is the question:
> Whether 'tis nobler in the mind to suffer
> The slings and arrows of outrageous fortune,
> Or to take arms against a sea of troubles,
> And by opposing end them? To die: to sleep;
> No more; and by a sleep to say we end
> The heart-ache and the thousand natural shocks

30   *"Seasons of sleep"*

> That flesh is heir to, 'tis a consummation
> Devoutly to be wish'd. To die, to sleep;
> To sleep: perchance to dream: ay, there's the rub;
> For in that sleep of death what dreams may come
> When we have shuffled off this mortal coil,
> Must give us pause: there's the respect
> That makes calamity of so long life. ... (3.1.58–70)

As literary scholars have long commented, in Shakespeare death is commonly presented as akin to sleep and here Hamlet also suggests the dreams that arise in death are inherently to be feared. As Filip Krajnik explains in his study of sleep in Shakespeare's plays, in this verse Hamlet presents the afterlife as a kind of dreaming and death synonymous with a sleep filled with dreams. He further extrapolates, "Dreams in the sleep of death are not seen as a reward – they are presented as a worse punishment than earthly nightmares."[58] However, as Krajnik also reminds us, the literary use of sleep as a metaphor for death was ancient and derived from classical mythology since the God of sleep, Hypnos, was brother to the God of Death, Thanatos. Both gods were sons of Nyx, the Goddess of the Night. Here the deep and intimate cultural understandings of sleep, death and the night are paramount and, since classical ideas and mythology continued to influence early modern literature, help explain the lingering notions of the close ties among death, sleep and the night. The first use of the literary metaphor of sleep as death appeared in Homer's *Iliad*. Alongside the work of Shakespeare, other early modern English writers to use this trope include John Donne in his *Holy Sonnet*, the Jesuit Robert Southwell in his poem *Saint Peter's Complaint* and also John Milton in *Paradise Lost*, amongst numerous others.[59]

Christianity further enhanced the close cultural associations between sleep and death. In early modern English religious culture dreaming was frequently conceived as a kind of soul-sleep in which the mind or soul wandered at will. For example, in the polemical pamphlet *The strange witch at Greenwich* (1650), the author wrote, "the bodies of the Saints are a sleepe in the Lord ... that they sleep with their Fathers, they go into their Graves as into their beds."[60] The idea of soul-sleep was one that appealed to Martin Luther and such early English reformers as William Tyndale and John Firth. However, it met with increasing criticism in Calvinist circles and in seventeenth-century English Protestant texts.[61] In spite of this controversy, the idea remained attractive and underlay English beliefs in dreams, death and the afterlife. Isaac Ambrose (1604–1664), a Cambridge-taught clergyman, wrote in 1650, "When all is done ... we sleep again and go from (our grave) the bed, to (that bed) our grave. *A sleep*? that is too quiet, it is nothing but a dream ... all our worldly pleasures are but waking dreams, so at last Death rouzeth our souls that have slept in sinne."[62]

"*Seasons of sleep*"   31

Figure 1.2 "Richard III." Engraving by Thomas Stothard after: James Neagle and William Shakespeare, Geo. Kearsley, London: 2 June 1804. Wellcome Library, London.

The close association between sleep and death was also familiar to members of the broader populace. Lady Sarah Cowper wrote in her diary:

> I am more weary of the Day, then of the night, yet 'tis the day wherein we seem to live, night and sleep is the image of Death, the Condition of the night is more agreeable to me than the transactions of the Day, why may I not then Chuse Death rather than this Life? Did I not believe and hope, there is a state better than Either, prepared for them yt Endure this; in Obedience to God.[63]

32 *"Seasons of sleep"*

Whilst Cowper confessed to prefer the night to the "transactions of the day" here she is using day as a metaphor for the material world and night/sleep to symbolize the afterlife promised to the elect. Elizabeth Isham (*bap.* 1608, *d.* 1654) another pious elite diarist, while meditating on her own death, consoled herself in her diary writing, "as for death it is but a sleepe and even in it I shalbe a conqueror."[64] Early modern discussions of night or sleep as a benign symbol representing the release from the material world may be understood to reflect the process of "nocturnalization" in which, according to historian Craig Koslofsky, night became a positive cultural symbol.[65] However, despite her wistful musings about the virtues of night and sleep, Cowper's sleep was often interrupted and uneasy.

It was perhaps the close association between sleep and death for early modern people that imbued the seasons of nocturnal repose with an acute sense of vulnerability and heightened anxiety. For since sleep, like death, was a state in which the body lay immobile, unprotected and exposed to all physical and supernatural dangers, the need for spiritual and bodily protection was paramount. Equally, in sleep bodies and souls were subject to the prevalent dangers of the night, ranging from the possibility of natural and supernatural assaults in the forms of murderers, robbers, ghosts, witches and, perhaps most terrifying, those of the Devil. As will be discussed in Chapter 4, the practice of night-time prayers before bed asking for spiritual and physical protection from God in sleep continued throughout the period, suggesting that early modern people continued to view sleep as an inherently vulnerable state. This common practice complicates Koslofsky's ideas about nocturnalization.

In writings of natural philosophy and medicine, early modern English models of the mind involved the complex and ambiguous workings of the "inner senses" that were believed to reside in the brain. The "inner senses" were "phantasy" (imagination), "common sense" (reason) and memory. Each of these faculties worked to regulate the functions of the mind and was involved in both waking and sleeping life. Of these faculties the most important in producing dreams was the imagination and, to a lesser extent, memory. As Robert Burton explained,

> The affections of these senses are sleep and waking, common to all sensible creatures. "Sleep is a rest or binding of the outward senses and of the common sense, for the preservation of body and soul" ... for when the common sense resteth, the outward senses rest also. The phantasy alone is free and his commander, reason: as appears by those imaginary dreams, which are of divers kinds, natural, divine, demoniacal, etc. which vary according to humors, diet, actions, objects, etc.[66]

According to early modern models of the mind, largely based on the works of Aristotle and Plato, all sensory stimuli passed through the faculty of memory into the imagination.[67] Dreams occurred when the imagination drew images and thoughts from the storehouse of memory to create chimeras of its own design. Consequently, Thomas Nashe wrote, "a dreame is nothing els but a bubling scum or froath of the fancie, which the day hath left undigested; or an after feast made of the fragments of idle imaginations."[68] Dreams, according to these writers, were therefore meaningless chimeras of the mind, delusions of the imagination, serving no purpose other than to befuddle the senses into thinking scenes perceived were in fact real.

Ideas about the role of the imagination varied slightly in the period, some writers enabled it full power over the "common sense" while others attributed it less agency in the production of dreams. However, during the mid-seventeenth century, the imagination came to be increasingly seen as an uncontrollable, dangerous force within the human mind. The opponents of "enthusiasm," such as the Cambridge Platonist, Henry More and the Arminian theologian and metaphysician, Moyse Amyraut, highlighted this tendency. As Chapter 3 will discuss, the response of these writers was directly linked to the rise of sectarian prophets and visionaries who mushroomed in the tumultuous period of the English Civil Wars and Interregnum. Concern with religious "enthusiasm" led some philosophers to question and others to seek to reconcile the nature of revealed religion, or at least to attempt to contain it within a specific set of rational criteria. Although mechanical philosophy was gaining ground, reaching perhaps its logical conclusions in the materialist philosophy of Thomas Hobbes, writers concerned with the spread of atheism sought to champion ideas of supernatural dreams and the role of the soul in sleep as proof of the immortality of the soul and subsequently of a world suffused with spiritual essence. These writers fought a delicate battle in print fending off the two extremes of "enthusiast" and "atheist" views of religious inspiration and perhaps sought a middle ground.

While the role of the imagination as a primary instigator of dreams was unquestioned by writers on dreams, the role of the soul in sleep was much more controversial. The problem was that if one ascribed too little agency to the soul then this accorded too much power to a lesser intellectual faculty or subordinated its divine nature to the material and profane workings of the body. As a result of seventeenth-century concerns with atheism and materialist philosophy, some writers such as the clergyman Philip Goodwin strongly asserted that the soul was active and fully engaged in the production of dreams:

> In their part Rationall and Intellectual. To compound the person of every Man like Gideons Souldier, he hath his Body as his Earthen Pitcher and his Soul as his Lamp therein. His body may be sleeping, when yet his Soul as his Lamp is burning. Yea as there is the Soul in a man, so there is Reason in the Soul ... In the dark night into divers Dreames man is led by the light of this candle, 'tis Reason in man as the endowment of the Soul, in and by which such Dreames are drawn out. (1658)[69]

34 *"Seasons of sleep"*

According to Goodwin, to divest the role of the soul in sleep was also to deny the potentially divine nature of dreams. As Chapter 3 will illustrate, Goodwin promoted the study of dreams as part of the pastoral care of the soul. He explained, "And if it were *laudable* in them, to look into Dreames to learn out the state of mens *bodies*, may it not be *commendable* in others, thereby to discover the case of mens *souls*."[70] Goodwin was not alone in viewing the soul as active in sleep. Joseph Hall (1574–1656), a prolific religious writer who was Bishop of Norwich and Exeter during the Civil Wars mused in his work, *The contemplations upon the history of the New Testament* (1614), "Give me a Sea that moves not, a Sun that shines not, an open Eye that sees not; and I shall yield there may be a Reasonable Soul that works not."[71]

A correct understanding of dreams was most useful for Christians because it gave insight into the soul in sleep as well as proof of its immortality. According to Goodwin, the soul was active in sleep and was the main instigator of dreams. However, the role of the soul in dreams was a controversial issue in seventeenth- and eighteenth-century writings on dreams. Writers such as Richard Haydock presented an alternate view suggesting that sleep is a "binding" of the faculties of sense and that dreams are the result of the soul putting together incoherent images from the fantasy. In Haydock's view, in sleep the soul works on the "phantasy" and stays in the body.[72] According to Henry More, "For what are *Dreams* but the Imaginations and perceptions of one asleep, which notwithstanding steal upon the Soul, or rise out of her without any consent of hers, as is most manifest in such as torment us and put us to extreme pain till we awake out of them."[73] The rational soul in More's schema was therefore inactive in sleep and overcome by the power of the imagination, which forced dreams into the mind without its consent. The co-existing theory of natural dreams as products of the body and mind's baser functions, based on the traditional ideas of Aristotle and Galen, deprived the soul of any agency in the production of dreams. This notion, according to Goodwin, was to divest the soul of its God-given merits, its immortality and to subordinate it to profane bodily impulses and lesser mental faculties. In effect the philosophical debate about the role of the soul in dreams derived from the assertions of Aristotle, who argued in his essay on dreams that they were the remnants of sense perceptions rising involuntarily in the mind during sleep.

The most famous debate on this topic was raised in the mid-eighteenth century between the writer Thomas Branch (*fl.* 1738–1753) and the Scottish philosopher Andrew Baxter (1687–1750).[74] In his work *An Enquiry into the Nature of the Human Soul* (1733), Baxter grappled with the problem of the soul and its involvement in dreams. According to Baxter, in sleep spirits injected dreams or images into the mind in what was a kind of possession. A participant in the growing critique of the many unresolved vagaries of humoral medicine, Baxter attempted to develop a new theory of dreaming. For him it seemed ridiculous that the soul should terrify itself in sleep with fearful dreams: "It is inconceivable what [sic] the soul could design by these extravagancies [dreams], always deceiving and often terrifying itself."[75] Since the soul could not act unless the individual was conscious, it followed that in sleep the soul retired and became inactive.[76] This difficulty is solved by Baxter's idea that "our dreams are prompted by separate immaterial Beings," who "act upon the matter of our bodies and prompt our sleeping visions."[77] Dreaming, Baxter radically asserts, is nothing "but possession in sleep" by spiritual beings.[78] Seen in this way, the mind itself was a porous entity, vulnerable to outside forces like spirits who mysteriously "injected" dreams into the sleeping mind.

Baxter's idea of dreaming as a form of "possession" was not surprisingly controversial. Thomas Branch launched the most overt critique in his work *Thoughts on dreaming* (1738). Branch argued that "this new Hypothesis," though "ingenious," was "unwarrantable, as well as unphilosophical," since it divested "the Soul of its active Power; and incapacitates it for the Exercise of its proper Functions."[79] Branch intended to show that *"our ordinary Dreams are not effected by Spirits*; but that the *Sensory is not immediately necessary to the Soul for producing the common Appearances of Dreaming."*[80] Branch extrapolated that during the day the "Soul, by its *imaginative Power*, forms Multitudes of Appearances and Scenes, which never existed together in the Mind before."[81] Therefore, it was possible that in sleep the soul took fragments of memory and made a conglomerate of compound images the result of which were dreams. He further speculated, "Have we two Sensories, one for sleeping the other for waking Use?"[82] This was a question that perplexed John Locke in his *Essay on Human Understanding* and led later thinkers to the idea of the unconscious. Although Branch did not entirely rule out supernatural dreams, he described the state of sleep as the "province of the imagination:"

> I look on Sleep as the Province of the Imagination; here it reigns. Corporeal Objects are shut out and cannot approach the Soul in this State, but myriads of incorporeal Ideas, presented by the Memory and the Imagination and principally the latter, afford it Exercise and Entertainment. It has a World of its own Creation and peopling to range in and converse with, tho' then imprisoned in a sleeping Body.[83]

Particularly during the long eighteenth century, the faculty of "fancy," or the imagination, was frequently portrayed as a kind of dangerous and uncontrolled wild force in the mind linked to delusion and madness, which freed itself in sleep and reigned unchecked by its "commander," reason. This was, as Chapter 3 will discuss, indicative of the growing debates about revealed religion and concern with religious "enthusiasm." The "wildness" of dreams themselves was evidence of the dangerous force of the imagination. David Hartley wrote, "There is a great Wildness and inconsistency in our Dreams."[84] Authors frequently argued that the imagination was deceptive and a dangerous generator of delusions, madness and flights of fancy in

36 *"Seasons of sleep"*

the human mind. Dreams in this schema were false perceptions of reality that deceived the senses into believing that what was perceived was real. John Trenchard (1669–1723), a landowner and publicist, commented on the problems of false perceptions in dreams in his work on *The natural history of superstition* (1709):

> 'Tis this Ignorance of Causes, & c. subjects us to mistake the Phantasms and Images of our own Brains (which have no existence any where else) for real Beings and subsisting without us, as in Dreams where we see Persons and Things, feel Pain and Pleasure, form Designs, hear and make Discourses and sometimes the Objects are represented so Lively to our Fancies and the Impressions so Strong, that it would be hard to distinguish them from Realities, if we did not find our selves in Bed.[85]

The danger for the individual was therefore to lose the ability to distinguish between reality and fantasy, resulting in madness and delusion or, by ascribing to dreams a supernatural origin and message, to succumb to the social dangers of "enthusiasm" and "superstition" – the twin evils of the enlightenment. As mentioned earlier, this was an argument made in the seventeenth century by Henry More, Meric Casaubon and Thomas Hobbes. In the eighteenth century, David Hume propagated the same critique of dreams in his most famous work, *An Enquiry Concerning Human Understanding* (1748).[86] Dreams, in this sense, were potential catalysts of disorder in the mind of the dreamer and, hence, dangerous for the mental health of the individual and, as Lucia Dacome noted, the "Mind Politic."[87]

Although dreams might act as problematic instigators and reflections of mental illness, they might be useful, according to some writers, by providing insight into the moral and psychological state of the dreamer. Early modern writers were well aware that natural dreams often contained daily preoccupations or "thoughts of the day." This was an idea that originated in the works of both Plato and Aristotle and was expounded by Scholastics and Neoplatonist authors during the early modern period in England and the Continent.[88] Additionally, the knowledge that natural dreams were also caused by daily preoccupations was more widely appreciated. The Elizabethan diplomat and Dean of Canterbury Nicholas Wotton (1479–1567) was renowned for his accurate predictive dreams. In a famous incident Wotton foresaw in a dream the incarceration and execution for treason of his nephew. Believing himself forewarned, Wotton managed to have his nephew arrested by the Queen on false pretences and so foiled his fate. His biographer, Izaak Walton, in 1670 commented, "Doubtless, the good Dean did well know, that common Dreams are but a senseless paraphrase on our waking thoughts; or, of the business of the day past; or, are the result of our over ingaged affections, when we betake ourselves to rest."[89] Walton himself was clearly rather perturbed by the faith the "good Dean" had in predictive dreams.

However, it was not simply thoughts we harbour during the day that were understood to influence dreams, but also the individual dreamer's occupation and personality. Moses Amyraut (1596–1664), a French Protestant theologian and metaphysician, whose much-admired work on divine dreams was translated into English in 1676, suggested that,

> Natural dreams are such as proceed from those employments of our life, to which we apply our selves with great intention of mind; for studious men dream of books, covetous men of money, Souldiers imagine they see battalions of foot and squadrons of horse and generally those who are delighted in any employment dream of things relating thereunto.[90]

Thus, a person's profession or private preoccupation gave rise to dreams based on his or her daily experiences. This rationale was drawn from the ancient practice of oneiromancy established by practitioners such as Artemidorus who advised dream interpreters to obtain information about the dreamer's occupation before attempting to interpret his or her dream.[91]

Early modern English writers also understood that our dreams are born of our wishes, desires and anxieties. In his *Republic*, Book IX, Plato suggested that,

> Some of our unnecessary pleasures and desires seem to me to be lawless. They are probably present in everyone, but they are held in check by the laws and by the better desires in alliance with reason. ...Those [desires] that are awakened in sleep, when the rest of the soul − the rational, gentle and ruling part − slumbers. Then the beastly and savage part, full of food and drink, casts off sleep and seeks to find a way to gratify itself. You know that there is nothing it won't dare to do at such a time, free of all control by shame or reason. It doesn't shrink from trying to have sex with a mother, as it supposes, or with anyone else at all, whether man, god or beast, it will commit any foul murder and there is no food it refuses to eat. In a word, it omits no act of folly or shamelessness.[92]

Long before Freud would posit a pathological view of dreams as expressing unconscious desires and anxieties, Plato speculated on the powerful unconscious forces in the human psyche. These ideas fundamentally influenced generations of western ideas of dreams and Plato's writings were revitalized and further developed in Neoplatonic thought in the early modern period. The notion that dreams revealed base desires and anxieties was therefore well known to those with an education in the period and may have seeped into wider understandings of dreams.

The idea that natural dreams revealed our daily preoccupations and "secret" wishes is evident in early modern English writings. Roger North (1651–1734), the English lawyer, politician and writer, explained, "Wee dream of some such and of which we are concerned as at the university

38 *"Seasons of sleep"*

boys dream of being at head: and folk that are marryed of being marryed again, & such like nonscence."[93] Thomas Tryon explored this notion in more detail and wrote that one of the uses of dreams was to understand better the "secret bent of our minds:"

> That since the *Heart of man is deceitful above all things*, therefore for him that would truly *know himself*, it has by the wise Doctors of *Morality* been always advised to take notice ... of his usual *Dreams*, there being scarce any thing that more discovers the secret bent of our minds and inclinations to *Vertue* or *Vice*, or this or that particular Evil, as *Pride, Covetousness, Sensuality* or the like, then these nocturnal sallies and reaches of the *Soul*, which are more free & undisguis'd & with less reserve than such as are manifested than we are awake.[94]

For some writers, therefore, dreams were useful for better understanding the self and helping to edify the soul against undesirable thoughts and unchristian vices. Inherent in the idea of dreams as mirrors to the soul is the underlying notion that sleep was a particularly vulnerable state, not just for the body but even more so for the soul. Our sinful thoughts, desires, wishes and anxieties of the day autonomously recur in the night, replaying in our dreams. Understood in this sense, dreams could be important sources of spiritual edification and introspection, potentially offering insight into the health of the soul.

Tryon was not alone in viewing dreams as providing useful insights into the self or soul of the dreamer. According to several other writers, a study of dreams offered insight into our secret "inclinations." Owen Felltham surmised, "Dreams are notable means of discovering our own inclinations. The wise man learns to know ourselves as well by the nights black mantle, as the searching beams of day."[95] Sir Thomas Browne also supported the idea of dreams as a significant "mirror to the self" and wrote in his essay on dreams:

> But the Phantasms of sleep do commonly walk in the great road of naturall & animal dreames: wherein the thoughts or actions of the day are acted over and echoed in the night. ... However dreames may be fallacious concerning outward events, yet may they bee truly significant at home, & whereby wee may more sensibly understand ourselves. Men act in sleep with some conformity unto their awakened senses, & consolations or discouragements may bee drawne from dreams, which intimately tell us ourselves.[96]

This idea continued into the eighteenth century and letters written by John Byrom to Joseph Addison printed in *The Spectator* in August 1714 reveal several ideas of the way dreams are produced by fears and anxieties as well as by thoughts of the day: "Dreams are certainly the Result of our waking

Thoughts and our daily Hopes and Fears are what give the Mind such nimble Relishes of Pleasure and such severe Touches of Pain, in its midnight Rambles."[97] David Hume also commented in *An Enquiry Concerning Human Understanding* (1748) that "several moralists have recommended it [dream interpretation] as an excellent method of becoming acquainted with our own hearts," indicating that the idea that dreams were potentially useful for understanding the self and secret "inclinations" was still circulating.[98]

"The febrile air:" Environmental factors and their effect on sleep and dreams

In the state of sleep not only were the body and mind subject to internal forces, both were also vulnerable to a host of external stimuli. From the sixteenth to the mid-eighteenth century, natural dreams were also conceptualized as being directly affected by environmental factors that had both positive and negative effects on the health of the sleeping individual. These factors included both physical and immaterial stimuli hidden from the naked eye, but nonetheless detrimental or beneficial to the sleeping individual. Included in the list of environmental stimuli influencing sleep and dreams were noises, air, temperature, beds, the position of the body, movements of the planets and the manipulations of spirits. Each of these factors was believed to have a profound effect on the quality of sleep and the overall health and dreams of men and women. In his 1791 medical dissertation on sleep, Samuel Forman Conover, a New Jersey physician, noted the importance of studying sleep to arrive at a better understanding of health: "An accurate knowledge of the effects of *sleep*, upon the human system, will enable us to see the propriety of fortifying the body, in the morning, with either the durable or diffusible stimuli, against the noxious quality of the air at certain seasons of the year."[99]

One of the most important environmental factors understood to affect the dreams and health of the individual was the air and temperature of the bedroom or place in which the person slept. Noxious fumes were believed to stifle the sleeping body and permeate the vulnerable pores of the skin, resulting in ill health and imminent disease. The surrounding air, its quality and heat were also said to influence dreams. This model of dreams drew on contemporary ideas about the symbiotic relationship between the macrocosm and the microcosm of the human body as vulnerable to the influences of the natural material world. Thomas Wright explained that natural dreams were caused by the effects of the "heavens" and "ayre" on the humours in the body.[100] These ideas continued throughout the period well into the eighteenth century when James Beattie wrote, "When the air is loaded with gross vapour, dreams are generally disagreeable to persons of a delicate constitution."[101] The quality of the air was thus understood to have a profound effect on both dreams and sleep.

40 *"Seasons of sleep"*

The spatial topography of bedrooms was considered another important facet of procuring good health and quiet sleep.[102] According to Thomas Cogan, the ideal place to sleep should be "somewhat dark, defended from the Sunne beames and from the light: it must be temperate in heate and cold, yet rather inclining to cold than heat ... for if wee sleepe in a place very hot, we are in danger to fall into a swoune, by reason of the contrariety of sleepe and heat."[103] Cogan's ideal sleeping conditions excluded excessive warmth on the assumption that, according to Lemnie, in sleep the body's warmth moved to the interior regions of the body to assist in concoction.[104] In sleep the body was already a cauldron of heat and vapours to which the added febrile air could potentially cause unnatural and unhealthy "swoons" and related ailments.[105] The position of the body in bed was also an important part of procuring pleasant sleep and dreams. In 1772 the anonymous author of *Directions and observations relative to food, exercise and sleep* advised sleeping on the right side, with the head "raised higher than other parts of the body" so that the vapours from "concoction" arising from the stomach were freely able to ascend to the brain.[106]

In addition to writing a treatise on dreams, Thomas Tryon wrote extensively on the importance of well-ventilated bedrooms for promoting the health of the sleeping inhabitants. An eclectic writer, vegetarian and promoter of general health, Tryon penned numerous works that emphasized the importance of clean beds and well-ventilated rooms for the overall preservation of health.[107] In *A treatise of cleanness in meats and drinks* (1682) Tryon included a section on the "excellence of good airs and the benefits of clean sweet beds:"

> Cleanness in Houses, especially in Beds, is a great Preserver of Health. Now Beds for the most part stand in Corners of Chambers and being ponderous close Substances, the refreshing Influences of the Air have no power to penetrate or destroy the gross Humidity that all such Places contract, where the Air hath not its free egress and regress. In these shady dull Places Beds are continued for many Years and hardly see the Sun or Elements. Besides, Beds suck in and receive all sorts of pernicious Excrements that are breathed forth by the Sweating of various sorts of People, which have Leprous and Languishing Diseases, which lie and die on them: The Beds, I say, receive all the several Vapours and Spirits and the same Beds are often continued for several Generations, without changing the Feathers, until the Ticks be rotten.[108]

Beds and bedrooms were consequently important contributors to good and bad health, which, like the porous body, were vulnerable to the noxious fumes of vapours and diseases circulating in the air. Interestingly, Tryon believed beds themselves were porous bodies that housed diseases as well as bugs in the mattresses and bed stands.

From Tryon's discussions we get a vivid picture of the unhealthiness of early modern beds and bedrooms. His various works on health also illustrate the fact that the immediate environment was perceived as a source of disease and discomfort for sleeping persons. Bed bugs, as Tryon notes, were a common hazard of early modern sleep, which, according to him, are germinated by the unclean excrements of the human body itself.[109] To combat the combined evils of unclean beds and noxious vapours in the bedroom, Tryon advised his readers to ventilate their bedrooms, destroy all bug-ridden beds and wash and clean the "woollens" and "linens" regularly "at least three or four times in a Year." Finally, for promoting the best sleep and overall health of the family, Tryon suggested that "moderate Clothing, hard Beds, Houses that stand so as that the pleasant Briezes of Wind may air and refresh them" are best.[110]

In addition to the physical environment, air and temperature of the sleeping individual, the planets were also believed to influence one's dreams. Both writers of dream treatises, Thomas Hill and Thomas Tryon, wrote of the influence of astrological forces in permeating and shaping the dreams of humankind. In *The moste pleasaunte arte of the interpretacion of dreames* (1576) Hill explained, "But well consideringe that the ayre is the outward cause of dreames, because in the first it receiveth the impression of the starres and after touchethe the bodies of men and beastes, whiche are altered of it yea in the daye tyme."[111] Considering the popularity of astrological medicine and contemporary beliefs about the macrocosm and microcosm, it is unsurprising that early modern medical ideas of natural dreams involved the influence of the planets. Tryon listed astrological factors as one of his seven-fold theory of dreams and wrote as follows:

> Others [dreams] are occasion'd by the influx of the Planets predominate in [the dreamer's] Nativity, or at such or such times by Direction, Transit, or the like, if we may believe the notions of Astrologers, whose science as far as modestly it contains its self within the Bounds of Nature with a Resignation alwayes to the over-ruling Pleasure of Omnipotency, seems not altogether to be contemned [sic].[112]

Richard Saunders (1613–1675) an astrologer-physician who published an astrological divination handbook that included a large section on oneiromancy, also accorded the planets an influence on dreams. In his lavishly illustrated work, *Physiognomie, chiromancie, metoposcopie* (1653), although he carefully disassociated himself from superstitious observations on dreams, Saunders included a section that explored "How to know the Dreams that Princes and other Persons have Dreamed, if extraordinary, by the Science of Chiromancy, joyning thereto the Secrets of Geomancy."[113] He also listed auspicious dates for dreams that depended on the position of sun, moon and planets as well as what particular dream symbols meant when occurring on particular astrological conjunctions.[114] In this way the planets were deemed

42   *"Seasons of sleep"*

to be additional external environmental forces, which were believed to influence the content of dreams.

Another significant external stimulus affecting dreams as well as the quality of sleep was the noises of the environment. As A. Roger Ekirch illustrates, early modern sleep was frequently interrupted by noises of the external world.[115] The noises of night watchmen calling in cities in the midnight hours, babies crying, animals baying, barking and bellowing, as well as the frightening noises of the weather – wind, thunder and lightning – all interrupted sleep and were believed to infiltrate the dreams of sleeping individuals. Conventional dream-lore dating back to Aristotle stated that night noises permeated the dreams of men and women, causing them to dream of what they unconsciously heard in sleep. Thomas Nashe summarized this notion in his discussion of the causes of night terrors, "Our dreames (the Ecchoes of the day) borrow of anie noyse we heare in the night. For example if in the dead of the night there be anie rumbling, knocking, or disturbance neere us, wee straight dreame of warres, of thunder."[116]

Noises heard in sleep were believed to affect dreams throughout the period. Joseph Addison remarked upon instances wherein the dreams of his readers were shaped and abruptly ended by the unwanted noises of chimney sweeps, watchmen and other "noisy slaves" in the early hours. He wrote in *The Spectator* on Wednesday, September 22, 1714,

> I have received numerous Complaints from several delicious Dreamers, desiring me to invent some Method for silencing those noisy Slaves, whose Occupations led them to take their early Rounds about the City in a Morning, doing a deal of Mischief and working strange Confusion in the Affairs of its Inhabitants. … A fair Lady was just upon the Point of being married to a young, handsome, rich, ingenious Nobleman, when an impertinent Tinker passing by, forbid the Banns; and an hopeful Youth, who had been newly advanced to great honour and Preferment, was forced by a neighbouring Cobbler to resign all for an old Song.[117]

Unfortunately for early modern folk, the noises of the night and early morning were a common complaint and led to intermittent sleep.[118] Elizabeth Drinker, an eighteenth-century diarist, wrote, "Did not sleep an hour all night" due to the "screaming in the street, howling of dogs and a thumping as I thought in our house."[119] More disturbing interruptions to sleep include the following nocturnal adventures that prevented an English traveller from sleeping in Scotland in 1677: "We might have rested, had not the mice rendezvoused over our faces."[120] In May 1705 Lady Cowper recounted that Sir Nicholas Armourer told her how "a Dolefull Bell:man used to disturb his sleep in the Night and throw him into some Melancholly Contemplations of Eternity."[121] The idea that noises directly influenced the content of dreams was also proved by experiments made on unknowing sleepers. James Beattie recounted a trick played on a sleeping soldier by his fellows, "I have heard of a gentleman in the army; whose imagination was so easily affected in sleep with impressions made on the outward senses, that his companions, by speaking softly in his ear, could cause him to dream of what they pleased."[122]

The physical position of the body in sleep was also believed to affect the quality of sleep, dreams and directly cause sleep disorders such as the "nightmare," "deade sleep" and "vigilance." According to most writers, drawing from Avicenna, the best position for the body at the outset of sleep was to sleep on the right side first and then move to the left side, after the "first sleep.[123] William Vaughan advised his reader to sleep "upon his right side, untill the meat which he hath eaten, be descended from the mouth of the stomack (which is on the left side) then let him sleepe upon his left side and upon his belly."[124] While this was ideal for those with strong digestive systems, persons suffering from "feeble digestion," according to Thomas Elyot, were advised to sleep on their bellies.[125] The theory of "concoction" and the humours dictated that for digestion to occur most "perfectly," the body had to be in the best possible position in sleep, allowing for a more "perfect sleep" and "quiet dreams." Sleeping on the back was "to be utterly abhorred" since this was believed to instigate the nightmare or *incubus,* a condition today known as sleep paralysis.[126]

Conclusion

The relationship of sleep, dreams and health in early modern medical and dream treatises was closely intertwined. Sleep was understood as the passive state in which natural dreams occurred while dreams themselves were the symptoms and products of good and bad health. From the sixteenth to the mid-eighteenth century, the ideas of the humours dominated models of health as well as underlying theories of sleep and dreams. Moderate sleep was viewed as part of the essential regimen of health whilst dreams themselves were fundamentally understood as products of the physiology of sleep and as useful clues to the imbalances of the four humours and hence of the overall physical and mental health of the individual.

Writings on sleep and dreams also reveal the porous model of the body and mind that were vulnerable to internal and external stimuli ranging from the inner senses, air, noises, the planets, supernatural beings and the physical surroundings of the sleeping individual. According to early modern medical writings, in sleep we are particularly vulnerable to a wide range of forces, which in turn infiltrate and directly influence our dreams. Underlying all ideas about natural dreams is the acute sense of the vulnerability of the early modern individual in sleep. Whilst we can seize a degree of control over diet and the length of sleep, we can control neither our dreams, nor autonomous internal and external forces. Within the framework of health, dreams offered important clues not only to the health of the body but also to that of the mind and soul. Writers who promoted a more psychological

44 *"Seasons of sleep"*

model of dreaming argued that dreams could also reveal the secret "inclinations" and preoccupations of the sleeping mind as well as providing significant insight into the moral or spiritual health of the soul.

In addition to ideas of natural dreams, the idea that dreams had a supernatural origin and offered insight into the future of the dreamer was persistent throughout the early modern period. English dreambooks, such as those authored by Thomas Hill and abridged editions of Artemidorus' *Oneirocritica,* appeared in the mid-sixteenth and seventeenth centuries, popularizing a model of dreams as lexicons to the fortunes of dreamers. The practice of oneiromancy and the popularity of dreambooks survived well into the eighteenth century, as the following chapter elucidates.

Notes

1 Lady Sarah Cowper, "Sarah Cowper's Diary," Volume 1, 1700–1702, Hertfordshire Archives and Local Studies, D/EP F29, edited by Adam Matthew Marlborough, *Defining Gender* (accessed 11 February 2015), fol. 141v, http://www.gender.amdigital.co.uk.myaccess.library.utoronto.ca/Documents/Details/Sarah%20Cowpers%20Diary%20Volume%201%2017001702.
2 *Ibid.,* 135; A. Roger Ekirch, *At Day's Close: Night in Times Past* (New York, London: W.W. Norton & Co., 2005), 332–33; "Sleep We Have Lost: Pre-Industrial Slumber in the British Isles," *The American Historical Review* 106, no. 2 (2001): 343–86.
3 Roger Schmidt, "Caffeine and the Coming of the Enlightenment," *Raritan* 23, no. 1 (Summer 2003): 129–49.
4 Sasha Handley, "Sociable Sleeping in Early Modern England, 1660–1760," *History* 98, no. 329 (January 2013): 79–104; *Sleep in early modern England* (London; New Haven: Yale University Press, 2016).
5 Galen, *On Diagnosis in Dreams,* translated by Lee Pearcy, 2008, (accessed 1 November 2009), http://www.ucl.ac.uk/~ucgajpd/medicina%20antiqua/tr_GalDreams.html. For an additional translation see: Steven M. Oberhelman, "Galen, On Diagnosis from Dreams," *Journal of the History of Medicine and Allied Sciences* 38 (1983): 36–47.
6 Galen, *Diagnosis in Dreams.*
7 Owen Felltham, *Resolves divine, moral, political* (London, 1677), 83. Note: the emphasis is Felltham's own.
8 Stanford Lehmberg, "Elyot, Sir Thomas (*c.* 1490–1546)," in *Oxford Dictionary of National Biography,* online edn., edited by Lawrence Goldman (Oxford: OUP, 2004), (accessed 30 November 2010), http://www.oxforddnb.com/view/article/8782.
9 Thomas Elyot, *The castle of healthe* … (Londoni, 1539), title page.
10 Thomas Cogan, *The haven of health chiefely gathered for the comfort of students and consequently of all those that have a care of their health* … (London, 1584); Nicholas Culpeper, *The English physitian, or An astrologo-physical discourse of the vulgar herbs of this nation being a compleat method of physick* … (London, 1652).
  PatrickCurry, "Culpeper, Nicholas (1616–1654)," in *Oxford Dictionary of National Biography,* online edn, edited by Lawrence Goldman (Oxford: OUP, 2004), (accessed 15 November 2010), http://www.oxforddnb.com/view/article/6882.
11 Thomas Hill, *The most pleasaunt arte of the interpretation of dreames whereunto is annexed sondrie problemes with apte aunsweares neare agreinge to the matter and very rare examples, not the like extant in the Englishe tongue* … (London, 1571),

partial copy; Thomas Hill, *The moste pleasuante arte of the interpretacion of dreames whereunto is annexed sundry problemes with apte aunsweares neare agreeing to the matter and very rare examples ...* (London, 1576).

12 Haydock, *Oneirologia*. E.P. Scarlett, "Richard Haydock: Being the Account of a Jacobean Physician Who is Also Known to History as 'The Sleeping Clergyman'," *Canadian Medical Association Journal* 60 (1949): 177–182; "An extract of Richard Haydock's *Oneirologia*," British Library, MS Landsdowne 489, fols. 129–32.

13 Thomas Tryon, *Treatise of dreams & visions* (London, 1689); *A treatise of dreams & visions ...* (London, 1695); *A treatise of dreams & visions ...* (London, 1700).

14 Anon, *Nocturnal revels: or, a general history of dreams ...* (London, 1706); *Nocturnal revels; or, an universal dream-book. ...* (London, 1749); *Nocturnal revels; or, a universal dream-book. ...* (London, 1750); *Nocturnal revels; or, a universal dream-book ...* (London, 1767); *Nocturnal revels: or, universal interpretor of dreams and visions ...* (London, 1789).

15 Mary Lindemann, *Medicine and Society in Early Modern Europe* (Cambridge: Cambridge University Press, 1999), 68.

16 Thomas Elyot, *The castle of health ...* (London, 1610), 70–72. The first edition of this text, as mentioned earlier, was printed in 1539.

17 Andrew Boorde, *The breviarie of health wherin doth folow, remedies, for all maner of sicknesses & diseases, the which may be in man or woman ...* (London, 1587), 65r.

18 Haydock, "Oneirologia," fol. 7r.

19 Patrick Woodland, 'Beale, John (*bap.* 1608, *d.* 1683)', *Oxford Dictionary of National Biography*, Oxford University Press, 2004; online edition, Jan 2008, (accessed 21 May 2015), http://www.oxforddnb.com.myaccess.library.utoronto.ca/view/article/1802.

20 John Beale, "Treatise on the Art of Interpreting Dreams," Undated, 25/19/1-28, in *The Hartlib Papers: A Complete Text and Image Database of the Papers of Samuel Hartlib (C.1600–1660)*, edited by Mark Greengrass, Michael Leslie and Michael Hannon, Held in Sheffield University Library, 2nd ed. (Sheffield, 2002), 25/19/9A.

21 Lindemann, *Medicine and Society*, 12.

22 Elyot, *Castle of health* (1610), 3.

23 Wilhelm Scribonius, *Naturall philosophy, or, A description of the world, namely, of angels, of man, of the heavens, of the ayre, of the earth, of the water and of the creatures in the whole world.* Translated by Daniel Widdowes (London, 1621), 50. Widdowes's translation was based on Scribonius' Latin work *Rerum naturalium doctrina methodica* first published in 1538. The English edition was published three times in the seventeenth century.

24 Hill, *Interpretacion of dreames* (1576), Bviii(r); Anon., *The problemes of Aristotle with other philosophers and phisitions. Wherein are contayned divers questions, with their answers, touching the estate of mans bodie* (Edinburgh, 1595), E4r- E5r; Thomas Cogan, *The haven of health ...* (London, 1636), 274; Francis De Valangin, *A treatise on diet, or the management of human life; by physicians called the six non-naturals ...* (London, 1768), 275–76; Anon., *Directions and observations relative to food exercise and sleep* (London, 1772), 9, 22–23.

25 Thomas Walkington, *The optick glasse of humors ...* (London, 1607), 29–30; William Vaughan, *Approved directions for health, both naturall and artificiall derived from the best physitians as well moderne as auncient ...* (London, 1612), 58–61; Levine Lemnie, *The touchstone of complexions: expedient and profitable for all such as bee desirous and carefull of their bodily health ...* (London, 1633), B1r-B2r, 90–95.

46 *"Seasons of sleep"*

26 Karl H. Dannenfeldt, "Sleep: Theory and Practice in the Late Renaissance," *Journal of the History of Medicine and Allied Sciences* 41, no. 4 (1986): 415.
27 Elyot, *Castle of health* (1610), 70.
28 Vaughan, *Approved directions for health,* 58; Ceri Davies, "Vaughan, Sir William (*c.* 1575–1641)," in *Oxford Dictionary of National Biography*, online edn, edited by Lawrence Goldman (Oxford: OUP, 2004), (accessed 1 December 2010), http://www.oxforddnb.com.myaccess.library.utoronto.ca/view/article/28151.
29 Lemnie, *Touchstone of complexions*, 95.
30 *Ibid.*
31 Hill, *Interpretacion of dreames* (1576), Cvii(r).
32 Haydock, fols. 4v-5r.
33 De Valangin, *Treatise on diet*, 269–70.
34 *Ibid.*
35 Scribonius, *Naturall philosophy*, 51.
36 Haydock, fol. 14.
37 Thomas Nashe, *The terrors of the night or, A discourse of apparitions* (London, 1594), Eiiii(v).
38 Cogan, *Haven of health* (1636), 268–70.
39 Hill, *Interpretacion of dreames* (1576), Diiii(v).
40 Tryon, *Treatise of dreams & visions* (1695), 11–12. The italics in this passage are Tryon's own.
41 Ann Marie Plane, *Dreams and the Invisible World in Colonial New England: Indians, Colonists and the Seventeenth Century* (Philadelphia, PA: University of Pennsylvania Press, 2014), 6.
42 *Ibid.*
43 Elyot, *Castle of health* (1610), 3.
44 *Ibid.*, 3–5.
45 *Ibid.*, 1–5; Boorde, *Breviarie of health,* 44v; Hill, *Interpretacion of dreames* (1576), Dv(v)-Dvi(r); Nashe, *Terrors of the night*, Ciiii(v); Walkington, *Optick glasse of humors,* 30; Thomas Wright, *The passions of the minde in generall. Corrected, enlarged and with sundry new discourses augmented* … (London, 1604), 65; Vaughan, *Approved directions for health*, 61–65; Helkiah Crooke, *Mikrokosmographia a description of the body of man* … (London, 1615), 500; Robert Burton, *The anatomy of melancholy*, edited by Holbrook Jackson (New York: NYRB, 2001), Part. I, 160; James Ferrand, *Erotomania or A treatise discoursing of the essence, causes, symptomes, prognosticks and cure of love, or erotique melancholy* (Oxford, 1640), 182–83; Felltham, *Resolves*, 83; Tryon, *Treatise of dreams & visions* (1695), 11–12; *A collection of miscellany letters, selected out of Mist's Weekly Journal*, Vol. 1 (London, 1722), 164.
46 Tryon, *Treatise of dreams & visions* (1695), 53–55.
47 Ralph Josselin, *The Diary of Ralph Josselin 1616–1683*, edited by Alan Macfarlane (London: Oxford University Press, 1976), 20.
48 Katherine Austen, "Book M," British Library, MS Add. 4454, fol. 25.
49 Cowper, "Diary," Vol. 1, fol. 141v.
50 Wright, *Passions of the minde*, 65.
51 Nashe, *Terrors of the night*, Eii(v)-Eiiii(r).
52 Haydock, fol. 8r.
53 De Valangin, *Treatise on diet*, 306–307.
54 Burton, *The anatomy of melancholy*, Part. I, 160.
55 Cogan, *Haven of health* (1636), 268–69.
56 Thomas Cheesman, *Death compared to sleep in a sermon preacht upon the occasion of the funeral of Mrs. Mary Allen, who died Feb. 18, anno Dom. 1695* … (London, 1695).
57 Cotton Mather, *Awakening thoughts on the sleep of death* … (Boston, 1712), 10.

58 Filip Krajnik, "In the Shadow of Night: Sleeping and Dreaming and Their Technical Roles in Shakespearian Drama" (Doctoral, Durham University, 2013), 236, (accessed 18 April 2016), http://etheses.dur.ac.uk/7764/.

59 *Ibid.*, 226–29; Garrett A. Sullivan, *Sleep, Romance and Human Embodiment: Vitality from Spenser to Milton* (Cambridge: Cambridge University Press, 2012), 121.

60 Hieronymus Magomastix, *The strange witch at Greenwich, (ghost, spirit, or hobgoblin) haunting a wench, late servant to a miser, suspected a murtherer of his late wife* ... (London, 1650), 14.

61 Peter Marshall, "'The Map of God's Word': Geographies of the Afterlife in Tudor and Early Stuart England," in *The Place of the Dead*, edited by Peter Marshall and Bruce Gordon (Cambridge: Cambridge University Press, 2000), 116–17.

62 Isaac Ambrose, *Ultima, = the last things in reference to the first and middle things: or certain meditations on life, death, judgement, hell, right purgatory and heaven* (London, 1650), 2–3.

63 Cowper, "Diary," Vol. 1, 1700–1702, fol. 20r.

64 Elizabeth Isham, "My Booke of Remembrance," edited by Elizabeth Clarke and Erica Longfellow, 34r, (accessed 29 April 2016), http://web.warwick.ac.uk/english/perdita/Isham/bor_p34r.htm.

65 Koslofsky, *Evening's Empire.*

66 Burton, *Anatomy of Melancholy*, Part. I, 160.

67 *Ibid.*, Part. I, 159–60; Thomas Hobbes, *Leviathan* (London: Penguin, 1985), 87–91; Thomas Branch, *Thoughts on dreaming* ... (London, 1738), 66.

68 Nashe, *Terrors of the night*, Ciii(v).

69 Philip Goodwin, *The mystery of dreames, historically discoursed* ... (London, 1658), B2v.

70 *Ibid.*, A3v.

71 Joseph Hall, *The contemplations upon the history of the New Testament, now complete: together with divers treatises reduced to the greater volume* (London, 1661), 488.

72 Richard Haydock, "'Oneirologia, or, a Brief Discourse of the Nature of Dreames," *Dramatic and Poetical Miscellany,* Folger Shakespeare Library, MS J.a.1. Vol. 5, f. 10.

73 Henry More, *Enthusiasmus triumphatus, or, A discourse of the nature, causes, kinds and cure, of enthusiasme...* (London, 1656), 3.

74 J. M. Scott, "Branch, Thomas (*fl.* 1738–1753)," revised by Robert Brown, in *Oxford Dictionary of National Biography*, online edn., edited by Lawrence Goldman (Oxford: OUP, 2004), (accessed 1 December 2010), http://www.oxforddnb.com/view/article/3247.

75 Andrew Baxter, *An enquiry into the nature of the human soul; wherein the immateriality of the soul is evinced from the principles of reason and philosophy* (London, 1733), 201.

76 *Ibid.*, 200.

77 *Ibid.,* 215.

78 *Ibid.*, 253.

79 Branch, *Thoughts on dreaming*, 3–6.

80 *Ibid.*, 5. Note: the italics are Branch's own.

81 *Ibid.*, 9.

82 *Ibid.*, 29.

83 *Ibid.*, 66.

84 David Hartley, *Observations on man, his frame, his duty and his expectations. In two parts* (London: London, 1749), 384.

85 John Trenchard, *The natural history of superstition* (London, 1709), 11.

48 *"Seasons of sleep"*

86 Hobbes, *Leviathan,* 90–97, 167–78, 344, 429; Henry More, *Enthusiasmus triumphatus, or, A discourse of the nature, causes, kinds and cure, of enthusiasme* (London, 1656), 2–6, 12, 16, 24–31; Meric Casaubon, *A treatise concerning enthusiasme, as it is an effect of nature: but is mistaken by many for either divine inspiration, or diabolical possession* (London, 1654), A1r, 3–10; Trenchard, *Natural history of superstition,* 1–20; David Hume, *An Enquiry Concerning Human Understanding,* edited by Eric Steinberg (Indianapolis: Hackett Pub. Co., 1977), 71–91.

87 Lucia Dacome, "'To What Purpose Does It Think': Dreams, Sick Bodies and Confused Minds in the Age of Reason," *History of Psychiatry* 15, no. 4 (2004): 395–416.

88 John M. Cooper ed., *Plato: Complete Works* (Indianapolis: Hacket Pub. Co., 1997), 269; J. Barnes ed. *The Complete Works of Aristotle,* Vol. 1 (New Jersey: Princeton University Press, 1984), 727–733.

89 Izaak Walton, *The lives of Dr. John Donne, Sir Henry Wotton, Mr Richard Hooker, Mr George Herbert …* (London, 1670), 15. This work was originally published in 1651.

90 Amyraut, *Discourse concerning divine dreams,* 15.

91 Artemidorus, *The Interpretation of Dreams: Oneirocritica,* translated by Robert J. White (Park Ridge, NJ: Noyes Classical Studies, 1975), 21.

92 John M. Cooper ed., *Plato: Complete Works* (Indianapolis: Hackett Pub. Co., 1997), 1180.

93 Roger North, "On Dreams," British Library, MS Add. 32526, fol. 16.

94 Tryon, *Treatise on dreams & visions* (1695), 6–7.

95 Felltham, *Resolves,* 82.

96 Thomas Browne, *The Major Works,* ed. Geoffrey Keynes, Vol. 1 (Oxford: Oxford University Press, 1964), 476–77.

97 Donald F. Bond ed., *The Spectator* Vol. 5. No. 585–635 (Oxford: Clarendon Press, 1965), 4.

98 Hume, *Enquiry Concerning Human Understanding,* 268.

99 Samuel Forman Conover, *An inaugural dissertation on sleep and dreams; their effects on the faculties of the mind and the causes of dreams …* (Philadelphia, 1791), 14.

100 Wright, *Passions of the minde,* 65.

101 James Beattie, *Dissertations moral and critical …* (London, 1783), 227.

102 Sasha Handley discusses the material culture of beds and bedrooms in her recent study, *Sleep in Early Modern England* (2016), 39–61.

103 Cogan, *Haven of health* (1636), 272–73.

104 Lemnie, *Touchstone of complexions,* 90.

105 Cogan, *Haven of health* (1636), 273.

106 *Directions and observations,* 23.

107 Thomas Tryon, *A treatise of cleanness in meats and drinks of the preparation of food, the excellency of good airs and the benefits of clean sweet beds also of the generation of bugs and their cure …* (London, 1682); *Healths grand preservative: or The womens best doctor …* (London, 1682); *The good house-wife made a doctor…* (London, 1692); *Miscellania: or, A collection of necessary, useful and profitable tracts on variety of subjects which for their excellency and benefit of mankind, are compiled in one volume …* (London, 1696).

108 Tryon, *Treatise of cleanness in meats,* 5.

109 *Ibid.,* 7.

110 *Ibid.,* 10.

111 Hill, *Interpretacion of dreames* (1576), Bvii(r).

112 Tryon, *Treatise of dreams & visions* (1695), 48–49.

"Seasons of sleep" 49

113 Richard Saunders, *Physiognomie and chiromancie, metoposcopie* ... (London, 1653), Chapter IX.
114 *Ibid.*, Book 2, 203–12.
115 Ekirch, "Sleep We Have Lost," 358.
116 Nashe, *Terrors of the night,* Ciiii(v).
117 Bond, *Spectator,* 41.
118 Ekirch, *At Day's Close,* 292–93.
119 Quoted in Ekirch, *At Day's Close,* 293.
120 *Ibid.*
121 Lady Sarah Cowper, "Diary," Volume 3, 1705–1706, Hertfordshire Archives and Local Studies, D/EP F31, *Perdita Manuscripts,* (accessed 12 February 2015), 35v, http://www.perditamanuscripts.amdigital.co.uk.myaccess.library.utoronto. ca/collections/doc-detailsearch.aspx?documentid=20823&searchmode= true&previous=0&dt=10140711280637808&aid=Women&id=2.
122 Beattie, *Dissertations moral and critical,* 217.
123 Avicenna had also written about dreams as useful for diagnosing illness in his *Canon of Medicine,* a commonly used textbook of medicine in the medieval period, believed to have been written in 1025 CE. For a discussion of the ideas of dreams in Acivenna, Aristotle and Scaliger, see, Kristine Louise Haugen, "Aristotle My Beloved: Poetry, Diagnosis and the Dreams of Julius Caesar Scaliger," *Renaissance Quarterly* 60, no. 3 (2007): 819–51.
124 Vaughan, *Approved directions for health,* 59.
125 Elyot, *Castle of health* (1610), 72.
126 *Ibid.*

2 Decoding dreams
Dreambooks and dream divination

Introduction

Particularly vivid and ominous dreams were frequently recorded in private early modern English writings. On the 24th November 1582, John Dee had the following dream: "Saterday night I dremed that I was deade and afterward my bowels wer taken out I walked and talked with diverse and among other with the Lord Thresorer [sic] who was com to my howse to burn my bokes when I was dead and thought he loked sourely on me."[1] Such narratives often recounted horrible nightmarish scenes of death, illness and suffering, as did John Dee's dream of being disembowelled, as well as anxious montages from everyday life, like those in Ralph Josselin's diary.[2] What is clear from such writings is that certain dreams were often recorded because the writer believed them especially auspicious. The abundant records of private dreams in journals, diaries and letters reveal to us the significance of the dream in a diversity of early modern lives. As Peter Burke, Charles Carlton, Patricia Crawford, Ann Plane and others have demonstrated, early modern dream narratives also provide some of the most direct avenues into the rich, deeply emotional, cultural and psychological landscapes of early modern men, women and, on the more rare occasions, children.[3]

Alongside the idea that the dream provided insight into individual health, the belief that dreams were predictive and could offer glimpses of the future of dreamers and their families was persistent in English culture throughout the early modern period. Evidence for belief in predictive dreams can be found in private writings as well as in the continued market for dreambooks, fortune-telling books, almanacs and other ephemeral publications featuring sections of oneiromancy, which circulated from the late sixteenth to the eighteenth century. A comparative study of printed handbooks of oneiromancy reveals that writers essentially copied, often *verbatim,* the dream interpretations of two works – Artemidorus' *Oneirocritica* (2nd century CE) and the most popular medieval dreambook, the *Somniale Danielis.* Little of the content of English dreambooks was therefore new and authors typically recycled dream interpretations from these perennial dreambooks with little modification. The evolution of dreambooks and the practice of oneiromancy in early modern England is therefore indicative of a legacy that represented the hybridization and vulgarization of Artemidorus and the *Somniale Danielis*. This demonstrates a long thread of continuity between classical and medieval oneiromancy and the early modern practice.

What was new in the period is that while publications of dreambooks remained steady from the sixteenth to the eighteenth century, these works were notably eclipsed and superseded by the new wave of ephemeral fortune-telling books and almanacs. The trade in handbooks of divination and almanacs flourished amidst the popular revival of a debased form of astrology. This lucrative industry was also reflective of the broader explosion of print culture in the seventeenth and eighteenth centuries. Another notable development included the evolution of dream divination from a learned practice, represented by the Humanist Greek and Latin editions of Artemidorus in the sixteenth century, to one that was made more accessible to a broader audience through vernacular, simplified and abridged editions of dreambooks. Yet such rudimentary dream interpretation handbooks were themselves the direct heirs of the medieval "dreambook proper," in particular the *Somniale Danielis*, which contained alphabetical lists of dreams with their brief interpretations. Dreambooks, almanacs and other fortune-telling books also shamelessly pilfered their content from the *Oneirocritica*, the *Somniale Danielis* or perhaps each other. Subsequently, there was little original content in published works of oneiromancy from the sixteenth to the eighteenth century. Overall, this suggests there was more continuity than change to the early modern practice of oneiromancy.

This chapter aims to present a more nuanced understanding of another of the major frameworks used to understand, decode and ascribe meaning to the dream – prediction or oneiromancy. Little work has been undertaken on studying the history, print culture and content of early modern dreambooks. By examining early modern English dreambooks and other works featuring oneiromancy, the chapter will trace the practice of oneiromancy from its classical and medieval roots and highlight the major techniques of divination used to decode the dream. Additionally, to shed new light on early modern understandings of dreams as well as people's predominant daily concerns, the most prominent dream symbols and their corresponding interpretations will be discussed, including the prevalent themes of death and the dead, love and sexuality, the dream body and gender.

Narratives of dreams appear in a diverse range of early modern private writings, such as those of the astrologer and physician Simon Forman (1552–1611); Archbishop William Laud (1573–1645); Nehemiah Wallington (1598–1658), a London turner; Katherine Austen (1629–1683); Alice Thornton (1626–1707) and Samuel Pepys (1633–1703), amongst countless others.[4] Each of these individuals recorded multiple dreams throughout the course of his or her life. While historians have studied dream narratives through the lens of modern psychology, fewer studies have sought to understand in depth how early modern dreamers themselves might have

52   *Decoding dreams*

understood their dreams.[5] A study of the dreams recorded by early modern English authors demonstrates how the idea that dreams could predict the future was prevalent from the sixteenth through to the eighteenth century, at least among the literate.

Dreams of death and the dead feature prominently in the private records of Ralph Josselin, Elias Ashmole, Katherine Austen and Alice Thornton, amongst others. The possibility that a dream might predict the death, illness or misfortune of a member of one's household or community seems to have haunted the conscious and unconscious minds of men and women. As not all dreams were necessarily significant and were subject to the laws of contraries and similitudes, oneiromancy required a specialized knowledge of the multifarious meanings of dream-symbols. For example, while the law of contraries held that dreams should be interpreted according to their opposite outcomes, the law of similitudes stipulated that certain dreams should be interpreted according to like symbols that predicted similar outcomes. A specific dream-symbol might have a positive or negative outcome that also depended on the age, wealth and gender as well as the social and marital status of the dreamer.

Dream divination handbooks therefore offered readers a valuable tool for decoding their dreams, giving easily referenced interpretations based on comprehensive lists of dream-symbols. Moreover, according to English writers of dreambooks, an accurate understanding of one's resolve or dreams allowed the individual to avert a potential disaster or strengthened one's the "patience" to endure it.[6] Thomas Hill gave this argument about the usefulness of dream divination in *The moste pleasuante arte of the interpretacion of dreames* (1576):

> What a comfort wil it be to hym that examining the cyrcumstances in their due tyme & order, shal prognosticate what such things portende. And thereby may solace himself with good happes and labour to prevent or hinder the imminent mysffortune, or at the least arme hymselfe so stronglye wyth patience as quietly to beare them.[7]

The desire to understand the meaning of dreams and the belief that they could predict the future helps to explain why diarists may have recorded certain dreams above others. Being at the mercy of death, disease, accidents and supernatural forces beyond their control, the drive to know the future and thereby to prepare for or change it, appears to have led many men and women to seek clues from their dreams. Belief in predictive dreams was simultaneously bolstered by both classical and biblical endorsements of dream interpretation. Records of dreams reveal another facet of the individual dreamer's sense of vulnerability to the combined forces of the unknown future. At the same time, some writers, such as Alice Thornton and Katherine Austen, viewed their experiences of prognostic dreams as a sign of God's providence and perennial care.[8]

As will be explored in Chapter 3, there is an inherent tension in records and discussions of predictive dreams in private writings as well as in dreambooks, fortune-telling books and other handbooks of divination and astrology. In many cases, individual diarists and authors sought to defend or reconcile the art against its critics who argued that to seek knowledge of the future was to contravene Providence and presumptuously seek knowledge that belonged to God alone. The root of the problem for writers and individuals concerned with irreligion was that the Bible warned against false prophecy and divination even while it, on the other hand, advocated for its orthodoxy. So too, the practice of oneiromancy as a form of pagan divination was a legacy of the ancient Greeks that some argued was superstitious, irreligious and unfit for Christians. Although authors such as Thomas Hill, Richard Saunders and William Lilly, amongst others, defended oneiromancy as an orthodox practice, supported by the Scriptures and classical writings, many early modern men and women remained wary of ascribing too much meaning to dreams. Yet outright rejections of predictive dreams were few and individuals themselves might oscillate between belief in and scepticism of the oracular function of dreams.

Despite ongoing concerns about the practice of dream divination, the evidence of private writings and continued market for dreambooks suggests the persistence of belief in predictive dreams. Unfortunately, in private memoirs only a few writers offer insight into how they interpreted their dreams: most men and women recorded their dreams without providing any reflection or interpretation. However, the numerous handbooks of dream divination that circulated in the period can provide more detail of early modern beliefs in prognostic dreams. While we have little evidence as to who precisely read and purchased English dreambooks, the fact that they continued to be printed well into the nineteenth century does suggest an ongoing interest in and market for them.[9] Moreover, as I will develop later in the chapter, the gendering of dreams in these handbooks, which include references to both men and women's dreams, indicates they catered to both male and female audiences. Similarly, the simple format, affordability and content of dreambooks suggest they were marketed at a broadly literate audience. However, as Adam Fox and other historians have suggested, early modern literacy was complex and the authors and audiences of "popular literature," including those of almanacs, chapbooks and dreambooks, are difficult to assess with any certainty.[10] The evidence of dreambooks, fortune-telling books, almanacs and courtesy books thus must be considered alongside other writings on dreams, including diaries, journals and letters. What becomes clear from a review of a broader collection of writings on dreams is that neither was belief in their predictive properties confined to the "popular" masses nor was scepticism solely the purview of the learned sort.

During this study, all extant English printed works that either featured or included sections of oneiromancy and discussions of prognostic dreams were compiled. These texts can be broadly categorized into five

54 *Decoding dreams*

genres: (1) dreambooks; (2) dream treatises; (3) fortune-telling books; (4) almanacs and (5) courtship books. Dreambooks included works that were primarily designed as handbooks of dream interpretation and incorporate, for example, the *Somniale Danielis* and the many English editions of Artemidorus' *Oneirocritica*. Dream treatises, on the other hand, were more serious semi-learned works that featured long discussions about the different categories of dreams, their causes and meanings. Significant dream treatises in the period include Thomas Tryon's *A treatise of dreams and visions* (1689) and Philip Goodwin's *The mystery of dreames, historically discoursed* (1658). However, these works paled in popularity to the flourishing genre of fortune-telling books, courtesy books and almanacs that, being introduced in the sixteenth century, grew exponentially, reaching their zenith in the long eighteenth century.

While dreambooks functioned solely as handbooks of dream interpretation, fortune-telling books, almanacs and courtship books appealed to a larger audience by offering a more diverse range of information. In addition to oneiromancy, fortune-telling books contained knowledge of a variety of divination techniques, including numerology, astrology, palmistry and moleoscopy (divination by moles on the face).[11] As part of the flourishing genre of chapbooks and prescriptive literature, courtship books were marketed as handbooks providing "delightful" and "profitable" instructions for a successful courtship while almanacs were designed as useful handbooks with all manner of practical information. These eclectic compendiums of knowledge included everything from directions for dream divination to lists of local fairs and markets, medical cures and astrological prognostications, some even including blank pages so they could be used as diaries or notebooks.[12]

Artemidorus and the *Oneirocritica*

English dreambooks typically recycled excerpts of dream interpretations from Artemidorus' original work the *Oneirocritica* and popular medieval manuals accredited to the biblical dream interpreter, Daniel. A comparison of early modern dreambooks and the *Oneirocritica* demonstrates that Artemidorus was essentially the forefather of premodern dreambooks.[13] A professional dream interpreter about whom little is known for certain, Artemidorus Daldianus (or Ephesius) is believed to have lived in the second century CE and was originally from Ephesus.[14] During his lifetime he wrote five collected books on dream interpretation. The first three were dedicated to Cassius Maximus while the last two were bequeathed to his son who was training as a professional oneiromancer. The compiled works became known as the *Oneirocritica* (or *Oneirokritikon* in Greek), perhaps the most influential dreambook in the western tradition.[15] This text offered readers not only an extensive compendium of dream symbols with their corresponding interpretations but also a detailed and sophisticated classification of

Decoding dreams 55

dreams along with instructions for practitioners concerning the rules and best practice of oneiromancy. As the classicist Robert J. White explained, Artemidorus' achievement was to present a systematic and rational practice of dream interpretation, which eradicated much of the prior "superstition and mysticism."[16] It was likely this rationalism and sophistication combined with the extensive dream interpretations that appealed to later writers and led to the perpetual popularity of the work as a handbook of oneiromancy.

Artemidorus' seven-fold theory of dreams was emulated by such later writers as Macrobius and was still subscribed to by early modern dreambooks and writings on dreams. The *Oneirocritica* divided dreams into two main categories: (1) *enhypnion* or meaningless things that occur in sleep and (2) *oneiros* – significant dreams. Artemidorus divided *oneiros* dreams into two further subcategories: (1) *theorematic* or predictive dreams that explicitly represented future events and (2) *allegorical* dreams, which contained glimpses of the future encoded in symbols that required an interpretation. *Allegorical* dreams were then subdivided into five categories: (1) *personal* (involving the self); (2) *alien* (involving others); (3) *common* (involving self and others); (4) *public* (involving public places) and (5) *cosmic* dreams (involving "cosmic" symbols such as planets, stars, etc., which predict "cosmic" outcomes).[17] According to this schema, only *allegorical* dreams required an interpretation as the *enhypnion* were meaningless and *theorematic* dreams were explicit representations of the future. The *Oneirocritica* was therefore an extensive and in-depth manual for interpreting *allegorical* dreams.

Originally written in Greek, the *Oneirocritica* most likely reached a Continental and English audience during the Renaissance, when texts lost to the West were reintroduced via the Middle East instigated by the Humanist revival of the classics. The earliest extant manuscript of Artemidorus derives from the eleventh century, although earlier Arabic translations survive from the ninth or tenth century.[18] The first printed Latin edition appeared in 1518 and was printed in Venice at the famous printing house of Andreas Torresanus de Asula (1451–1529) and Heredi di Aldo Manuzio.[19] However, the most authoritative edition of Artemidorus circulating in the sixteenth century was the Latin translation by the Saxon Humanist scholar Janus Cornarius (1500–1558) and published by Hieronymus Froben in 1539. Froben reprinted this edition in 1544 and another version was issued from the Parisian printing house of S. Gryphium in 1546.[20] While these editions were confined to a learned audience, other German, French and Italian translations were published in the sixteenth century making Artemidorus more widely accessible.

Continental Humanist editions of the *Oneirocritica* circulated amongst the educated in early modern England. It is likely that the Froben 1539 edition of Artemidorus was the copy that Thomas Hill consulted for *The moste pleasaunte arte of the interpretacion of dreames* (1576), which was essentially an English translation of Books 1 to 4 of the *Oneirocritica*. Hill may have had access to this edition of Artemidorus in the library of John Dee, whom he thanked for his earlier education in *The contemplation of*

56   *Decoding dreams*

mankind (1571).[21] Dee had a substantial library with over 2,000 titles at his house at Mortlake. In the self-compiled index of his collection, Dee records owning "Artemidoriy de somnys lay 8o frob 1539."[22] According to Francis R. Johnson, Dee was known to take on students and allow scholars to consult with and use his library. It is therefore possible that Hill was given access to Dee's collection and consulted the work of Artemidorus at Mortlake.[23] Interestingly, rare copies of early sixteenth-century Latin editions of Artemidorus, including the 1518 edition by the Aldine Press and the 1604 edition printed in Paris by Marc Orry were sold in exclusive English book sales in the late eighteenth century, demonstrating how such scholarly editions had by this time become valuable curios for book collectors and antiquarians.[24] However, during the seventeenth and eighteenth centuries, far more popular were the English translations of Artemidorus.

Demonstrative of an ongoing interest in dream interpretation and inspired by the growing appetite for cheap, simplified, vernacular handbooks of divination and astrology, the first English edition of Artemidorus' classic dreambook appeared in 1606 as *The judgement, or exposition of dreames*. This work was published by R. Braddock for William Jones in London at the "signe of the Gun" and was translated by R.W., possibly Robert Wood a prolific seventeenth-century translator of French and Latin works.[25] This edition presented a brief two-page overview of Artemidorus' extensive discussion and classification of dreams from Book 1 of the *Oneirocritica* and then proceeded directly into the dream interpretations. The work was a lasting success. Between 1606 and 1786 there were 26 editions of Artemidorus' *The Interpretation of Dreams* published in England. However, of these only 14 editions have survived to the present day.

While early modern English dreambooks, fortune-telling works, almanacs and courtship books copied examples of dream interpretations from Artemidorus, they largely ignored his sophisticated system of dream classification and extensive commentary on dreams. Instead, English works presented grossly simplified versions of the *Oneirocritica*, following the format of the medieval "dreambook proper" and the *Somniale Danielis* – to dream of x signifies y. In this way English authors of oneiromancy fused the two dreambooks, appropriating the extensive dreams contained in the *Oneirocritica* and presenting them in the simplified format of the *Somniale Danielis*. Furthermore, these works simplified the original content, omitting the lengthy explanations for particular dream interpretations offered by Artemidorus and emulating the simpler format of the *Somniale Danielis*, synthesizing the best of both works into a more accessible system of dream interpretation.

Somniale Danielis

Equal to the influence of Artemidorus on English dreambooks, is that of the *Somniale Danielis*. This work was the most popular medieval handbook of dream interpretation. Scholars believe the original was written in the fourth

Decoding dreams 57

Figure 2.1 "The power of counsel." Engraving by Adrian Collaert after Jan van der Straet, Antwerp, 1567/1605. Wellcome Library, London.

century in Greek, which was then translated into Latin and a plethora of vernacular languages from the ninth to the sixteenth century. The popularity of the *Somniale Danielis* in the medieval world is illustrated by the fact that scholars have identified over 70 surviving manuscripts of this text in Latin, French, German, English and Welsh, representing, according to the medievalist Lawrence T. Martin, "nearly every area of Europe."[26] The fact that this work was translated into vernacular languages suggests that it was adapted for a lay audience.

The work itself slowly evolved over the centuries. As Steven Kruger explains, these manuals circulated extensively in the Middle Ages in manuscript form, with different authors often adding dreams so that multiple editions and versions exist. The *Somniale Danielis* was a "dreambook proper," a medieval genre of dreambooks that interpreted dreams, often alphabetically, based on the content of the dream.[27] Authors of medieval dreambooks sought to establish credibility for their texts by ascribing them to biblical figures: consequently, these works were bolstered by the strong tradition of prophetic and predictive dreams in the Bible.[28] A typical example of the content and format in this work is as follows:

> A man to be [turned] in to a beste [beast] by-toknith offence of God.
> A man that thynkyth beastis and sayle hym, his ennemyes shul trauaylyn hym.

58   *Decoding dreams*

A ffoure-footid beste betokeneth that thyn ennemyes shul be glad be-forn the[e].
To have a long berd [beard] by-toknith streng[t]h.
To se[e] a berd bi-toknyth grete harme.
A man that dremeth, that byrdys [birds] ffyghten with hym, it be-tokneth wrath [sic].[29]

Here we can see the simple format of the text. The basic model of "this dream means this outcome" in medieval dreambooks was one authors of early modern English dreambooks, including Thomas Hill, emulated.[30]

Besides the *Oneirocritica*, the *Somniale Danielis* was the main original source of dream interpretations contained in seventeenth- and eighteenth-century English dreambooks and fortune-telling books. A detailed comparison of the dream interpretations in fifteenth- and sixteenth-century Latin and English manuscripts of the *Somniale Danielis* and seventeenth- and eighteenth-century dreambooks, fortune-telling works, courtesy books and almanacs clearly demonstrates this fact. For example, the 1556 English edition of the *Somniale Danielis*, (entitled simply *Daniels dreams)*, lists the following dream interpretations: "A man that dreameth that he goeth to wed a mayde, betokeneth anguyshe ... to dreame to wed a whyfe, betokeneth harme ... to speake with a kynge, or an emperoure, betokeneth dygntye."[31] The popular fortune-telling book, *Dr Flamstead's and Mr Partridge's new Fortune Book* (1729), explains that dreaming of marrying a woman or being at a wedding signifies loss and damage due to the death of a friend while speaking to a king in a dream was good.[32] As another example, *The compleat book of knowledge* (1698) included interpretations for dreams including "to have a long beard," "to shoot a bow," "to see your friends and relations dead" and "to play with dogs" along with a plethora of others that appear in the earlier editions of the *Somniale Danielis*.[33] Similarly, notably recurring dream symbols often found in seventeenth- and eighteenth-century dreambooks, "to fly," "to fall down a hill," "to see serpents attack you" and "to see friends are well," all appear in English fifteenth- and sixteenth-century versions of the *Somniale Danielis*.[34] Another possibility is that these works may have simply copied each other.[35] What is also revealing is that the perennial oneirocritic symbol of losing one's teeth, (which was believed to indicate the death or loss of friends and family), found in most early modern dream interpretations, is also found in both Artemidorus and the *Somniale Danielis*, perhaps suggesting that the original source of the latter was in fact the former.[36] That is to say, it is entirely possible that the *Somniale Danielis* itself was an heir of the *Oneirocritica*, which, through the disparate translations and additions of various authors, was altered considerably from its original form.

Almanacs

Capitalizing on the vibrant interest in astrological handbooks, almanacs and fortune-telling books were abundant in the periods of the late sixteenth to eighteenth centuries. Bernard Capp estimated that in the 1660s sales of almanacs alone averaged around 400,000 copies annually.[37] Showing no indication of decline, fortune-telling books also thrived in the period and were widely available for purchase from booksellers in the cities and travelling itinerant chapmen around the countryside.[38] The culture from which dreambooks, almanacs and fortune-telling books emerged is one in which interest in divination flourished. Astrology, alchemy, palmistry, moleoscopy and other specialized forms of divination were enormously popular in the period and the art of dream interpretation was inextricably bound with these diverse practices. While historians such as Keith Thomas have suggested that astrology declined in the late seventeenth century, the trade in astrological works and divination handbooks suggests otherwise.[39] Rather than a process of "disenchantment," the evidence of a growing appetite and market in divination handbooks points to a process of continuity (rather than change) that some historians have labelled the "re-enchantment" of the world.[40] Further evidence of the close connections between astrology and oneiromancy was that numerous astrologers such as John Dee, Samuel Jeake of Rye, Elias Ashmole and William Lilly also recorded their own dreams in their private diaries alongside astrological sigils and horary questions.[41] Not only did astrologers subscribe to this practice, Archbishop William Laud also recorded numerous dreams in his diary alongside notations of astrological signs and the position of the planets.[42]

One of the most popular almanacs to offer dream interpretation was the *Erra Pater: The book of knowledge*. This work, ascribed to Erra Pater "a Jew bourne in Jewry," had circulated in manuscript form in the medieval period and was posthumously ascribed to William Lilly in the eighteenth century, perhaps to give it an additional readership and bolstered credibility.[43] Earlier versions of the *Erra Pater* were short works of 24 to 48 pages that included astrological-medical prognostications "for ever" with lists of fairs and markets as well as lucky and unlucky days for bloodletting, business and weather. The first extant edition was published by Robert Wyer in 1540 and was entitled, *The pronostycacyon for ever of Erra Pater: A Jewe borne in Jewery, a Doctour in Astronomye and Physycke Profytable to kepe the bodye in helth*.[44] This edition was reprinted in 1545, 1550, 1554, 1555 and 1562. Thereafter editions appeared regularly, typically every four to five years. The popularity of this almanac is demonstrated by the fact that from 1540 to 1800 there are 28 extant editions of the *Erra Pater*, which were published by various printers, amended and expanded. At the cost of one to three shillings, this almanac was easily affordable for most readers and, as Bernard Capp explained, was aimed at the "bottom end of the market."[45]

During the eighteenth century, the *Erra Pater* was vastly expanded and an array of new sections were added, most notably sections on astrology, oneiromancy and palmistry. While the perpetual prognostication and farmer's calendar remained a standard feature, the work evolved into a larger compendium of practical and divinatory knowledge.[46] Eighteenth-century editions of the *Erra Pater* appeared in 1703, 1712 and 1720, being regularly printed

60 *Decoding dreams*

thereafter. The first edition to include dream interpretation was published in 1720 by T. Norris, which grew from 48 to 168 pages and was extended into four main subdivisions: (1) astrology and health; (2) prognostications "for ever" with medical recipes; (3) physiognomy, palmistry, moleoscopy and oneiromancy; and (4) the farmer's calendar, including weather prognostications, husbandry and "the compleat and experienc'd farrier and cow-leach."[47]

In the section of oneiromancy, like other similar works, the *Erra Pater* simply listed dreams with short interpretations. For example, "To dream you fly in the Air, signifies a speedy journey, or some hasty News."[48] The dreams that are interpreted are almost identical to those included in *The true fortune teller* (1686), *Aristotle's legacy* (1699) and *The High Dutch Fortune-teller* (1750) as well as the *Somniale Danielis*. This suggests that the author(s) of the *Erra Pater* copied dream symbols either directly from other contemporary works or from an earlier manuscript edition of the *Somniale Danielis*. Although dream interpretation was by no means the most heralded feature of this popular almanac, the introduction of a section of oneiromancy in the eighteenth century suggests that it had become a popular addition to almanacs, reflecting a growing appetite and interest in oneiromancy.

No doubt seeking to capitalize on the success of the *Erra Pater*, *The compleat book of knowledge* appeared in 1698 and, like its predecessor, contained an assortment of information including: summaries of astrology, lists of local markets, fairs and roads and perpetual prophecies. According to the preface of the 1698 edition, the work was designed to satisfy the insatiable curiosity of "the Soul of Man" and impart the "hidden Secrets of Art and Nature" concealed by the "Antients" to those of "the meanest Capacities."[49] The segment of dream interpretation was notably longer than in other almanacs and a total of 309 dreams were interpreted. Presumably to reinforce its credibility, the excerpts of oneiromancy were celebrated as deriving from "the wisdom of the ancients" and "collected alphabetically out of approved authors." As with the majority of dream interpretations featured in fortune-telling works and almanacs, the author drew from Artemidorus; yet the *Oneirocritica's* dream symbols were helpfully alphabetically reorganized for greater ease of reference, emulating the medieval "dream alphabet" or "dreambook proper."[50]

Tapping into the growing market for astrological works and almanacs, fortune-telling books also proliferated in the period. Dream divination became a staple feature in these ephemeral works. Popular titles to incorporate dream divination include: John Booker's *The Dutch Fortune-teller* (1650); J.S., *The true fortune-teller* (1686); *Aristotle's legacy: or, his golden cabinet of secrets opened* (1699); *The High Dutch Fortune-teller* (1700) and *The entertaining fortune book* (1755). Each of these works went through multiple editions in the period.[51] Often anonymously authored, or ascribed to famous astrologers such as John Booker and William Lilly, these handbooks were typically 24 pages with cheap, recycled woodcut images. Fortune-books incorporated a conglomerate of short sections of dream interpretation, palmistry, astrology and moleoscopy, frequently including the "wheel of fortune," which was

Decoding dreams 61

a table for using dice to divine answers to general questions. The sections of oneiromancy listed random dream symbols with brief interpretations and were designed as concise reference guides to dreams. Several tracts, such as *The true fortune teller* (1698), like almanacs or dreambooks, included an additional section on "exemplary dreams and their interpretations." These excerpts narrated dreams from classical histories, such as the dream of Nero's mother or the wife of Julius Caesar, as well as the Bible and were presumably included for the entertainment of the reader and edification of oneiromancy.[52] A close comparison of the dream interpretations of each of these texts also demonstrates that the authors copied them directly from either Artemidorus or versions of the *Somniale Danielis*. For example, *The High Dutch Fortune Teller* (1700) explained that a dream of being bitten by a snake indicated "danger will befall you by secret and subtle enemies."[53] This dream interpretation appeared in both Artemidorus' *Oneirocritica* and late medieval copies of the *Somniale Danielis* as well as *The true fortune teller* (1686) and *The High Dutch Fortune Teller* (1750), amongst others. Another possibility is that fortune-telling works simply pilfered excerpts of oneiromancy directly from other contemporary dreambooks, popular almanacs and fortune-telling books.

Another genre of works to include sections of dream interpretation was courtesy books or courtship manuals. These were designed as handbooks of social etiquette that gave useful advice on proper and effective methods of courtship, letter writing and social etiquette for men and women, as well as techniques of divination.[54] Several titles contained excerpts of dream interpretation alongside the art of wooing and more practical skills such as carving roasts and impressing one's loved one with poetry and letters. In these works dream interpretation was advertised as a useful means of obtaining insight into one's present or future romantic relationships. *The art of courtship or school of delight* (1686) contained two pages of dream interpretations including the following example, "To dream a Ring drops off ones Finger, denoteth a disapointment in Love."[55] Other popular courtship books such as *Wit's cabinet* (first printed in 1698), followed a similar formula with sections on oneiromancy appearing alongside palmistry and moleoscopy as well as the "Whole Art of Love, with the best Method of Wooing and making Complemental Letters."[56] This work offered a more extensive section on dream interpretation with 11 pages containing 97 dreams, which were all borrowed from the *Oneirocritica*.[57] Overall, courtesy and courtship books presented themselves as useful "companions" for both "gentlemen and ladies" that imparted "pearls of Love and Eloquence" to their readers.[58] Dream interpretation was marketed in these cheap publications as part of the essential toolkit of love and courtship.

Dreambooks

In addition to the English translation of Artemidorus, other dreambooks proliferated in the period. Some of the most popular manuals in early modern

62 *Decoding dreams*

England include the works of Thomas Hill and those ascribed to the astrologers William Lilly, *A groatsworth of wit for a penny, or the interpretation of dreames* (1670) and John Booker, *The history of dreams, interpreted* (1670). Frederick Hendrick van Hove (1628–1698), a Dutch writer and artist resident in London, has been credited with another dream interpretation manual, the *Oniropolus, or dreams interpreter* (1680); however, as an engraver he was only responsible for creating the woodcut on the title-page.[59] The close links between oneiromancy and astrology are evident from the fact that numerous authors of dream handbooks were attributed to practicing astrologers. William Lilly (1602–1681) was one of the most famous astrologers of the seventeenth century and his almanacs and astrological prophecies were widely read by a broad audience, including the soldiers of the New Model Army and members of the elite. His works often sold out quickly so that even his critics were unable to obtain copies to study for their own use in planning a printed attack.[60] Lilly's *A groatsworth of wit for a penny, or, the interpretation of dreams* was first printed in 1670 and reprinted in 1750, 1770 and 1780. This tract was a brief compendium of astrological lore aimed at both men and women with basic literacy. The manual included two sections on dreams entitled "how a man or a maid by their Dreams may know whether they shall have them they love or no" and "the signification of Dreams."[61] Like many other contemporary fortune-telling books, this work included other "profitable" advice on: "how a man may get money in hard times," "how a man may obtain the love of his mistress" and "how they may know what planets they are born under." Lilly's interpretations of dreams drew directly from Artemidorus and simply listed each dream with a brief interpretation as the following excerpt illustrates.

> If you dream you see men with Bills & swords with writing in their hands, then beware, of being arrested the next day. If you dream of a Snake or Serpent and that they come near to hurt you, then look well to your self for there are private enemies seeking to destroy you and yours: if you dream you go up to the top of an Hill, then the next day you will put an end to some great business which you have long desired to finish, or else other good fortune will fall out; but if you dream that you fall down again before you get to the Hill top then your Suit will be lost, if you dream of troubled waters and that you fall into the water, then you may look to hear bad news the next day.[62]

Lilly assures readers these dreams predict what will happen "always the Day following." According to him, a correct understanding of predictive dreams was most "profitable" since one might "pray to Almighty God" and "prevent the danger that might have fallen on him."[63] With numerous reprints and being both cheap and accessible, Lilly's dreambook was a success. However, due to the fact that several works were posthumously accredited to Lilly, it is also possible that this work was merely marketed as one of his works to attract a greater readership.

Thomas Hill's most pleasant art of dream interpretation

While editions of Artemidorus and the *Somniale Danielis* circulated widely in the period of the sixteenth century, the only native English dreambooks were those of Thomas Hill, whose works represent an important transition between learned dreambooks and the more widely accessible simplified handbooks that emerged in the seventeenth and eighteenth centuries. Hill produced two dream interpretation manuals – a shorter dreambook *A little treatise of the interpretation of dreams* (1567) and the substantially longer *The moste pleasaunte arte of the interpretacion of dreames* (1576). Emerging from the trade in lay scientific works in the mid- to late sixteenth century, Hill's dreambooks pioneered a model that combined the specialized oneirocritic knowledge of classical authors and medical theories of natural dreams with popular techniques of dream interpretation. While historians have briefly studied Hill's larger dream treatise, to date no extensive studies have been made of both texts. As Peter Holland argued, Hill's 1576 dreambook "is the most substantial attempt in English Renaissance writing to produce an account of dream theory."[64] As such, a close study of Hill's dreambooks offers us important insight into both the emergent early modern practice of oneiromancy and the way that dreams were interpreted and understood within the framework of prediction.

Thomas Hill (1528–1572/6) was a prolific writer and transcriber of lay scientific works. He produced handbooks on a variety of topics, including gardening, astrology, palmistry, dreams, arithmetic, midwifery and physiognomy. Hill's overall aim was to provide vernacular handbooks that distilled learned and popular lore for a wider audience, making knowledge previously confined to the learned minority more accessible. This aim also extended to his two extant dream divination handbooks, *A little treatise of the interpretation of dreams* (1567) and *The moste pleasaunte arte of the interpretacion of dreames* (first edition 1559, extant only in a 1576 edition). In these two dream handbooks Hill offered readers a novel synthesis of learned and popular theories about dreams and their interpretation, drawing from Artemidorus, Galen, Aristotle and Averroes, as well as medieval dreambooks ascribed to the biblical dream interpreters Daniel, Solomon and Joseph.

Although Peter Holland asserts that Hill's *The moste pleasaunte arte of the interpretacion of dreames* relied heavily on the writings and dream theories of Aristotle and Averroes, in fact it draws more extensively on the work of Artemidorus and was fundamentally concerned with being a practical handbook of dream interpretation rather than a detailed summary of dream theories.[65] Based largely on the *Oneirocritica*, Hill's 1576 dreambook was designed as a guide for helping readers to learn "the moste pleasaunte arte of the interpretacion of dreames." Dream divination in Hill's text is presented as both a serious, learned practice and simultaneously a "pleasaunte" pastime for the reader's leisure. In this way, Hill attempted to adapt the classical practice of oneiromancy, as one of the divinatory sciences, to the needs of a broader early modern English audience, also seeking to appeal to the

64   *Decoding dreams*

emerging interest in fortune-telling tracts and debased astrological works. Hill's approach to dream interpretation, evident in his shorter dreambook with its blending of learned and popular works and simplified format, was a model for later dreambooks.

Techniques of dream divination

To provide a more nuanced understanding of the framework of predictive dreams, the following section will outline the common techniques of dream interpretation with its many obtuse rules and methods, such as the law of contraries and similitudes, astrological computations and the importance of the time and date on which the dream was experienced. A closer examination of the methods of dream interpretation and dreams listed in printed works helps to reveal the overall culture of dream interpretation and to highlight dreams that were considered most common and significant.

Although many of the dreams featured in English dreambooks were taken from Artemidorus or the *Somniale Danielis*, the fact that they were adapted to and popular with English audiences suggests particular dream symbols were universally recurring dreams that resonated with an early modern audience. As Lyndal Roper and Daniel Pick discuss in their important study, while interpretations and understandings of dreams do evolve or "oscillate" in time and are undoubtedly shaped by culture and experience, dreams themselves may be posited as a psychological experience that changes little and reveals a manifestation of the universal nature of the human psyche and evidence of a "basic humanity."[66] The continuation of similar dream symbols in dreambooks across the centuries from the *Oneirocritica* to seventeenth- and eighteenth-century dreambooks adds weight to arguments about a universal experience of dreaming.[67] For example, the dream of teeth falling out, which appeared in the *Oneirocritica*, featured prominently in early modern English dream books and is still experienced today. Numerous other dreams listed in premodern dream books are not dissimilar to common modern dreams.

However, as dreams are simultaneously encoded and shaped by culture, it is also apparent that there are dreams in premodern dreambooks that would be unheard of or extremely rare today. A dream of shooting a bow, fighting with swords, donning a "tonacle," paying court to kings and queens or working in mills, which might be common to persons living in the early modern period, would be less likely to occur today. If we accept the premise that the content of dreams is born from our daily lives and preoccupations, arising from our conscious and unconscious thoughts, then it follows that dreams reveal significant insight into the individual psyche in addition to culture. According to psychoanalytical theories of dreams, dreams contain two layers – the *manifest* and *latent content*. The *latent content* of dreams pertains to the individual emotional and psychic life while the *manifest content* draws from and expresses experiences and content from daily life and culture. This two-fold nature of dreams, as a result, can offer historians a unique avenue into gaining significant insight into individual experiences and emotions as well as demonstrating the influence of culture and daily experience on both.[68]

Authors of early modern English dreambooks modified the classical and medieval content of earlier works to cater to a contemporary audience: dreams that were no longer relevant or acceptable to a Christian English audience, such as those of the Greco-Roman gods or sex, were omitted. Similarly, outdated occupations such as gladiators and slaves were modernized, so that a dream of a gladiator became one of a warrior or soldier while a dream of a slave became one of a servant. The translator of the first English edition of Artemidorus explained to the reader, "For whatsoever I sawe to bee nothing agreeable to our times and which was no wayes necessary I left out: seeing that in the worke it selfe there are many superstitions of the Pagans, which wold have bin ridiculous at this present."[69] In addition to demonstrating the shifting lexicons and sensibilities of early modern people, this also illustrates how authors modified and adapted older texts for a more modern readership.

While many works simply listed dreams with their interpretations, some authors attempted to present a more serious art of dream interpretation that followed the rules outlined by Artemidorus. The qualities and knowledge of the dream interpreter were important facets of the *Oneirocritica's* overall schema of dream interpretation. The most extensive discussion can be found in *The moste pleasaunte arte of the interpretacion of dreames* (1576) of Thomas Hill who drew directly from Artemidorus to outline the qualities requisite for a successful practitioner of dream divination. In Book 1 of the *Oneirocritica* Artemidorus advised that an accurate dream interpretation required that the interpreter "know the dreamer's identity, occupation, birth, financial status, state of health and age."[70] According to Hill, "it shalbe necessarye for the interpretoure to consider and knowe what the persone tradeth or occupyeth, & of what birth hee is & what possessions he hath & what state he is in for the healthe of the bodye & of what age he is also which seeth the dreame."[71] Artemidorus' schema of dream divination also stipulated that the actual interpretation and outcome of a particular dream narrative varied depending on the age, sex, marital status, profession, health and wealth of the dreamer. For example he wrote,

> To have hair that is long and beautiful and to be proud of it, is good, especially for a woman. For women, for the sake of beauty, sometimes use the hair of others. It is also good for a wise man, a priest, a prophet, a king, a ruler and for stage performers, since it is customary for some of these men to let their hair grow long. It is the profession of the others that lets them grow their hair long. It is also auspicious for other men, but less so. For it simply signifies riches, not pleasant but involving trouble, since the grooming of long hair demands great care and attention.[72]

66 *Decoding dreams*

A dream interpreter, according to both Artemidorus and Hill, must also know the complete narrative of the dream without any omissions or fabrications.[73] Above all, Hill urges that "none also but the wise and discret parsons, may rightlye discerne and Judge of Dreames."[74] Dreams that occur to individuals "whose spirites are occupied" with "irrationall imaginations," or who are "overcharged" with "the burthen of meate or drinckes, or superfluous humors," are not true, but rather are "named vain dreams, no true signifiers of matters to come but rather shewers of the present affections and desiers of the body."[75] This example shows how authors such as Hill were able to reconcile the frameworks of health and prediction. Hill draws the emphasis on the body as a site where the humours and soul could be corrupted from contemporary Christianized readings of Galen. This understanding of the relationship among dreams, the body and health is largely absent from Artemidorus, yet these ideas are present in Aristotle and early modern medical writings on dreams.

Other works of dream interpretation were more circumspect with advice on the best practice of oneiromancy. Most almanacs, courtship and fortune-telling books, such as the *Erra Pater* (1720), *Wit's cabinet* (1698) and *Aristotle's legacy* (1699), would launch into lists of dreams with their corresponding interpretations.[76] English dreambooks such as the *Oniropolus* (1680) also followed suit and interpreted dreams in verse without any guidance on the practice itself. In English editions of Artemidorus, much of the author's original discussion of dream interpretation as a professional practice was condensed or omitted altogether leaving readers with little advice on how best to interpret dreams. In the epistle to the reader it was explained that one should not "regard any Dream each particular wherof [sic] one cannot entirely remember." Before interpreting any dream, the interpreter should therefore "have perfect remembrance of the beginning, the midle [sic], the end and al the circumstances of his Dreame." Additionally, the interpreter should "have regard to the Qualities of the persons according to which Dreames, arise divers effects."[77] However, the translator does not mention the cardinal rule of Artemidorus – a correct dream interpretation depended on the sex, marital status, wealth and age of the dreamer. Although Hill's dream manual and English editions of Artemidorus include some details and discussions of the art of dream interpretation, most works simply listed dreams with their concise interpretation showing how the art of oneiromancy was vastly simplified and catered to the casual reader interested in a quick guide to dream interpretation.

The "law of similitudes" and "law of contraries"

According to early modern theories, dream divination was believed to rest on two principal rules, the "law of similitudes" and the "law of contraries." Artemidorus had originally established the law of similitudes, which stipulated that certain dream symbols corresponded to similar outcomes, persons and meanings. The head signified the head of household, while the limbs symbolized the children and members of the household. Similarly, as the following example from Thomas Hill's dream treatise illustrates, certain dreams could be easily interpreted, such as to steer a ship well was fortunate and portended good, while tempests at sea indicated evil and harm:

> He that thinketh in his dreame, to governe a shippe wel and wyselye, signifyeth goode to all personnes. For not without feare and labour it is governed and brought to any port. But if they be vexed with tempestes or come to shyppewracke, it doth portende a myghtye evill or harme to ensue which hath often bene observed.[78]

Hill includes another example, a dream of marriage equals death, since "marriage is also similar to death and is represented by death" in dreams.[79] The astute interpreter of dreams therefore "ought to bee a moste arteficiall judger, which well knoweth similitudes, in that all dreams fall not out right, for in this case everye one maye easelye judge those dreames as the same happneth of the notes. ... Also he ought to know how to discusse from like to like."[80] This meant that a correct interpretation of certain dreams corresponded to its similar meaning.

The "law of contraries" or "law of antithesis" also derived from Artemidorus, who wrote in Book 2 of the *Oneirocritica*, "fulfillments are always contrary to dream images. ... Weeping and mourning for a dead man or for anyone else and grief itself foretell rightly and logically that one will rejoice in something and take delight in a successful business venture."[81] This law may also have been disseminated through the popular medieval dreambooks accredited to Daniel, Joseph and Solomon. For example, according to the *Somniale Danielis* (and much repeated in seventeenth- and eighteenth-century dreambooks, almanacs and fortune-telling books), to dream of a "ded body and ther-with speke," to see "a man hangd" and "to se him silfe sike" signified joy and gladness – interpretations that are opposite their logical meaning.[82] It is easy to see how this rule complicated the art of dream interpretation for early modern men and women interested in decoding their dreams. According to it, particular dream-symbols corresponded not to their obvious interpretation, but rather to the opposite outcome. The death of friends, for example, indicated they were in good health and vice versa.[83]

Other contemporary writers also demonstrated an awareness of the law of contraries. Reginald Scot recounted an English proverbial joke in *The discoverie of witchcraft* (1584): "Albeit that here in England, this Proverbe hath beene current; to wit, Dreames proove contrarie: according to the answer of the priests boy to his master, who told his said boy that he drempt he kissed his taile: yea maister (saith he) but dreames proove contrarie, you must kisse mine."[84] Thomas Nashe derisively criticized the practice of dream interpretation in his work *The terrors of the night* (1594):

> Those that will harken any more after Dreames, I referre them to Artimidorus, Synesius, & Cardan, with many others which onely I have

68   *Decoding dreams*

heard by their names, but I thanke God had never the plodding patience to reade, for if they bee no better than some of them I have perused, every weatherwise old wife might write better. What sense is there that the yoalke of an egge should signifie gold, or dreaming of Beares, of fire, or water, debate and anger, that everything must bee interpreted backward as Witches say their Pater-noster, good being the character of bad and bad of good.[85]

A broader knowledge of the law of contraries shows how these rules pervaded and complicated the art of oneiromancy so that an accurate interpretation required a specialized knowledge of dream-symbols and their encoded meanings.

The temporality of the dream

The time, day and season in which dreams occurred were important indicators of the truth-value of the dream. According to Thomas Hill, morning dreams were widely believed to be more fortuitous. The power of morning dreams was a common belief in England and is related to the Galenic model of health and the physiology of sleep. Steven Kruger traced this idea to twelfth-century writings on dreams, particularly those by Adelard of Bath, Gregory of Tours and Guillaume de Conches.[86] Yet, as the cleric and Hartlib Circle member John Beale noted in his unpublished seventeenth-century treatise on dreams, this idea can actually be found in the writings of Tertullian. As a result, Beale concluded that it was necessary "To distinguish the Morning dreames, as more apt to bee significant, Then such as befall in our first Slumbers."[87] The credibility of morning dreams was based on the idea that after midnight and towards dawn the body had completed digestion, allowing the soul to commune more freely with spirits. Emulating Aristotle, Hill explained,

> Why dreames which are caused in the morning, be parfiter and to more reason, then the others in the night tyme. To which the philosopher answeareth that in the morning the middle devision betweene the common sence and the Organe reservative is sufficient quiet, throughe whiche the fumes of the meat elevated then, are sufficiente weake and of this cause trewer and parfytter dreames.[88]

Reginald Scot also acknowledged this belief stating, "dreames in the dead of night are commonlie preposterous and monstrous," while in the morning "when the grosse humors be spent, there happen more pleasant and certaine dreames, the blood being more pure than at other times."[89] John Beale also suggested that both the body and soul were in a purified state just before waking: "That the Morning dreames beare the greatest importance. For that the conteste & distemper of the humours beeing rebated & better qualifyed in the foregoeing parts of sleepe. The spirite is more purifyed, & (by a while of cessation from wakeing functions) more habilitated to attend a spirituall intercourse for divination."[90] This is another example of the way that approaches to dreams were reconciled so that the frameworks of health and prediction were complementary rather than contradictory. Astrological principles also helped to determine the truth-value of dreams; it was believed that the virtue of the morning dream was also due to the movements of the sun and moon. With the nearing of the dawn and the proximity of the sun, dreams themselves were accordingly more likely to be true: "for that the sonne is the authour of the true and constante thinges," Hill explained.[91]

The significance of morning dreams is supported by evidence from private writings. Early modern English diarists frequently recorded the time of their dreams and proximity to morning, indicating an awareness that morning dreams were more potent and true. The astrologer Elias Ashmole was careful to note the approximate time of his dreams in his diary, as did William Laud, who wrote in one entry, "Monday. This morning between four and five of the clock, lying at Hampton Court, I dreamed that I was going out in haste."[92] Ralph Josselin noted in his diary entry for 5 October 1656, "I dreamed in the night towards the lords day morning of many things, at length of the unrulines of souldiers in quartering."[93]

In addition to the temporal occurrence of the dream, the season and precise date were also significant factors in assessing its truth-value. Hill advised his readers, "men have truer dreames in the Sommer and the Wynter then in the Springe and the Harveste."[94] This was because summer and winter were longer, more stable seasons, while spring and autumn were transitory and therefore ambiguous. Based on contemporary notions of the influence of the planets, moon and sun on dreams, Hill also emphasized that the astrological position of the sun and moon influenced when the dream would be fulfilled:

> And if in the Kalendes of any moneth, or in the entrance of the Sonne into anye signe then within a moneth. And if in the same way of the Sunnes enteraunce, eyther into the Solstice or Equinoctiall, then shall the effecte ensue within three monethes. And if in the houre of the full Moone or Chaunge, then within two dayes after. And if at the Sun rysinge on the Sondaye; then within seven dayes after.[95]

Dreams associated with specific feast days were also considered especially fortuitous.

According to Hill, dreams were particularly "marvelous" when they occurred on Christmas day, "the day of the salutation of the virgin Marye" and on Easter, the "daye of the resurrection."[96] The influence of the Christian liturgy is evident here in shaping early modern ideas of dream divination, as is the close relationship between oneiromancy and other divinatory sciences, such as astrology.

70   *Decoding dreams*

Astrological dream interpretation

The diary entries of John Dee, Elias Ashmole, William Lilly and Samuel Jeake of Rye suggest that another method for interpreting dreams rested on a synthesis of astrology and oneiromancy.[97] These diarists would often record their dream along with the position of the moon and planets with horary questions and astrological sigils. Elias Ashmole would frequently record a dream followed by a horary question as to whether the dream was true or indicated a specific outcome. In 22 June 1646 he wrote,

> A dream:
> Morning/that Mrs Thorn[borough]: lay upon a bed with me and ex[erci]sed some love to me and that she did really love me, [also] that I felt her [blank] and it seemd to be closed up and no entrance had been made there.
> A note of an horary question:
> 8 a clock this morning I proposed whether this dream was true.[98]

As will be discussed later, records of dreams of sex, though rare, do exist in the early modern period suggesting that premodern people were no strangers to sexual dreams. The record of Ashmole's dream, apart from demonstrating this fact, also shows how individuals with astrological training or knowledge could utilize the tools of astrology to understand their dreams. Uncertain as to whether his dream was fortuitous or not, Ashmole sought guidance from the stars.

The close link between astrology and dream interpretation is also supported by the fact that several astrologers published dreambooks or included sections of oneiromancy in their astrological handbooks. In addition to publishing astrological prophecies and almanacs and purportedly *A groatsworth of wit for a penny, or the dreams interpreter* (1670), William Lilly also produced a lengthy handbook of astrology and divination that included sections of oneiromancy alongside other methods of divination. Lilly's most important work, *Christian astrology* (1647), contained two chapters on astrological dream divination.[99] As Patrick Curry explains, this work was the first major "textbook" of astrology published in English.[100] Lilly's handbook included an exhaustive selection of information on a wide range of astrological practices and divinatory techniques, including palmistry and oneiromancy. According to Lilly and based on the ideas of Guido Bonatus, a thirteenth-century Italian astrologer, dreams should be interpreted in light of whichever astrological houses and planets were ascendant when the dream occurred. For example, Lilly explains if "a good Planet [is] in the ninth, no ill shall happen by the Dream: a good Planet in the ascendant signifies the same."[101] Astrological interpretations of dreams were new neither to the period nor to England and can be traced to medieval "dreamlunars." As Steven Kruger explained, these dreambooks interpreted dreams according not to their content but rather to the position of the moon at the time of the dream.[102]

In addition to an annual almanac and fortune-telling book, the physician and astrologer Richard Saunders (1613–1675) also published an important handbook of astrology in English in 1653, which was reprinted in 1671. Saunders' *Physiognomie and chiromancie, metoposcopie* was an expensive folio volume with numerous illustrations, introduced and endorsed by contemporary astrologers William Lilly and George Wharton. The intricate detail of the diagrams and extensive discussions of a variety of divination techniques in addition to the significant expense of the work indicates that it was marketed at a wealthier and perhaps professional astrological audience.[103] The handbook distilled earlier and contemporary English, Scottish and Continental writings on astrology and drew from such authors as Michael Scot (1175–1232), Paracelsus (1493–1541), Girolamo Cardano (1501–1576), Giambattista Della Porta (1535?-1615) and Robert Fludd (1574–1637), amongst others.[104] The work explained in detail the practice of "chiromancy," better known as palmistry, as well as moleoscopy, metoposcopy (divination by the lines on the face), astrology and oneiromancy. Saunders' discussion of dream divination is extensive. He, like Lilly, provides an astrological method of interpreting dreams so that the meaning and outcome of the dream depended on the astrological signs and position of the planets ascendant at the time.[105] Although his introduction to the chapters on oneiromancy is rather apologetic, noting the many "conjectures" and "imaginations" written about dreams, he proceeds to outline a serious practice of astrological dream divination.[106] According to Saunders, the meaning and truth of a dream depended on the day and lunar calendar it occurred on as well as the astrological conjunctions in motion at that specific time. Following the methods of Cornelius Agrippa, Saunders then corresponded the date of the dream with the days of creation. For example, if a dream falls on "the first day of the Moon or the first night wherein it was creator by the Eternal for to give it light" then "all the dreams that any one shall dream, shall be very true and shall happen to the satisfaction and joy of the parties." However, if a dream falls on the "second night or second day" then "the dreams of the night are unprofitable."[107] From Saunders' perspective, the significance and meaning of the dream depended less on its content and more on whichever astrological events were in motion at that exact time.

For contemporaries, astrology was therefore another means to interpret one's dreams. This method was a continuation of oneirocritic techniques popularized in medieval dreamlunars and disseminated amongst the learned through the work of Cornelius Agrippa. In early modern England astrological dream divination was primarily endorsed in semi-learned astrological works but occasionally featured in fortune-telling books and almanacs. Evidence for a practice of astrological dream interpretation can also be found in the medical notebooks of Richard Napier and Simon Foreman, both astrologer-physicians. Some of Napier and Foreman's

72 *Decoding dreams*

patients sought consultations about their dreams asking the physicians to cast horary questions about whether their dreams were true or not. For example, on 8 July 1596 Mrs. Avis Allen consulted Foreman about a dream she had recently had. She asked him to divine whether the dream indicated her sick boy would live or die.[108] Similarly, Robert Watson of Bucksted consulted Foreman in March 1597 about whether the treasure he had dreamt of was actually located in Crowborrow Common in Bucksted.[109] The motif of dreaming of treasure was a common urban legend in the period and led many hopeful dreamers to scour the countryside for hidden deposits of gold they believed had been revealed in a dream.[110] Foreman also used astrology to interpret and divine his own dreams. In March 1597 he dreamt that he saw Anne (Agnes) Young and her mother dressed in white. He cast a horoscope to determine whether Ralph Walworth (possibly the husband), was dead or would soon die.[111] These records strongly suggest that men and women consulted astrologers for dream interpretations and that astrologers themselves might also use astrological oneiromancy to divine the prognostic meaning and status of their own dreams. Astrology was therefore another powerful tool for divining and decoding the dream.

Gendering dream interpretation

Emulating Artemidorus, in some works the interpretation of the dream depended on the gender of the dreamer. Thomas Hill's 1567 shorter dreambook, *A little treatise on the interpretation of dreams,* provides further insight into sixteenth-century practices of oneiromancy. Published by William Copland and at only 48 pages (8vo), this simplified dreambook was designed by Hill as a quick, easily referenced, dictionary of dream interpretation. Within this handbook, 161 dreams are interpreted, including everything from dreaming of one's teeth falling out, to animals and the dead, to eating fish. The first section of the dreambook briefly discusses the kinds of dreams, the qualities of the ideal "expounder of dreams" and summarizes Aristotle's views of dreams. Following this shorter section is a longer one that includes brief summaries of dreams with their interpretations and predictive outcomes. In this dreambook, the interpretations of dreams are taken from another dreambook circulating at the time, which was ascribed to Joseph.[112]

Like Hill's *The moste pleasaunte arte of the interpretacion of dreames* (1576), this earlier handbook is gendered, with the default dreamer being male. Hill's longer dream treatise refers mostly to the interpretation of men's dreams, or alternately the significance of dreams according to the fortunes of men. In his earlier, shorter dreambook, of the 161 dreams that are interpreted, only six refer to a female dreamer. The few dreams that are significant for female dreamers contain what may have been viewed as particularly female dream motifs such as giving birth and the moon.[113] For example, according to Hill, if a woman dreamt of giving birth to a peach tree, this indicated she would give birth to a son "of honeste conditions," yet this child would live only a short time.[114] Men's dreams of women appear more frequently in the text as well as interpretations of dreams that relate to the significant women in the male dreamer's life, such as his mother, wife and daughter. For a man to dream he marries a widow indicated "the compassinge of olde matters or businessess," while to dream your wife married another man indicated divorce or the "alteratione of actions."[115] More positively, to dream one opens a new door predicted that the male dreamer would marry a "wiffe proffitable unto hime."[116] Dreams that predicted unfaithful wives were also included. To dream one saw a ram indicated an adulterous woman and to dream a ram "smote" you with its horns predicted the male dreamer would marry a woman who would "after playe the harlott." On the other hand, to dream one rode a "fayre Mare," denoted a happy and prosperous marriage with a wealthy wife.[117] In this way, dreams were a useful way of foretelling whether one would get married and whether one's wife would be faithful. While women figure as important symbols in dreams and as significant for the outcome of dreams, on the whole, Hill's dreambooks are gendered with the default dreamer being male. This, combined with evidence from other similar works, suggests that whilst Maureen Perkins found that dreambooks were aimed at a predominantly female audience in the nineteenth century, those of the sixteenth, seventeenth and eighteenth were marketed at both male and female readers and catered to a predominantly male audience.[118]

Although many dreambooks and other works with excerpts of oneiro-mancy tended to follow the model of the *Somniale Danielis* – "to dream of ... means ..." – without including the gender of the dreamer, there is a slight shift towards interpreting women's dreams in the seventeenth and eighteenth centuries. A statistical study of references to the gender of the dreamer from the thirteenth to the eighteenth century demonstrates that in works before 1600 the dreams of men were dominant. Manuscript and print editions of the *Somniale Danielis* include dream interpretations of anywhere from 59 to 232 total dreams. Of these none referred to women's dreams and in manuscripts before 1500 a total of 41 refer explicitly to men's dreams.[119] In *Daniels dreams* (1556), of the 59 dreams interpreted none referred to a female dreamer while 17 refer clearly to a male dreamer. This pattern shifted in the later seventeenth century and dreams pertaining to women begin to appear in dreambooks. In the *Oniropolus* (1680) a total of 213 dreams are interpreted: while 23 refer to a male dreamer, 8 women's dreams are inter-preted. Similarly, *Wit's cabinet* (1698) offered readers interpretations of 97 dreams of which 30 are men's and 7 women's dreams. Printed handbooks and excerpts of oneiromancy in the seventeenth century thus begin to cater to both a male and a female audience.

In eighteenth-century works there is a slight increase in the ratio of men's to women's dreams. In the *High Dutch Fortune Teller* (1700), of a total of 34 dreams only one referred explicitly to a male dreamer while four inter-preted women's dreams. *Dr Flamstead's and Mr Partridge's New Fortune Book* (1730) gave interpretations for 107 dreams. Men's dreams accounted

74   *Decoding dreams*

for 14 of these, while women's accounted only for 6 dreams. *The High Dutch Fortune Teller* (1750) interpreted 13 dreams, which were all gender-neutral, while the 1730 edition of the *Erra Pater* included one male-specific dream and three female-specific dreams out of 39. At the end of the century the anonymously authored fortune-telling book, *Dreams and Moles* (1780) interpreted 119 dreams of which 11 were men's and 12 women's.

Overall, a study of the references to the gender of the dreamer suggests that the targeted audience of dreambooks and similar works before the sixteenth century was predominantly male, while the seventeenth and eighteenth centuries saw a slight shift towards catering for a female readership. At no point however, do dreambooks and sections of oneiromancy seem to appeal solely to female readers, even in the late eighteenth century. This suggests that, based on Perkins' assertions about dreambooks becoming linked with a female readership and oneiromancy with femininity in the nineteenth century, this was a nineteenth-century development. Moreover, while a small percentage of the dreams interpreted in works of oneiromancy do refer explicitly to the gender of the dreamer, the larger percentage are gender-neutral, suggesting that the majority of dreams were designed to cater to both a male and female audience. In this way, dreambooks and other works that provided advice on interpreting dreams could appeal to a larger audience and market interested in interpreting dreams as oracles to the future. This trend also suggests that in the early modern period, the art of oneiromancy was considered either a gender-neutral or even a more masculine practice.

In dreambooks and other excerpts of oneiromancy, certain dream motifs, such as to give birth, are frequently gendered. For example, *Aristotle's legacy* (1699) explains that "for a Woman to Dream she is with Child, Denotes Sorrow and hard Labour; but to dream she is delivered, the contrary."[120] Patricia Crawford has examined women's dreams in the early modern period and suggests that they reveal women's preoccupations with motherhood, lactation and children.[121] However, a detailed comparison of women and men's dreams actually reveals a more complex range of themes that are less gender specific and traverse the spectrum of gendered roles. Women, like men, also had dreams that concerned the death of household members and friends as well as dreams that featured concerns about family business and assets. Alice Thornton, the fifth child of Charles Wandesford, Lord Deputy of Ireland, noted several dreams in her autobiography. In 1660 she recorded this warning dream: "For that very morning, before the balyes came, I dreamed for a certaine that Nettleton had sent his bailys to drive all our goods and to seize on all we had, for the debt which Mr. Thornton ingaged. And I was in deepe concerne as soone as I wakned out of sleepe affter it."[122] When she woke from her dream, Thornton summoned her maid, Jane Flower, to ask her if indeed the "baileys" had arrived. Incredulously, Flower asked Thornton how she knew this and whether anyone had already told her. Thornton answered, "None; but my God gave me warning in a dreame which I had dreamt this morning."[123] Women, like men, therefore experienced dreams that were believed to forewarn of events that were detrimental to the family estate or business.

Katherine Austen, a London diarist and poet, also recorded in her journal, "Book M," several of her own dreams as well as those of others she believed to be predictive. Indicative of her own reservations about dreams and an awareness of contemporary debates about dream divination, Austen included a lengthy discussion of the tendency of some to be misled by irrational fears and their consequent engagement in "superstitious" observations by dreams.[124] This shows that individuals might oscillate between belief and disbelief, demonstrating a more complex spectrum of contemporary views of dreams. The following is an example of one of Austen's dreams, an entry from November 1664:

> It pleased God to take away an honest servant Williame Chandeler, who had dwelt in my house almost Ten yeares. He served me ffaithfully. I trust he is gone to a better service ... He was buried 11: Nov: aged 38 yeares. ffoure nightes before he died I dreamet I saw him fall downe dead before me. And I did see him die. Tho when I waket I hopet he wud not die, And he comeing downe the night before he died and thought himself pretty well. Death came upon him in the space of 3 howeres, when before that he thought he might doe well. But after the minister had prayed with him and he setled what he had to say to his friends, he died all the way. And was apprehensive of every decay. His coffe left him. Noe ses he I shal bid you goodnight.[125]

As can be seen from the excerpt, Austen believed this dream presaged the imminent death of her longstanding servant, Williame Chandeler, whose death she foresaw in the dream four nights before.

Austen documented several other dreams that she believed were predictive, including a lengthy one involving her late husband, which she interpreted as an augury of the outcome of her battles over her husband's estate.[126] Like Alice Thornton, Austen experienced dreams that she believed forewarned of future outcomes related to her family estate. In her dream in which she was attending a wedding, Austen climbed some stairs to a room where she found her husband "discoursing with a gentleman." Austen left the room, descending "a few steps" and then she saw her husband again. After asking him how he could have left the room without her seeing him, she, "forgetting my Muffe," went up the back stairs, "but I had not gone up above 8: or 9: steps but I waket."[127] This dream stayed with Austen and she was convinced the number of stairs she ascended and descended were significant. On reflection, she wrote in her journal,

> This ran in my minde divers dayes afterwards and I concluded, the first paire of staires signified to me to the end of Janr and the second was so

76 *Decoding dreams*

> many dayes in febr: and then something wud fall out to me. And indeed I was troubled that some unhappy adventure wud come, as I indreaded every day wishing ffebr out. It came to pase that on the 9th of feb: I was appointed to be that day at the commencement of parliament: And when I came into the Roome it was the same as I saw in my Dreame, the situation of the Roome the same with the Table. And as soone as I cast my eye on Sr John Birkenhead, I was confident he was the very same man I saw my Hus: with.
>
> This busines was a weading: for it was a Contract, a Confederacy to take away our estate. And I shall noe more be of that opinion gennerally observed in Dreames that a weading foretels a burnig and a burnig a weading. But that it is danger of Conspiracy against one, as this was to us.[128]

Austen is unusual in recording and writing about how she interpreted her dream. For this reason, as Patricia Crawford has shown, this excerpt offers a rare glimpse into the mental worlds of early modern women.[129] For the history of dreams, such an interpretation also shows how dreams were interpreted within predictive frameworks. Austen believed dreams were encoded clues to the future that predicted important events in the dreamer's life. In Austen's view, this dream offered foresight into the outcome of the legal battles over her estate following the death of her husband.[130]

In the aforementioned excerpt, Austen also shows an awareness of the popular notion that a dream of a wedding or marriage indicated a death.[131] As was mentioned earlier in the chapter, this interpretation was based on the law of similitudes, which stipulated that particular dream-symbols indicated similar or like outcomes. What is also clear from Austen's writings on dreams is that, like Thornton, Austen believed she was privileged to have had these predictive dreams as warnings from God.[132] The idea that God sent warning dreams derived from the Bible and unquestionably helped bolster early modern belief in predictive dreams. Such dreams were often interpreted as proof of God's providence, grace and mercy. In this way, Austen and Thornton were able to reconcile their Christian beliefs with the practice of oneiromancy.

Above all, these records demonstrate that women's dreams were much more complex than previously asserted. Women's writings also reveal a sophisticated knowledge of contemporary dream theories and ideas about the different kinds of dreams. Although it is true that women did dream of childbirth, children and pregnancy, they more often dreamt of other non-gendered themes such as death, disease and threats to the family estate. A closer inspection of women's dreams thus reveals a more diverse and complex mosaic of women's preoccupations and inner lives. According to dreambooks and the dream interpretation schema of Artemidorus, particular dreams should be interpreted differently depending on the gender of the dreamer.

The dream body

In addition to the notion that the gender of the dreamer determined the meaning and significance of the dream, oneiromancy was further complicated by ideas about the symbolic relationship between the dream body and the social body. One of Artemidorus' most influential theories about dream interpretation was the idea that the dream body corresponded to the social body. This was a schema of oneiromancy linked to the law of similitudes that was emulated in Hill's dreambooks as well as in other later seventeenth-century fortune-telling tracts. In Book 1 of the *Oneirocritica*, Artemidorus explained,

> But those [dreams] which involve the body or a part of the body, or external objects such as beds, boxes, or baskets, as well as other articles of furniture ... although they are personal, often have the tendency to affect others too, depending on the closeness of the relationship. For example, the head indicates one's Father; the foot indicates a slave; the right hand indicates one's Father, son, friend or brother; the left hand indicates one's parents, wife or children.[133]

Book 1 is devoted to a detailed study of dream interpretations based on the particular body parts appearing in the dream. The major organs acted as symbols for the dreamer's immediate family, with the heart and lungs signifying the male dreamer's wife, while the liver indicated the son. The gallbladder was a symbol for women in the dreamer's life and the belly and guts signified his or her children.[134] Thomas Hill included this list of dream-symbols, transcribing it almost *verbatim* from Artemidorus, yet notably omitting the section on the penis and groin. According to Artemidorus, the genitals "indicate one's parents, wife, or children."[135]

One of the most pervasive and commonly interpreted dreams was that of one's teeth falling out. Artemidorus interpreted this dream as signifying the death and injury of significant people in the dreamer's life. According to him, the upper teeth represented "the more important and excellent members of the dreamer's household" while the lower referred to "those who are less important." Teeth on the right side of the mouth signified men and the left, women. In some cases the side of the mouth also signified the age of those persons symbolized. The right side represented older men and women while the left, younger persons.[136] Consequently, dreams in which teeth fell out were interpreted based on which specific tooth was involved and its position in the mouth. If, for example, a tooth on the top left fell out this indicated that a significant young female of the dreamer's household would die or be injured.

Early modern dreambooks, fortune-telling books, almanacs and courtship books copied this interpretation yet simplified the original system considerably. Rather than give details about the age or sex of the dreamer

78 *Decoding dreams*

depending on the position of the dream teeth, they simply interpreted the dream as signifying the death of a friend or family member. According to *Aristotle's legacy* (1699), for example, to dream one's eyes or teeth fell out indicated the sickness or death of one's children, friends or relations.[137] Similarly, *The compleat book of knowledge* (1698) also explained that to lose one's teeth signified "the Death of some near Relation or intimate Friend."[138] In the eighteenth century, these interpretations changed little. The *Erra Pater* (1753) explained that "to dream your Teeth are drawn, or dropt out, denotes the loss of Children or other Relations."[139]

English editions of the *Somniale Danielis* also followed the interpretation of Artemidorus regarding dreams of teeth, adding further evidence to the possible origins of the popular dreambook deriving from the *Oneirocritica*. In *Daniels dreams* is written "to dreame that thou leese thye teeth, thou shalte leese a frinde, for one of thy kynne shall dye."[140] Above all, these recurring interpretations of teeth falling out across the period of the sixteenth to the eighteenth century suggest that Artemidorus' system of oneiromancy and his idea about the dream body corresponding to the social body were still widely circulating in early modern dreambooks well into the eighteenth century.

Love and sexuality

Sexuality and sexual dreams were discussed in detail in the original *Oneirocritica*. Artemidorus offered interpretations of dreams about sodomy, sex with one's mother, masturbation, homosexual sex, sex with gods and goddesses, necrophilia and bestiality.[141] In both Hill's dream treatise and later seventeenth-century English translations of Artemidorus, these dreams are most often omitted, indicating the early modern belief that such topics were unfit for a Christian audience. Yet, in his section on sexual dreams, Hill includes Artemidorus' interpretations of dreams involving visiting brothels, having sex with known and unknown women, sex with one's wife, sex with one's servant, sex with one's brother and adultery.[142] However, Hill omits discussions about dreams involving sex with one's mother, kissing one's own penis, fellatio with one's self, homosexuality, sex with gods/goddesses, sex with the moon, necrophilia and bestiality.[143] English editions of Artemidorus also omitted these sections, skipping over all sexual dreams to the section on dreaming of sleep.[144]

While dream interpretation handbooks contained few examples of sexual dreams, this is not to say that early modern men and women did not have sexual dreams. Elias Ashmole recorded several dreams he had of the women he was courting in his personal diary that leave little doubt about their sexual nature.[145] Samuel Pepys also wrote of the intense pleasure he derived from a dream, "which I think is the best that ever was dreamed – which was, that I had my Lady Castlemayne in my armes and was admitted to use all the dalliance I desired with her."[146]

Death and the dead

In addition to sexual dreams, death, dying and the dead are important themes in early modern English dreambooks. These were not only significant dream-symbols but also occurred as common outcomes of dreams in Artemidorus' schema of oneiromancy. Dreaming of death often foretold marriage and "if a married man dreams that he is dead, it means he will be separated from his wife. It also indicates that associates, friends and brothers will part and be separated from one another."[147] Thomas Hill explained,

> And to a man not havinge a wyfe, it foreshewethe Mariage to ensue. For that mariages and death be thoughte both as the endes to men and do alwayes shewe a lyke together. So that to sicke personnes to marry a wyfe and to keepe the Brydale, signifieth deathe to ensue. For that the same happen to both, in that feastes be kept as well at the Burialles, as at the Marriages.[148]

Dreaming of eagles, teeth falling out and the dead stealing your possessions and clothes also signified death to the dreamer.[149] Similarly, "to dreame that he seeth his mother deade declareth joye" and "to see the majestye of God, signifyeth death or a most greevouse syknesse."[150]

In Hill's *A little treatise of the interpretation of dreams* (1567) dreams of the dead and those signifying death and illness are pervasive. For example, to dream one saw a "foul figure" in a mirror indicated sickness, while to dream one went to hell foretold a long sickness and eventual death.[151] Of the 161 dreams contained in his dreambook, 27 pertained to dreams of the familiar and strange dead. It was believed to be less dangerous to see the familiar dead, one's parents in particular, as these dreams foretold more positive outcomes, whereas to dream of the unknown dead, was particularly ominous.[152] Similarly, to dream one's friends were dead predicted "good or lesser evils" than dreaming one's enemies were dead, which was particularly ominous.[153] Dreams of tombs or graves were also significant. To dream "to dresse or trime thye grave signifieth that eyther thow (which so dreameth) or some of thine, shalbe greatlie spokine of and commended longe after." Additionally, to dream one saw a grave full of "Serpentes" indicated "the elders of hime or his predicessours weare wicked parsons."[154] Examples of dreams that foretold the deaths of dreamers or their families and friends included being called by the dead, having the dead steal one's clothes, seeing the dead sleeping and having a ship enter one's house and leave again.[155] The deaths of children were also predicted through dreams. If a woman dreamt of giving birth to fish, this indicated she would give birth to a "dumb" child who would die soon after. Similarly, to dream of one's teeth falling out, with much pain and blood, predicted the death of one's wife or daughter.[156] According to Hill's 1567 dreambook, dreams of the dead were particularly significant and numerous dreams were believed to portend death.

80 *Decoding dreams*

Early modern diarists recorded certain dreams that unquestionably lingered in their conscious minds; dreams of death, in particular, are frequently documented. Archbishop Laud recorded his first dream in his diary on 14 December 1623: "Sunday night, I did dream that the Lord Keeper [John Williams, Bishop of Lincoln (d.1625)] was dead: that I passed by one of his men, that was about a monument for him; that I heard him say, his lower lip was infinitely swelled and fallen and he rotten already."[157] In November 1660, Samuel Pepys dreamt that his wife had died after he quarrelled with her over whether the dog should stay in the house, so that he "slept ill all night." Thomas Vaughan dreamt frequently of his dead wife and saw one particular dream as presaging his own death.[158]

Records of dreams that accurately foretold the death of the dreamer or members of his or her household and community are also common in private writings of the period. Samuel Pepys wrote in his diary how the wife of an acquaintance correctly dreamt both of her uncle's death and her own.[159] John Aubrey also noted several men and women whose dreams predicted death in his *Miscellanies* (1696). One of the most striking examples referred to a time when his neighbour, Old Farmer Good, dreamt that he met with a dead friend, who warned him "that if he rose out of his bed, that he would die." The farmer's death occurred as the dream foretold: "he awaked and rose to make Water and was immediately seized with a shivering Fit and died of an Ague, aged 84."[160] Ralph Josselin believed dreams could tell the future and recorded no less than 34 descriptions of his own in his diary, including several from his wife and children.[161] The following entry in his diary for 30 June 1654 shows Josselin's reflections on a dream he believed predicted the deaths of his wife and children.

> I had a sad dreame in '48, of the death of wife and children, none left but Jane afterwards in '49. I buried Mary and Ralph: in '51: I dreamed 3 branches of a hedge growing in my house cutt downe sprouted again, which I feared as a continuence of the trouble of my first dreame, but I hope god intends by this wife and so I am persuaded that intended, that the 3 children god had taken from mee, he would make up again out of this stocke and now god hath graciously bestowed 2 upon me and hopes of their life.[162]

As a powerful and pervasive facet of everyday life, dreams of death and the dead were common experiences that reveal a deep collective anxiety about individual mortality and the death of loved ones. Since it was widely accepted that dreams could serve as either oracles of the future or providential warnings from God, particular dreams were cautiously heeded and recorded in private writings. Dreambooks and other works including oneiromancy offered readers the tools to decode the hidden meaning of their dreams, allowing readers to navigate the complex laws and techniques of oneiromancy and to interpret dreams themselves without the guidance of a professional dream interpreter.

Conclusion

Although more lengthy discourses on dreams continued to appear in the seventeenth and eighteenth centuries, including those written by Thomas Tryon, Philip Goodwin and others, they were far outpaced by the sheer numbers of popular dreambooks, almanacs and chapbooks. The ongoing persistence of these cheaper, more ephemeral publications and the popularity of an abridged, debased English edition of Artemidorus in the seventeenth century, shows there was a marked interest in handbooks that interpreted dreams within the framework of prediction. Even if we may never know who precisely read these works, or how they were utilized, the simplified content and format suggests they were marketed for a broad literate audience. Similarly, the interpretation of men's and, to a lesser extent, women's dreams in the early modern English dreambooks and other works point to oneiromancy as a predominantly masculine practice that, in the eighteenth century, slowly shifted towards a more gender-neutral one. The language of dreambooks was also frequently genderless, allowing the contents of dreams to be interpreted by males and females alike.

In addition to the framework of prediction, spiritual frameworks of dreams were equally pervasive in early modern England. However, the idea that God, angels or the Devil sent supernatural dreams in sleep was also highly contested in the period, particularly during the Interregnum, as a response to the claims of radical sectarians to divine dreams. Writers concerned with the spread of "enthusiasm" and false claims to divine inspiration began to assert a medicalized theory of dreams. In response to the contested subject of divine dreams, writers such as Philip Goodwin and John Beale defended contemporary ideas of dreams as both meaningful and divine, as I will explore in the following chapter.

Notes

1 John Dee, *The Private Diary of Dr. John Dee and the Catalogue of His Library of Manuscripts,* edited by James Orchard Halliwell (London: Camden Society, 1842), 17–18.
2 Ralph Josselin, *The Diary of Ralph Josselin,* edited by Alan Macfarlane (London: Oxford University Press, 1976), 617.
3 Peter Burke, *Varieties of Cultural History* (Cambridge: Polity Press, 1997), 23–42; Charles Carlton, "The Dream Life of Archbishop Laud," *History Today* (December 1986): 9–14; Carole Levin, *Dreaming in the English Renaissance: Politics and Desire in Court and Culture* (New York: Palgrave Macmillan, 2008); Ann Marie Plane, *Dreams and the Invisible World in Colonial New England: Indians, Colonists and the Seventeenth Century* (Philadelphia, PA: University of Pennsylvania Press, 2014); Ann Marie Plane and Leslie Tuttle, eds., *Dreams, Dreamers and Visions: The Early Modern Atlantic World* (Philadelphia, PA: University of Pennsylvania Press, 2013).
4 Dee, *Diary*, 10, 29; Simon Forman, Notebooks, Bodleian Library, MS Ashmole 1472, fols. 808, 809, 812, 814; William Laud, *The Works of the Most Reverend Father in God, William Laud, D.D.*, edited by James Bliss. Vol. 3 (Oxford: John

82 Decoding dreams

Henry Parker, 1975), 144, 200, 217, 224–25; Nehemiah Wallington, *The Notebooks of Nehemiah Wallington, 1618–1654: A Selection*, edited by David Booy (Aldershot: Ashgate, 2007), 20, 29, 50, 153, 177, 192, 325, 330–33; Josselin, *Diary*, 20, 187–88, 309–10, 325, 333–34; Elias Ashmole, *Elias Ashmole, His Autobiographical and Historical Notes, His Correspondences and Other Contemporary Sources Relating to His Life and Work* (Oxford: Clarendon Press, 1966), 386, 424, 442, 452, 454, 467; Katherine Austen, "Book M, "British Library, MS Add. 4454, 3r-3v, 7r-8r, 10r-17r, 21r-22r, 24r-26r, 31v-33v, 38v, 54r, 60v-61r, 63v-65r; Alice Thornton, *The Autobiography of Mrs. Alice Thornton of East Newton, Co. York*, Surtees Society Durham Publications (Durham: Andrews and Co., 1875), 23, 136–57, 169; Samuel Pepys, *The Diary of Samuel Pepys: A New and Complete Transcription*, edited by Robert. Latham and William. Matthews, 11 Vols. (Berkeley, CA: University of California Press, 1970) Vol. 1, 162; Vol. 2, 226; Vol. 3, 250; 14–15, 43, 235; Vol. 5, 8, 108; Vol. 6, 51–52, 145, 191; Vol. 7, 287, 299.
5 Carlton, "The Dream Life of Archbishop Laud," *History Today* 36, no. 12 (December 1986): 9–14; Reid Barbour, "Liturgy and Dreams in Seventeenth-Century England," *Modern Philology* 88, no. 3 (February 1991): 227–42; Burke, *Varieties of Cultural History*, 23–42; Crawford, "Women's Dreams in Early Modern England,"129–41.
6 William Lilly, *A groats worth of wit for a penny, or, The interpretation of dreams* (London, 1670), 5. While Lilly was listed as the author of this work it is possible, given the discrepancy between this and his other works, that the publishers ascribed this work to Lilly as a marketing ploy.
7 Thomas Hill, *The moste pleasuante arte of the interpretacion of dreames whereunto is annexed sundry problemes with apte aunsweares neare agreeing to the matter and very rare examples, not like the extant in the English tongue ...* (London, 1576), Avi(r)-Avi(v).
8 Austen, MS Add. 4454, fols. 54r, 60v, 64r, 66v-97r; Thornton, 136–37.
9 Perkins, "The Meaning of Dream Books." A close reading of Perkins' study suggests that she was actually discussing fortune-telling books that included sections of dream interpretation, rather than dreambooks as I define them.
10 Adam Fox, *Oral and Literate Culture in England, 1500–1700* (Clarendon Press, 2000); "Ballads, Libels and Popular Ridicule in Jacobean England," *Past & Present* 145 (November 1994): 47–83; Diane Purkiss, *Literature, Gender and Politics during the English Civil War* (Cambridge: Cambridge University Press, 2005); Andrew Hadfield, *Literature and Censorship in Renaissance England* (Houndmills, Basingstoke, Hampshire; New York: Palgrave, 2001); M.E. Fissell, "Readers, Texts and Contexts: Vernacular Medical Works in Early Modern England," in *The Popularization of Medicine 1650–1850* (London: Routledge, 1992), 72–96; Barry Reay, "Popular Literature in Seventeenth-century England," *Journal of Peasant Studies* 10, no. 4 (1983): 243–49.
11 See for example: Anon., *Oniropolus, or dreams interpreter* (London, 1680); Anon., *Aristotle's legacy: or, his golden cabinet of secrets opened* (London, 1699); Anon., *The High Dutch fortune-teller* (London, 1700); *The Old Egyptian fortune-teller's last legacy* (London, 1775).
12 Keith Thomas, *Religion and the Decline of Magic* (London: Penguin, 1991), 347. See also for example: Samuel Strangehopes, *A book of knowledge. In four parts* (London, 1679); Anon., *The compleat book of knowledge* (London, 1698).
13 Artemidorus also influenced Middle Eastern and Islamic dreambooks and practices of oneiromancy. See: Kelly Bulkeley, "Reflections on the dream traditions of Islam," *Sleep and Hypnosis* 4 (2002): 1–11; Steven M. Oberhelman, *The Oneirocriticon of Achmet: A Medieval Greek and Arabic Treatise on the Interpretation of Dreams* (Lubbock, TX, USA: Texas Tech University Press, 1991),

Decoding dreams 83

Introduction; Roger A. Pack, "On Artemidorus and His Arabic Translator," *Transactions and Proceedings of the American Philological Association* 98 (January 1, 1967): 313–26; Franz Rosenthal, "From Arabic Books and Manuscripts XII: The Arabic Translation of Artemidorus," *Journal of the American Oriental Society* 85, no. 2 (April 1, 1965): 139–44. For an excellent study of modern day Islamic dream theories and practices in Egypt see: Amira Mittermaier, *Dreams That Matter: Egyptian Landscapes of the Imagination* (Berkeley: University of California Press, 2011).

14 Artemidorus, *Artemidorus' Oneirocritica: Text, Translation and Commentary* trans. Daniel E. Harris-McCoy (Oxford: Oxford University Press, 2012), 1–2. For an interesting comparison between the writings of Artemidorus and Sigmund Freud see: S.R.F. Price, "The Future of Dreams: From Freud to Artemidorus," *Past and Present* 113 (1986): 3–37.

15 Dreambooks had actually existed since the earliest records of civilization. The earliest known dreambook was found in Egypt and has been ascribed to the Pharaoh Merikere in 2076 BCE. [C.W. O'Nell, *Dreams, Culture and the Individual* (San Francisco: Chandler and Sharp, 1976), 33. See also: Lyndal Roper and Daniel Pick, eds., *Dreams and History: The Interpretation of Dreams from Ancient Greece to Modern Psychoanalysis* (London: Routledge, 2004); M. Andrew Holowchak, *Ancient Science and Dreams: Oneirology in Greco-Roman Antiquity* (New York; Oxford: University Press of America, 2002); Susan Parman, *Dream and Culture: An Anthropological Study of the Western Intellectual Tradition* (New York: Praeger, 1991); Barbara Tedlock, *Dreaming: An Anthropological and Psychological Interpretation* (Cambridge: Cambridge University Press, 1987), J. Donald Hughes, "Dream Interpretation in Ancient Civilizations," *Dreaming* 10, no. 1 (2000): 7–18].

16 Artemidorus Daldianus, *The Interpretation of Dreams: Oneirocritica*, translated by Robert J. White (Park Ridge, NJ: Noyes Classical Studies, 1975), 15.

17 Artemidorus, *Oneirocritica* (2012), 47–55.

18 Price, 31–32; Manfred Landfester, "Artemidorus of Daldis (Lydia)/Artemidorus of Ephesus." *Brill's New Pauly Supplements I - Volume 2: Dictionary of Greek and Latin Authors and Texts*, edited by Manfred Landfester and Brigitte Egger (Brill Online, 2015), (accessed October 8, 2015), <http://referenceworks.brillonline.com/entries/brill-s-new-pauly-supplements-i-2/artemidorus-of-daldis-lydiaartemidorus-of-ephesus-COM_0036>; Rosenthal, "From Arabic Books and Manuscripts XII;" Pack, "On Artemidorus and His Arabic Translator"; Luther H. Martin, "Artemidorus: Dream Theory in Late Antiquity," *The Second Century: A Journal of Early Christian Studies* 8, no. 2 (Summer 1991): 97–108.

19 Artemidorus, *Artemidori De somniorum interpretatione libri quinq[ue]. De insomniis, quod Synesii cuiusdam nomine circu[m]fertur* (Venetiis, 1518).

20 *Artemidori Daldiani ... De somniorum interpretatione, libri quinq[ue]/ iam primum à Iano Cornario medico physico Francofordensi, Latina lingua conscripti* trans. Janus Cornarius (Basileae, 1539); *Artemidori Daldiani ... De somniorum interpretatione, libri quinq[ue]/ iam primum à Iano Cornario medico physico Francofordensi, Latina lingua conscripti* trans. Janus Cornarius (Basileae, 1544); *Artemidori Daldiani ... De somniorum interpretatione, libri quinq[ue],/ iam primum à Iano Cornario medico physico Francofordensi, Latina lingua conscripti* (Lugduni, 1546).

21 Julian Roberts and Andrew G., Watson, eds., *John Dee's Library Catalogue* (London: The Bibliographical Society, 1990), 1103, 1198, B237, B240. This speculation is based on the fact that Hill thanks Dee in his work *The contemplation of mankinde* (1571):

> Some what I have seene by experience, all that thou hast here, gathered oute of the best wryters: muche more I have reade and the best of that, I also give thee. So many as shall receyve any fruit or commoditie by me, let them give

84 *Decoding dreams*

> thankes unto the worshipfull and high learned man, Mayster Dee, by whose helpe and ayde at the beginning, I receyved such monuments and principles, as gave me great light unto this knowledge and unto whome also thou art greatly bound: for that he wisheth well unto his Countrie men and hath taken great paynes to do his Countrie good. [Thomas Hill, *The contemplation of mankinde* (London, 1571), Aiv(r)–Aiv(v)].

22 Roberts and Watson, *John Dee's Library Catalogue*, 1103, 1198, B237, B240.
23 Francis R. Johnson, *Astronomical Thought in Renaissance England: A Study of the English Scientific Writings from 1500 to 1645* (Baltimore: The Johns Hopkins Press, 1937), 41–42.
24 Edward Harwood, *A View of the Various Editions of the Greek and Roman Classics, with Remarks* (London, 1790), 86. Note: the 1518 edition sold for 15 shillings while the 1604 French edition sold for a pound and a shilling.
25 Artemidorus, *The judgement, or exposition of dreames …* (London: 1606).
26 Lawrence T. Martin, 'The Earliest Versions of the Latin "Somniale Danielis,"' *Manuscripta* XXIII (1979), 131.
27 S.F. Kruger, *Dreaming in the Middle Ages* (Cambridge: Cambridge University Press, 1992), 10. The "dreambook proper" was the only kind of dreambook that interpreted dreams specifically based on their content. Other kinds of dreambooks defined by Kruger, include the "Dreambook lunar," which interpreted dreams depending on the position of the moon and disregarded the content of the dream and the "dream alphabet" or "chancebook" that interpreted dreams organized alphabetically, according to a random process (Kruger, *Dreaming*, 8–10).
28 Kruger, *Dreaming*, 10.
29 Steven R. Fischer, ed., *The Complete Medieval Dreambook* (Bern und Frankfurt am Main: Peter Lang, 1982), 24–25, 30–32.
30 See for example, Hill's *The moste pleasaunte arte of the interpretacion of dreames* (1576), Nvi(v)–Pvi(v); *A most briefe and pleasant treatise of the interpretation of sundrie dreames intituled to be Josephs and sundry other dreames out of the worke of the wise Salomon* (1601, 1626).
31 *Daniels Dreames*, Aii(r).
32 *Dr. Flamstead's and Mr. Patridge's New Fortune-Book* (London, 1729), 118–19.
33 *The compleat book of knowledge* (1698), 78, 80, 83, 84.
34 Steven R. Fischer ed., *The Complete Medieval Dreambook*. 73, 68, 134–35.
35 Compare for example the dream symbols contained in *Aristotle's Legacy, The compleat book of knowledge* and *William Lilly's A groatsworth of wit for a penny*.
36 See for example: *Ibid.*, 146–47, *Daniels Dreames*, Aii(v); Artemidorus, *Oneirocritica* (1975), 44–46; Hill (1567), Civ(v); *Aristotle's Legacy,* 15; *High Dutch Fortune Teller*, 23; *True Fortune Teller*, 109; *Erra Pater* (1753), Book 3, 74.
37 Bernard Capp, *English Almanacs 1500–1800* (New York: Cornell University Press, 1979), 23.
38 Victor Neuburg, *Popular Literature: a history and guide* (Middlesex: Penguin, 1977), 1–2.
39 Thomas, 338, 414–44, 769, 772.
40 Alexandra Walsham, "The Reformation and 'the Disenchantment of the World' Reassessed," *The Historical Journal* 51, no. 2 (2008): 497–528; Alex Owen, *The Place of Enchantment: British Occultism and the Culture of the Modern* (Chicago: Chicago University Press, 2004); Willem de Blécourt and Owen Davies, *Witchcraft Continued: Popular Magic in Modern Europe* (Manchester, New York: Manchester University Press, 2004); Owen Davies, *Witchcraft, Magic and Culture 1736–1951* (Manchester: Manchester University Press, 1999); Wouter J. Hanegraaff, "How Magic Survived the Disenchantment of the World," *Religion* 33 (2003): 357–80; Robert Scribner, "The Reformation,

Popular Magic and the 'Disenchantment of the World,'" *Journal of Interdisciplinary Studies* 23, no. 3 (Winter 1993): 475–94.

41 Dee, *The Private Diary of Dr. John Dee*, 10, 31, 19; Ashmole, *Elias Ashmole, His Autobiographical and Historical Notes*, 353, 372, 376; William Lilly, *The Life of William Lilly: Student of Astrology* (London: The Folklore Society, 1974), 4.; M. Hunter and E.A. Gregory eds., *An astrological diary of the seventeenth century, Samuel Jeake of Rye* (Oxford: Oxford University Press, 1988), 143.

42 Laud, *The Works of William Laud*, 246.

43 Thomas, *Religion and the Decline of Magic*, 350.

44 Erra Pater, *The pronostycacyon for ever of Erra Pater: a Jewe borne in Jewery, a doctour in astronomye and physycke profytable to kepe the bodye in helth* (London, 1540). Note: Robert Wyer published six editions of this work between 1540 and 1562.

45 Bernard Capp, *Astrology and the Popular Press: English Almanacs 1500–1800* (London: Faber and Faber, 1979), 31. See: William Lilly, *The Book of Knowledge; Treating of the Wisdom of the Ancients. In Four Parts.* (London, 1753); William Lilly, *The Book of Knowledge, Treating of the Wisdom of the Ancients, in Four Parts* (Glasgow, 1780); *The compleat book of knowledge* (London, 1698).

46 Roy Porter, *The Popularization of Medicine* (London: Routledge, 2013), 73.

47 Erra Pater, *The Book of Knowledge: Treating of the Wisdom of the Ancients ... Made English by W. Lilly* (London, 1720).

48 *Ibid.*, 73.

49 *The compleat book of knowledge* (1698), preface.

50 Kruger, *Dreaming in the Middle Ages*, 9.

51 Anon., *Aristotle's legacy: or, his golden cabinet of secrets opened* (London, 1699); Mother (Ursula) Shipton, *Mother Shipton's legacy. Or, a favorite fortune-book in which is given a pleasing interpretation of dreams* (York, 1797); Anon., *The High Dutch Fortune-teller ...* (London, 1700); J.S., *The true fortune-teller, or, Guide to knowledge Discovering the whole art of chiromancy, physiognomy, metoposcopy and astrology ...* (London, 1698); Anon, *The entertaining fortune book, as to what relates to good or bad fortune in either sex* (London, 1755); John Booker, *The Dutch fortune-teller* (London, 1650).

52 *The true fortune teller*, 102.

53 *The High Dutch Fortune-teller*, 23.

54 See for example, *Wits cabinet or a companion for young men and ladies* (London, 1684); *Wits cabinet: a companion for gentlemen and ladies* (London, 1715); Anon., *The art of courtship, or, the school of delight* (London, 1686); *A new academy of complements: or, the lover's secretary* (London, 1727); L. G., *The amorous gallant's tongue tipp'd with golden expressions: or, the art of courtship refined, being the best and newest academy* (London, 1741).

55 *The art of courtship*, B4r.

56 *Wits Cabinet*, (1715), frontspage.

57 *Ibid.*, 1–11.

58 *Ibid.*, preface.

59 Thomas Hill, *The most pleasaunt arte of the interpretation of dreames* (London, 1571); Thomas Hill, *A most briefe and pleasant treatise of the interpretation of sundrie dreames intituled to be Josephs* (London, 1601); William Lilly, *A groatsworth of wit for a penny, or the interpretation of dreams* (London, 1670); John Booker, *The history of dreams, or, dreams interpreted* (London, 1670); Frederick Hendrick van Hove, *Oniropolus, or dreams interpreter ..* (London, 1680).

60 Patrick Curry, "Lilly, William (1602–1681)," in *Oxford Dictionary of National Biography*, online ed., edited by Lawrence Goldman, (Oxford: OUP, 2004), (accessed 12 May 2011), http://www.oxforddnb.com/view/article/16661.

61 Lilly, *Groatsworth of wit for a penny*.

86 Decoding dreams

62 *Ibid.*, 5.
63 *Ibid.*
64 Peter Holland, "'The Interpretation of Dreams' in the Renaissance," in *Reading Dreams: The Interpretation of Dreams from Chaucer to Shakespeare,* edited by Peter Brown (Oxford: Oxford University Press, 1999), 142.
65 *Ibid.*
66 Roper and Pick, 15.
67 *Ibid.*, 4, 7.
68 For an excellent study of the relationship between dreams, culture and psyche see: Jeanette Marie Mageo, *Dreaming and the Self: New Perspectives on Subjectivity, Identity and Emotion* (New York: State University of New York Press, 2003). Ann Plane also discusses this issue in the introduction to her important study of dreams in early modern America. Plane, *Dreams and the Invisible World in Colonial New England.*
69 Artemidorus, (1606), epistle.
70 Artemidorus, *The Interpretation of Dreams: Oneirocritica,* translated by Robert J. White (Park Ridge, NJ: Noyes Classical Studies, 1975), 21.
71 Hill, *Interpretacion of dreames* (1576), Bvi(r).
72 Artemidorus, *Oneirocritica* (1975), 26.
73 *Ibid.*, 22; Hill, *Interpretacion of dreames* (1576), Bvi(r).
74 *Ibid.*, Aii(r)–Aii(v).
75 *Ibid.*
76 *Erra Pater* (1720), 60; *Wit's cabinet* (1698), A4r; *Aristotle's legacy* (1699), 14.
77 Artemidorus (1606), Epistle.
78 Hill, *Interpretacion of dreames* (1576), Lv(r).
79 Artemidorus, *Oneirocritica* (1975), 130; Hill, *Interpretacion of dreames* (1576), Niii(v)–Niiii(r).
80 *Ibid.*, Biiii(v).
81 Artemidorus, *Oneirocritica* (1975), 130. Luther H. Martin, "Artemidorus: Dream Theory in Late Antiquity," *The Second Century: A Journal of Early Christian Studies* 8, no. 2 (Summer 1991): 103. Note: in Artemidorus, as Luther H. Martin explains, this law was known as the "law of antithesis" or "law of opposites" [Martin, 103].
82 Fischer, *The complete medieval dreambook* (Bern, 1982).
83 Hill, *Interpretacion of dreames* (1576), Niiii(v).
84 Reginald Scot, *The discoverie of witchcraft* (London, 1584), 183.
85 Thomas Nashe, *The terrors of the night or, A discourse of apparitions* (London, 1594), Diii(v).
86 Kruger, *Dreaming,* 72.
87 John Beale, "Treatise on the Art of Interpreting Dreams," Undated, 25/19/1-28, in Mark Greengrass, Michael Leslie and Michael Hannon eds, *The Hartlib Papers: A Complete Text and Image Database of the Papers of Samuel Hartlib (C.1600–1660),* Held in Sheffield University Library, 2nd ed. (Sheffield, 2002), 25/19/8B.
88 Hill, *Interpretacion of dreames* (1576), Ci(v).
89 Scot, *Discoverie of witchcraft,* 183. Here Scot is referring to the ideas of Giambattista della Porta in his work, *Magiae naturalis* (1558).
90 Beale, "Treatise on the Art of Interpreting Dreams," 25/19/10A.
91 Hill, *Interpretacion of dreames* (1576), Dviii(r).
92 Laud, *Works,* 364; Ashmole, *His Autobiographical and Historical Notes,* 386, 442, 456.
93 Josselin, *Diary,* 364.
94 Hill, *Interpretacion of dreames* (1576), Dvii(v)–Dviii(r).
95 *Ibid.*, Eii(r).
96 *Ibid.*

Decoding dreams 87

97 Dee, *The Private Diary of Dr. John Dee*, 10, 31, 19; Ashmole, *Elias Ashmole, His Autobiographical and Historical Notes*, 353, 372, 376; Lilly, *Life of William Lilly: Student of Astrology*, 4.; M. Hunter and E.A. Gregory eds., *An astrological diary of the seventeenth century, Samuel Jeake of Rye* (Oxford: Oxford University Press, 1988), 143.

98 Ashmole, 386.

99 Lilly, *Christian astrology*, 434–37.

100 Patrick Curry, "Lilly, William (1602–1681)."

101 Lilly, *Christian astrology*, 435.

102 Kruger, *Dreaming in the Middle Ages*, 8.

103 M. H. Porter, "Saunders, Richard (1613–1675)," in *Oxford Dictionary of National Biography*, online edn, edited by Lawrence Goldman (Oxford: OUP, 2004), (accessed 2 February 2013), http://www.oxforddnb.com.myaccess.library.utoronto.ca/view/article/24702. Saunders' other notable works include: *Two groatsworth of wit for a penny. Or the English fortune-teller* … (London, 1675); *Saunders Physiognomie and chiromancie, metoposcopie* … (London, 1671) as well as the annual almanac *Apollo Anglicanus,* which was printed annually from 1653 to his death.

104 Porter, "Saunders, Richard (1613–1675)."

105 Saunders (1653), 201–36.

106 *Ibid.,* 201.

107 *Ibid.,* 203.

108 Lauren Kassell (ed.) et al."CASE537 (Normalised Version)," *Casebooks Project,* (accessed 7 July 2016), http://www.magicandmedicine.hps.cam.ac.uk/view/case/normalised/CASE537?sort=date&order=asc&t=26&tm=3&ntl=1.

109 Kassell, "CASE1299 (Normalised Version)," *Casebooks Project,* (accessed 7 July 2016), http://www.magicandmedicine.hps.cam.ac.uk/view/case/normalised/CASE1299?sort=date&order=asc&t=26&tm=3&ntl=1.

110 See for example the story of the Peddler of Swaffham in, Abraham de la Pryme, *The Diary of Abraham de la Pryme, the Yorkshire Antiquary* (Durham: Andrews and Company, 1870), 219–20. More stories about persons getting rich and finding treasure through a dream can be found here: http://www.pitt.edu/~dash/type1645.html#swaffham.

111 Kassell, "CASE1407 (Normalised Version)," *Casebooks Project,* (accessed 7 July 2016), http://www.magicandmedicine.hps.cam.ac.uk/view/case/normalised/CASE1407?sort=date&order=asc&t=26&tm=3&ntl=1.

112 Unfortunately, a comparison between Hill's 1567 dreambook and others circulating at the time (which may no longer be extant) is beyond the scope of this dissertation. Yet this would certainly help shed light on the original source(s) for Hill's text.

113 Hill, *Interpretation of dreams* (1567), Biv(v), Bvii(r)-Bvii(v), Cvi(v).

114 *Ibid.,* Cvi(v).

115 *Ibid.,* Bviii(v)-Biv(r).

116 *Ibid.,* Bv(r).

117 *Ibid.,* Ci(r), Bvii(v).

118 Perkins, "The Meaning of Dream Books."

119 See: Fischer, *The complete medieval dreambook.*

120 Aristotle's Legacy (1699), 16.

121 Crawford, "Women's Dreams in Early Modern England."

122 Thornton, *Autobiography*, 136–37.

123 *Ibid.,* 137.

124 Austen wrote, again quoting Jeremy Taylor, Sermon IX, "Of Godly Fear;" Part III, *Eniautos,* 114–24:

> But fear is Dul and sluggish, miserable and foolish. And from henc proceeds Observation of signes and of unlucky dayes and erra pater. If men doe listen to

88   *Decoding dreams*

wispers of fear and have not reason and observation enough to confute trifles they shal be affrighted with the noise of Birds and the Night Raven. And every old woman shal be a prophetes. And the events of our affaires which should be managed by the conduct of counsel, of reason and religion, shal by these vaine observations, succeed by chance, by ominous Birds, by the faling of the salt, or the decay of reason, of wisdome and the just religion of a man. And to these trifling superstitions may be reduced observations of Dreams, on unsecure expectation of evills that never shal happen.

[Austen, MS Add. 4454, fol. 25r]

125 *Ibid.*, fol. 38v.
126 Austen, MS Add. 4454, fols. 60v–61r.
127 *Ibid.*
128 *Ibid.*
129 Patricia Crawford, "Women's Dreams in Early Modern England," *History Workshop Journal* 49 (2000): 134.
130 For further details of her legal battles over property see, Barbara J. Todd, "Property and a Woman's Place."
131 Barbara Todd has interpreted and transcribed Austen's use of "burnig" to mean "burying" which makes more sense since in dreambooks to dream of a death foretold a wedding. There is no mention of the nature of that death in dreambooks.
132 Austen, MS Add. 4454, fol. 54r, 60v, 64r, 66v–97r.
133 Artemidorus, *Oneirocritica* (1975), 17.
134 *Ibid.*
135 *Ibid.*, 17, 38–39.
136 *Ibid.*, 44.
137 *Aristotle's legacy*, 15.
138 *The compleat book of knowledge* (1698), 95.
139 *Erra Pater* (1753), 74.
140 *Daniel's dreams*, Aii(v).
141 *Ibid.*, 58–66.
142 Hill, *Interpretacion of dreames* (1576), Lv(r)–Lvii(r).
143 Artemidorus, *Oneirocritica* (1975), 58–66.
144 See for example any seventeenth- or eighteenth-century English edition of Artemidorus, e.g. *The interpretation of dreames, digested into five books by that ancient and excellent philosopher, Artimedorus …* (London, 1644).
145 Ashmole, *His Autobiographical and Historical Notes*, 386.
146 Pepys, *Diary*, Vol. 6, 191.
147 Artemidorus, *Oneirocritica* (1975), 126.
148 Hill, *Moste pleasaunte art* (1576), Niiii(r).
149 *Ibid.*, Mv(v), Mvi(v), Nv(r).
150 Hill, *Interpretation of dreams* (1567), Pi(r).
151 *Ibid.*, Bii(r).
152 *Ibid.*, Biii(r).
153 *Ibid.*
154 *Ibid.*, Cvi(v)-Cvii(r).
155 *Ibid.*, Bii(r), Bii(v), Bv(v).
156 *Ibid.*, Bvii(r)-Bvii(v), Civ(v).
157 Laud, *Works*, 144.
158 Pepys, *Diary*, Vol. 1, 284–285; Vaughan, MS Sloane 1741, fols. 10, 90, 91, 103, 104.
159 Pepys, *Diary*, Vol. 5, 8.
160 John Aubrey, *Miscellanies* (London, 1696), 74.
161 Josselin, *Diary*, 183.
162 *Ibid.*, 325.

3 "Nocturnal whispers of the Allmighty"

Spiritual dreams and the discernment of spirits

On the 7th of January 1654, Anna Trapnel, the self-proclaimed prophet and daughter of a London shipwright, was waiting outside a chamber in Whitehall for the verdict on a Welsh radical minister. Sitting beside a fireplace, "being as it were seized by the Lord, she was carryed forth in the Spirit of prayer and singing from noon to night" until she was taken in by a Mr. Roberts where for 12 days she ate little and lay in a trance. Whilst in her trance, Trapnel experienced several "Visions and Revelations touching the Government of the Nation, the Parl. Army and Ministry and ... had a most strange Vision of horns; she saw fair Horns which were 4 Powers: the first was that of the Bishops, which first Horn she saw broke in two and thrown aside: then appeared the second Horn and joyned to it an head and although it seemed to bee more white then the first, yet it endeavouring to get aloft it was suddenly pulled down to piece."[1]

Trapnel had risen to fame by accurately predicting the arrival of the New Model Army into London weeks before its actual arrival in 1647. From this day forth her reputation grew as a true prophet whose visions correctly prophesied the outcome of the battle of Dunbar and many other events of the Civil Wars.[2] Trapnel represents one of many lay visionaries who emerged into the limelight as messengers from God, freed by the increased policy of toleration in the period 1642 to 1660 and driven by a sense of a divine mission.

As I will show in this chapter, during the seventeenth century several writers contested belief in prognostic dreams in response to the increasingly public profile of sectarian visionaries and the growing popularity of handbooks of divination. These critics drew from the frameworks of spiritual dreams and health to undermine both dream divination and claims to divine dreams as irreligious and superstitious follies. While before the Civil War critics focused on attacking oneiromancy alongside other practices such as astrology, after 1650 they became more concerned with false prophecies and visions. Writers such as the scholars Henry More (1614–1687), Meric Casaubon (1599–1671) and John Spencer (*bap.* 1630, *d.* 1693) used Robert Burton's pathology of "religious melancholy" to relegate claims to divine dreams as symptomatic of religious madness and "enthusiasm."[3] Within

90 *"Nocturnal whispers of the Allmighty"*

this new schema dreams became reinscribed into a discourse of "enthusiasm" and pathologies of madness that in the eighteenth century would challenge Christian ideas of revealed religion. However, while some writers sought to negate the significance of divine dreams, others, such as Philip Goodwin, sought to present a more positive view, seeing dreams not as prophetic revelations but rather as spiritually edifying experiences sent from God to strengthen individual faith and cultivate a closer relationship with his faithful. The category of spiritual dreams has therefore a complex history. Underlying the discourses and experiences of divine dreams was the inherent and longstanding problem of spiritual discernment – how to distinguish between supernatural and natural, divine from diabolic dreams.

Yet, the contested significance and meaning of dreams as divine visions was neither unique to England nor to this period but shows rather another continued facet of cultural ideas, attitudes and debates about dreams in early modern Europe. Debates about the discernment of dreams were a longstanding issue in Christian theology and part of the discernment of spirits (*discretio spirituum*).[4] The contested meaning of supernatural dreams was unresolved in these earlier periods and continued to be a serious issue for the Church throughout the medieval period, particularly during the Great Schism when female visionaries such as Catherine of Siena (1347–1380) and Bridget of Sweden (1303–1373) became embroiled in Church politics. In the fifteenth century the Church and secular rulers were alarmed by the political and spiritual power of visionaries such as Jeanne d'Arc (1412–1431) in France and Margery Kempe (1373–1438?) and later Elizabeth Barton, the Nun of Kent (1506?-1534) in England, amongst numerous others. These visionaries drew substantial followings and held both social and spiritual authority in their communities, solely due to their claim of divine visions.[5] The problem of divine dreams as sources of spiritual and political authority was therefore not unique to seventeenth-century England.

The emergence of sectarian visionaries during the English Revolution, seen against the background of the Radical Reformation on the Continent, made divine dreams a source of particular concern. The growing apprehension of writers with an unhindered belief in divine dreams was further triggered by the potential influence visionaries had over a wider community through the medium of print. Consequently, several writers such as Thomas Hobbes viewed them as catalysts of social disorder. Moreover, during the period from 1640 to 1690 England was subject to an unprecedented period of political and social instability. The combination of religious tolerance and political radicalism, in addition to the sporadic lapses in censorship and social stability, opened up a veritable Pandora's Box of religious radicalism. In a climate of social, political and religious disorder, groups such as the Fifth Monarchists, Anabaptists, Quakers and others emerged into the public sphere. Drawing strength from the Christian prophetic tradition and their conviction that they were living in the last days, visionaries believed they were sent to warn the English people of God's impending judgment. Charismatic visionaries such as Elizabeth Poole, Arise Evans, Anna Trapnel and others popularized their ecstatic millenarian visions both in print and at public gatherings.[6] The problem with these eschatological dreams lay in their means to empower lay visionaries and give credibility to their "seditious" messages. Moreover, by virtue of their claims to divine dreams, visionaries were able to transgress the limitations of their social status and gender, enabling men and women to speak in public about religion and politics in a way usually denied to them.

Underlying the problem of divine dreams was the ongoing issue of discernment and authentication. The ambivalent biblical view on dreams and the promise of an outpouring of prophesies, dreams and visions in Job and Acts at the dawn of the Apocalypse meant that authorities could neither simply discredit nor discount claims to divine dreams. Thus visionaries such as Elinor Channel and Arise Evans were able to gain access to Parliament and even have private audiences with Charles I and Oliver Cromwell.[7] Yet the Scripture's warning not to trust false prophets and co-existing medical theories of dreams as meaningless "flights of fancy" and melancholic delusion, combined with the equally powerful tradition of demonic dreams, further complicated the issue of supernatural dreams. Enmeshed in the problem of dreams was therefore the complex issue of spiritual discernment. Were visionaries truly inspired by God or were they merely suffering from mental illnesses, or alternately from demonic illusions? Contemporary views made divine dreams a site where the sacred and profane, natural and supernatural converged and where the borders were inherently porous and fundamentally ambiguous. What was ultimately at stake in debates about and claims to visions was power and authority, which in a climate of political and religious instability conferred on the visionary the liminal and exalted social status of God's herald.

Furthermore, the events of the Radical Reformation shifted the discourse on spiritual dreams away from classical oneirocritic ideas towards an understanding that was solely based on an exegesis of the Bible. Reformers rejected both Macrobius and Artemidorus' complex system of dream discernment in favour of a system that divided dreams into the more fundamental categories of natural, divine and demonic dreams. This was based on a simplification of Augustine's tripartite system and reflective of the new emphasis on the Bible as the only reliable and authentic source of truth. While Galen's ideas of natural dreams continued to be endorsed throughout the period, understandings of supernatural dreams were the source of heated debates about access to the divine. Inherent in this discourse was the idea of the dream as a liminal experience that bridged the human and divine, natural and supernatural worlds. Additionally, in a time of inherent crisis, both political and social, the dream lay at the centre of the ongoing confessional struggle delineating orthodoxy and authority.

While this study is primarily concerned with discussions of the broader ideas and more commonplace experiences of dreams, visions or supernatural

92 *"Nocturnal whispers of the Allmighty"*

dreams were an inherently linked and controversial facet of belief. The connection between dreams and visions derives from the ambiguous distinctions made between them in records of private dreams as well as those publicized in print. The dividing lines between the two were fundamentally blurred and often a matter of opinion. An individual, for example, might genuinely have believed that he/she had experienced a "vision" or divinely inspired dream, whilst others in their community or commentators in print might define the experience as a natural or even diabolic dream. Since the problem of discernment was at the very heart of debates about dreams and persisted throughout the period, this explains most especially why dreams were a source of controversy. Dreams might also be relegated to the more ambiguous category of the preternatural, the liminal spaces between the human and divine, angelic and demonic, natural and supernatural. A dream, for example, might derive from the Devil, a supernatural being, but the revelation contained was ultimately a trick or sleight of hand, which contained false information. Proponents of this preternatural category of dreams sought to undermine the power of the Devil and negate his ability to imitate God and possess omniscient knowledge of the future. Even if such a dream did indeed contain a true prophecy of future events, authors such as Philip Goodwin argued that the Devil obtained such divine insight through centuries of observation and a preternatural knowledge of human actions and behaviour. Since a variety of ideas of dreams co-existed, categories of dreams therefore existed along a spectrum, complimentary, ambiguous and often overlapping.

In premodern England divine dreams or visions were merely one sub-category of dreams – highly contested and often politicized, fabricated and formulaic. As I have sought to demonstrate, early modern people believed there were several different kinds of dreams with varying causes, meanings and significances. Dreams, for example, could be categorized as "natural" or "supernatural" or they might also be further sub-divided into "true" or "vain" and "angelic," "demonic" or "divine" dreams. Similarly, while a dreamer might conceive a particular dream as being a "vision" others might argue it was in fact a "natural," "demonic" or "vain" dream. To make matters more complicated categories of dreams frequently overlapped and were ambiguous. In spite of the numerous treatises on dreams published in the period, some of which attempted to codify dreams into discreet categories, the problem remained unresolved. Thomas Tryon remarked in the late seventeenth century:

> I call it neglected study; for though not a few of the Antients and some of the latter times have written concerning Dreams, as Aristotle, Themistius, Artemidorus, Carden, & c. yet did they not sufficiently comprehend the true Nature, Sourse, Original Radix thereof, nor the real Distinctions that are to be made of them and whence each kind do proceed; but have treated of the same so Darkly and at Random,

"Nocturnal whispers of the Allmighty" 93

with so little assurance and probability … whereof they have made large Volumes, which do but render those that mind them, more anxious and perplexed than before.[8]

As critics bewailed, the broader populace lacked the skill and learning to properly distinguish between different kinds of dreams and were consequently unaware of the subtleties of dream codification.[9] Similarly, the nuanced language and typologies of dreams contained in learned works and treatises on dreams and discernment were unavailable to all but a handful of educated men and thus their contents were lost to the broader community. Understandings of supernatural dreams were further reshaped and complicated by the religious reformations of the sixteenth and seventeenth centuries.

Dreams and the Reformation

English discussions of supernatural dreams were unquestionably influenced by Continental reformers' writings, which were catalysed by the events of the Radical Reformation. As in England, Europe experienced periods of social and political disorder as well as religious radicalism. This created a powerful forum for visionaries, the most famous being the Anabaptists, Zwickau Prophets and Dreamers, amongst others. The sixteenth and seventeenth centuries witnessed the emergence of numerous wars in Europe that arose in the wake of the Protestant Reformation. The period known as the Wars of Religion resulted in the deaths, suffering, impoverishment and displacement of countless communities and individuals across Europe. Although a plethora of small local conflicts erupted in the period, affecting only specific regional communities, several significant larger European wars flared up into wholesale warfare, affecting the lives of all those living within Europe's borders. In particular, the period witnessed the French Wars of Religion (1562–1598), Revolt of the Netherlands (1568–1648) and Thirty Years War (1618–1648). Spanning from Denmark to Hungary, warfare engulfed Europe in the early modern period, fundamentally influencing and destabilizing its political, social and cultural landscape. For this reason the early modern period has been understood as one of inherent crisis.

The tumultuous and schismatic rupture of the traditional church and subsequent questioning of orthodox theology during the sixteenth-century religious reformations led to the reappraisal of all facets of spirituality and lived religion. Dreams and visions were at the heart of debates about access to the divine and claims to spiritual authority within the community of believers. The theological fissures left by the Protestant Reformation and the splintering of Christendom into diffuse confessions led to the emergence of more radical forms of Protestantism that emphasized the Spirit over the Word. Fringe groups such as the Anabaptists, with their emphasis on dreams and visions as sources of spiritual authority and knowledge, forced

94 *"Nocturnal whispers of the Allmighty"*

members of the magisterial confessions to grapple with the slippery problem of dreams and visions.

The Protestant emphasis on the Word of God as the most powerful source of Christian truth and knowledge and the eradication of the traditional roles of the Priest and Church as mediators between humans and the divine left space for individuals to seize access to the divine themselves. No longer was there a need for a conduit between man and God, humanity and the divine. Similarly, the collapse of the moderating infrastructure of the Church and such bodies as the Church Courts allowed visionaries and dreamers free reign over claims to divine inspiration. Horrified by the Pandora's box of radical messages and visions of the sectarian visionaries and fearing further disruptions to the social and political order, the political and spiritual leaders of Europe and England faced the schismatic spiritual force they themselves had unwittingly unleashed.

At the heart of the problem of dreams was their liminal status between the human and the divine, God and the Devil as well as the natural and supernatural worlds. The inherent difficulty, as intellectuals and religious writers soon realized, was the longstanding issue of the discernment of spirits, in particular the problem of distinguishing natural from supernatural, divine from demonic dreams. However, as mentioned earlier, the ambiguity of dreams and the difficulty of discerning between natural and supernatural dreams was a longstanding problem of the Christian Church. Since the origins of Christianity, Christian writers, including the Church Fathers and canonical writers Thomas Aquinas and St. Augustine, had grappled with the issue of discernment. This too was a legacy of the ancient Greeks that had been discussed by the most formative classical philosophers, in particular Aristotle, Cicero and Plato. Later oneirocritic writers such as Artemidorus and Macrobius had attempted to bring order and clarity to the problem of dreams, both presenting a sophisticated and comprehensive schema of dreams that saw them as both prognostic and meaningful. However, both authors managed to circumvent the underlying contentious issue of origins.

The medieval period saw the continuation of theological discussions of supernatural dreams. Such debates, like later early modern ones, were instigated by the prominence of visionaries at large in the communities of the faithful and exerting influence on ecclesiastical as well as secular circles. As part of a vibrant medieval spirituality, divine dreams or visions as they were simultaneously termed, featured in the hagiographies and mystical lives of the medieval saints. As a mark of sanctity and a special grace, visions also led medieval mystics to influence Church politics and seek to impart their messages to religious and secular leaders. Such was the story of Catherine of Siena, Bridget of Sweden and Hildegard von Bingham. These influential female visionaries left a rich legacy of mystical writings and deeply imprinted the lives of their followers and communities. Inextricably tied to the problem of visions and supernatural dreams was the issue of women's roles within the Church. Ordinarily exempt from rising above the normative role of women in the Church and society, as some historians have argued, female mystics and visionaries were able to transgress their social limits and were elevated to a sanctified special status in their communities. However, if visions gave women a voice, they also brought the threat of censure.

Nevertheless, men also appeared in communities claiming mystical visions and elicited suspicion, censure and the heavy hand of the Church and state. Perhaps most infamous in England was William Hacket, an illiterate malt-maker from Northamptonshire, who in July 1591 proclaimed himself the messiah bringing Presbyterianism to England. Since his prophecies claimed that Elizabeth I had forfeited her crown through her support for episcopacy, Hacket and his two disciples were soon executed for treason by authorities, who remained wary of his potential to spread sedition and disorder.[10] In addition to the continuity of men and women's claims to divine visions and revelations throughout the premodern period, the concerns and claims of authorities were remarkably unchanging. Since the majority of people lacked the education necessary for understanding learned treatises on dreams, the issue of dream discernment was never fully resolved and the subtlety of philosophical, epistemological and theological ideas about dreams were lost on the broader populace.

The ongoing problem of dream discernment was instigated and exacerbated by the ambiguous legacy of the Bible. A ubiquitous and powerful cultural force in the confessional period thanks to the efforts of reformers and members of the ministering churches alike, the Bible was read, heard, interpreted and often memorized in daily life, regardless of one's confession. Unlike the classical discourses on dreams, the Bible was far more accessible and commonly viewed as the ultimate guide to truth and knowledge. However, on the subject of dreams it imparted a morass of contradictory views. On the one hand it endorsed dream interpretation, most notably in the stories of Daniel and Joseph. Additionally, the Bible promised that in the Last Days God would send dreams and visions to both men and women: "And it shall come to pass afterward, [that] I will pour out my spirit upon all flesh; and your sons and your daughters shall prophesy, your old men shall dream dreams, your young men shall see visions" (Joel 2:28) as well as "And he said, Hear now my words: If there be a prophet among you, [I] the LORD will make myself known unto him in a vision, [and] will speak unto him in a dream" (Num. 12:16). Conversely, the Christian Bible warned against false prophets and dreams: "For in the multitude of dreams and many words [there are] also [divers] vanities: but fear thou God" (Eccles. 5:7) and "Thou shalt not hearken unto the words of that prophet, or that dreamer of dreams" (Deut. 13:3). This conflicting message about dreams and visions remained at the centre of early modern debates concerning their credibility and origins.

The power of the immediate, vivid and highly visceral experience of a numanistic dream often caused individuals to fervently believe themselves gifted with a divine message and fundamentally convinced them of their special spiritual status. Claims to divine visions or supernatural dreams

Figure 3.1 "The three kings are told in a dream not to return to the land of Herod." Engraving. Wellcome Library, London.

further bestowed considerable spiritual authority on visionaries within their communities. With their anti-governmental and radical spiritual messages, threats to the social and political order via visionaries were long recognized by authorities. As Peter Marshall noted, the movement surrounding Elizabeth Barton or the Nun of Kent seriously threatened Henry VIII's reformation and restructuring of the English Church.[11] The mass social uprising and subsequent flocking of influential members of the Church and state to Barton led to a swift reprisal. This led to further legislation and a general suspicion of visionaries and supernatural dreams in the Elizabethan and Stuart periods. In the later sixteenth century, William Hacket's claims to be the messiah and politically charged prophetic messages earned him, in the mere space of a fortnight, the horrific death relegated for those who committed treason – being hanged, drawn and quartered. On the Continent, the undisguised political messages of Lucia de Leon also instigated Spanish authorities to carefully monitor the dreams of the visionary and the movements of her supporters.[12]

During the religious wars of the sixteenth and seventeenth centuries other visionaries emerged to lead popular movements and uprisings that left authorities apprehensive about the potential consequences of an unquestioned belief in the dream as a medium to the divine. Martin Luther and other reformers and secular leaders responded harshly to radical religious movements, particularly in the wake of the Münster Rebellion from 1534–1535. In 1534 an Anabaptist group led by Jan van Leiden and Jan Matthijs took over the city and expelled all Catholics, declaring it the New Jerusalem. After the death of Matthijs and based on a series of visions, Leiden proclaimed himself the successor of David and King of Münster. He then instituted polygamy and a form of religious communism, much to the horror of all. This led to the successful siege of the city by Catholic forces under the control of the bishop, Count Franz von Waldeck. The sect was harshly punished and its leaders, including Leiden, were tortured and publically executed, their bodies displayed in metal cages for all to see.[13] This incident served for all thereafter as a warning of the dangers of religious radicalism and an unmitigated belief in divine dreams.

The emphasis of new fringe groups such as the Anabaptists, amongst others, on the authority of the Holy Spirit or inner light over the Word and their reliance on dreams as sources of spiritual truth and social power directed reformers to reconsider the dream. This drove some to suggest that God had ceased sending revelations through dreams – that the divine message was complete and revelations no longer occurred. These writers, including Luther, promoted a more cautious approach to dreams and warned of mistaking natural for supernatural and demonic for divine dreams. As historians have demonstrated, supernatural dreams and apocalyptic visions flourish in periods of political and social crisis.[14] In the absence of authority and order, the masses often turned to charismatic leaders claiming divine inspiration and the prophetic gifts made manifest in dreams and visions. The Anabaptists were joined on the Continent and in England by a legion of other radical visionaries affiliated with Protestant fringe groups, heralding their dreams as the ultimate proof of their spiritual authority and claiming to offer insight into God's divine plan.

Reformers' writings on dreams

Martin Luther's reliance on the Bible as the sole source of all knowledge about dreams and his rejection of the classics was highly influential on both Continental and English learned understandings of dreams. Philip Goodwin, in particular, quoted extensively from Luther's writings in his significant spiritual treatise on dreams, *The mystery of dreames, historically discoursed* (1658). Luther himself wrote at length about dreams in his commentaries on Genesis, particularly chapters 15 to 41, since dreams, visions and prophecies proliferated in the stories of Jacob and Joseph. In response to the growth of radical visionaries and prophets on the Continent as well to the events at Münster, Luther presented a fundamentally cautious view of dreams and visions. In his schema, divine revelations could be put into three broad categories and ranked in order of significance: (1) When God spoke "mouth to mouth" or "face to face" as he did to Moses (Num. 12:6–8), (2) visions/apparitions and (3) dreams. According to

Luther's commentary on Genesis 15:1, "it is a vision or a form of apparition when God appears to people when they are awake, not as in dreams" while "dreams are on a level below this. Scripture often mentions them. Even though a man is asleep and is not making use of his sense organs, some images present themselves to his mind while the body is sleeping and the sense organs are resting."[15]

Luther was unusual in clearly demarcating dreams from visions and the Bible itself often conflated the two, for example in Job 33:15, "In a dream, in a vision of the night, when deep sleep falleth upon men." In a later commentary on Genesis 40:16–19 he further explained that the "grade of dreams" may be sub-divided into divine, diabolic and "physical" dreams. Divine dreams were "sure impressions sent by God and have attached to them not only the interpretation but also trust and belief on the part of those to whom they are shown." "Diabolic" dreams originated from the Devil, while

Figure 3.2 "Songe de St. Joseph." Engraved By: Anton Raphaël Mengs after Jean-Baptiste Joseph Wicar and Francois Morel. Wellcome Library, London.

in "physical" dreams Luther deferred to the expertise of doctors "from which they conclude what the nature of the constitution of the blood or the whole body is." The last two types of dreams were meaningless; only divine dreams were worthy of note.[16] This categorization of dreams was by no means novel and drew from the ideas of the Stoics, Tertullian, Augustine and Thomas Aquinas.[17] What is noteworthy in Luther's epistemology of dreams is that he ignores the writings of Macrobius, Artemidorus and other classical authors in favour of a purely Christian schema based on a Scriptural exegesis. This was an approach emulated by later early modern English authors such as Philip Goodwin and John Beale, reflecting the influence of Luther's writings. Moreover, Luther's fellow reformers including Philip Melanchthon and Caspar Peucer also followed his lead, overtly rejecting the classification of Macrobius and adopting Augustine's tripartite system.[18]

While the problem of discernment was longstanding, the Reformation fundamentally influenced early modern understandings of dreams by shifting accepted notions away from classical models and more firmly towards one that was fundamentally Christian, Protestant and based on Scripture. This in turn cultivated an even more problematic status of spiritual dreams that would divide Protestant writers into two camps – those who believed divine dreams had ceased with the end of the New Testament and those who asserted that prophetic dreams continued. Finally, divine dreams also became inscribed into the language and discourse surrounding providence and prognostic dreams were seen by both Protestant writers and their communities not simply as manifestations of God's continued revelation but also as signs of his special providence and part of the pious Christian's spiritual toolkit. The Reformation therefore significantly altered the language through which dreams were discussed and in turn shaped popular beliefs in dreams.

Unlike several other Protestant authors, such as Melanchthon and Peucer, Luther did not deny that divine dreams might indeed continue. However, he himself was deeply suspicious of dreams. Interestingly, Luther writes in his lectures on Genesis that he had made a "pact" with God "that He should not send me visions or dreams or even angels. For I am content with this gift which I have, Holy Scripture." This was because Luther distrusted his ability to discern between true dreams and demonic illusions disguised as revelations: "For I am influenced by that infinite multitude of illusions, deceptions and impostures by which the world was horribly deceived." He further extrapolates, "for I am not qualified to have dreams or to explain them nor do I seek this ability or knowledge for myself." According to Luther, the "gifts" of the Word and the Sacraments were enough since it was impossible to be deceived by them.[19] On his own experiences of dreams he revealed that "I do, indeed, have dreams from time to time, which move me somewhat, but I think little of them and I have made a pact with my Lord that I want to believe Moses and the Prophets."[20] Even more illuminating

100   *"Nocturnal whispers of the Allmighty"*

is a later commentary in which Luther vividly portrayed his many struggles with "fanatical spirits" who promised him dreams:

> I have often stated that at the beginning of my cause I always asked the Lord not to send me dreams, visions, or angels. For many fanatical spirits attacked me, one of whom boasted of dreams, another of visions and another of revelations with which they were striving to instruct me. But I replied that I was not seeking such revelations and that if any were offered, I would put no trust in them. And I prayed ardently to God that He might give me the sure meaning and understanding of Holy Scripture. For if I have the Word, I know that I am proceeding on the right way and cannot easily be deceived or go wrong. Indeed, I prefer the understanding of David to prophetic visions, which I do not think that David greatly desired. But see what a sure meaning of Scripture he has.[21]

Despite his own deep distrust of dreams, Luther did not rule out that this "gift" belonged to others: "But, as I said, this reason is peculiar to me and I would not dare to prescribe anything for others."[22] Furthermore, he noted that the continuity of divine dreams was supported by Scripture in Joel 2:28 and Numbers 12:6–8.[23] If indeed divine dreams continued, the difficulty was in distinguishing between divine and demonic dreams.

In his discussions of dreams Luther attempted to provide some practical advice on the problem of discernment and warned his readers to be wary of the Devil's false dreams. He explained that the Devil often sent dreams in the guise of the divine to deceive the faithful: "But because superstition and curiosity plague the hearts of men in various ways, Satan also often mocks men on this account. Therefore it is not always easy to make a distinction."[24] Moreover, the Devil possessed the ability to send dreams that were in fact true and prescient since he was "trained and equipped with an infinite number of God's government and he likewise knows the wishes, purposes and plans of men and even governs them ... so predictions about the future are easy for him." However, this was not to suggest that the Devil had an equal power to that of God: his "true" dreams were ultimately acts of legerdemain or sleights of hand. Luther also argued that the Devil was unable to see into the hearts of men "for faith and God's Word is a dark cloud to him into which he cannot penetrate with his light."[25] Here Luther is in effect compressing demonic dreams into the category of the preternatural. While such dreams derive from the Devil, a supernatural being, according to Luther the message they contained and the revealed futurity derived not from supernatural prescience but rather from a preternatural ability to understand human motivation.

According to Luther, divine dreams could also be discerned by their agreement with the Scriptures and by the emotional impressions they imprinted in the soul: "through the dreams from God an impression of such a nature is made on the hearts that not only the intellect but also the will is troubled beyond normal."[26] Divine dreams "agitated the heart" and moved the soul with the sheer force of their godly nature. Additionally, dreams that derived from God, like the Word, "never depart without accomplishing their purpose." Luther also believed that divine dreams were typically accompanied by their corresponding interpretations: God "implants dreams in the mind, at the same time [he] adds an interpretation and execution." Thus, true dreams were both fulfilled and explained by a corresponding interpretation that was most often attached to the dream or other times communicated via a divinely inspired dream interpreter, such as Daniel or Joseph. Such interpreters were able to decode the dream and "teach its significance under the illumination of the Holy Spirit."[27] Above all, according to Luther, divine dreams must agree with Scripture and "if they are not in harmony with the Word or destroy faith, they are of Satan."[28] Thus, Luther concluded that the Anabaptists at Münster "godless err in their interpretation and understanding of dreams, just as they talk nonsense when they explain signs and prodigies; for they neither observe nor have the Word."[29]

Luther's ideas were highly influential in shaping Protestant views of dreams: his emphasis on the Bible as the sole source of truth in understanding and categorizing dreams was adopted by other Protestant writers both in England and the Continent. Philip Goodwin cited Luther as an authority on dreams and wrote, "For writings Polemicall, read Luther, who hath large and learned Disputations and Dilucidations of Dreams, discussing how they may be discriminated and to what to them may be appropriated."[30] John Beale also adopted Luther's approach, explicitly rejecting the dream classification system of Macrobius in favour of one that was reinforced by an exegesis of the Bible. Compared to writings of John Calvin, who wrote little on the subject, Luther wrote extensively about dreams in his commentaries on Genesis and saw them as a significant source of spiritual edification and God's continuing revelation. Thus, while he vociferously advocated a cautious approach to heeding dreams and visions, Luther warned that it was a "great ingratitude to slight these faces of God."[31] Additionally, as can be seen by his frequent references to Anabaptists and *Schwärmers*, Luther's in-depth discussions of the problem of the discernment of dreams were a response to the spread of claims to divinely inspired revelations amongst fringe groups of Protestants.

John Calvin was much more circumspect on the subject of dreams; however, he presented a view of dreams in accordance with Luther's conclusions. In his *Commentaries on the Book of Daniel,* Calvin advocated for a prudent approach to dreams as both meaningful and divine. Like many other contemporaries, Calvin asserted that there are various causes and types of dreams and loosely divided them into natural, preternatural and supernatural categories. Calvin sternly warned his readers that to ascribe all dreams with divine agency "would be foolish and puerile ... as we see some persons never passing by a single one without a conjecture and thus making themselves ridiculous."[32] Calvin also emphasized that many dreams

102 *"Nocturnal whispers of the Allmighty"*

are in fact natural and caused by either thoughts of the day, intemperance or the natural functions of the body.

Like Luther, Calvin was reluctant to rule out completely the possibility of divine dreams and wrote: "As there are many natural causes for dreams, it would be quite out of character to be seeking for divine agency or fixed reason in them all; and on the other hand, it is sufficiently evident that some dreams are under divine regulation."[33] Similarly, Calvin rejected the classification scheme of Macrobius and commented, "The distinction made by Macrobius is worthy of notice; although he ignorantly confounds species and genera, through being a person of imperfect judgment, who strung together in rhapsodies whatever he read, without either discrimination or arrangement."[34] While Calvin considered the writings of Aristotle and Cicero with more esteem, he condemned them for denying outright the possibility of divine agency in dreams. Above all, Calvin referred to the Bible as the most reliable authority on dreams. He explained that although God sometimes sent dreams that explicitly revealed the future, the deity typically sent "allegorical" and "obscure" dreams, which required an interpretation. "Hence God often speaks in enigmas by dreams, until the interpretation is added. And such was Nebuchadnezzar's dream." He further extrapolates,

> We must hold generally that the art of conjecturing from dreams is rash and foolish; there is, indeed, a certain fixed interpretation of dreams, … yet as we shall afterwards see, this ought not to be ascribed to a sure science, but to God's singular gift. As therefore, a prophet will not gather what he has to say from fixed reasonings, but will explain God's oracles, so also he who will interpret dreams correctly, will not follow certain distinct rules; but if God has explained the meaning of the dream, he will then undertake the office of interpreting it according to his endowment with this gift. Properly speaking, these two things are opposite to each other and do not mutually agree, general and perpetual science and special revelation. Since God claims this power of opening by means of a dream, what he has engraven on the minds of men, hence art and science cannot obtain it, but a revelation from the spirit must be waited for.[35]

Calvin's views of supernatural dreams were remarkably in accordance with the ideas of Martin Luther. Like Luther, Calvin advocated for a judicious view of dreams, acknowledging that there are various kinds of dreams that can be broadly defined as natural and supernatural. To heed natural dreams as divine was both "rash" and "ridiculous" while divine dreams were a "gift" sent by God. These dreams were often encoded and required an interpretation that was believed to accompany the dream. This prudent view of dreams and overt rejection of classical models in favour of a system reliant on an exegesis of Scripture pervaded religious writings on dreams in the period of the reformations. Calvin's writings, like those of Luther, filtered into English discourses on dreams and were adopted by writers such as Philip Goodwin, who sought an orthodox and Protestant view of dreams.

Spiritual dreams in early modern England

In early modern England, as on the Continent, the religious reformations led to a destabilization of society and sporadic periods of civil warfare. Although supernatural dreams had been a cause for concern before this period, the emergence of radical Protestant fringe groups often centring around visionaries and their claims to supernaturally inspired dreams led to the reappraisal of dreams as forms of divine inspiration. The emergence of sectarian visionaries was made more problematic by the marshalling of print to spread their messages. While some authors such as Philip Goodwin sought to reappropriate dreams productively within a more orthodox Protestant system of spiritual introspection, allowing for the continuity of divine dreams, others, perturbed by the seditious messages and audacity of sectarians, argued that divine dreams had ceased with the end of the New Testament. In response to what they perceived as the growth of "enthusiasm" in the populace, a "gangrene" in society that threatened to infect the body politic and sicken society, writers such as Henry More, Meric Casaubon, Robert Burton and others argued that such persons were in fact delusional, mad and suffering from an acute specialized form of melancholy. The older dichotomy and close boundaries between dreams and madness, natural and supernatural dreams were thus collapsed and dreams became more intrinsically incorporated into a pathology of religious madness.

English debates about supernatural dreams appeared in a range of printed works directly and indirectly dealing with the problem of prognostic dreams, including works of demonology, philosophy, anti-astrology and anti-enthusiasm. In this way, published attacks against false beliefs in dreams were part of a broader concern with the spread of witchcraft, astrology, superstition and irreligion. Overall, with the exception of Thomas Nashe's *The terrors of the night* (1594), few works took dreams as their sole, or main, target. However, erroneous beliefs about predictive and prophetic dreams were an important part of broader anxieties concerning irreligion and social disorder.

Discussions about dream divination were a significant part of demonological works since divination was considered one of the key practices of witchcraft according to authors such as Reginald Scot, William Perkins, John Cotta and Thomas Ady. While Reginald Scot's *The discoverie of witchcraft* (1584) and Thomas Ady's *A candle in the dark* (1655) offered a sceptical view of witchcraft, demonological tracts by William Perkins and John Cotta sought to prove the real existence of witches.[36] In both strands of demonology, dream divination was condemned as either a real act of witchcraft or as a vain, superstitious practice. The perceived close relationship between

104   *"Nocturnal whispers of the Allmighty"*

dream divination and witchcraft becomes evident in Thomas Ady's *A candle in the dark* where he explained,

> Seeing it is manifest by the Scriptures, as appeareth in this second description of a Witch, that he that useth divination is a Witch and one main pretence in giving Divinations, was Dreams and Visions of the night, then it may bee supposed that he that telleth a Dream to his neighbour, thereby fore-telling things to come, useth Divinations and ought to be censured as a Witch, or else must needs bee a Prophet.[37]

For demonologists, the problem of dream divination was therefore that it was perceived as practicing witchcraft and, subsequently, as an act performed in league with the Devil. William Perkins explained: "Divining by the second sort [natural dreams] is superstitious, having no ground from God's word; so foretelling by this third sort [demonic dreams] is that Witchcraft, directly condemned ... where men are forbidden to prophecie by them, or to regard them."[38] According to Perkins and other writers, most people were unable to discern natural from divine or demonic dreams.[39]

In addition to works of demonology, criticisms of popular belief in dreams appeared in anti-astrological and anti-prophetic tracts published by clerics, statesmen and intellectuals. Public attacks on astrology and oneiromancy appeared in Sir John Melton's *The astrologaster-or figure-caster* (1620) and John Gaule's *Pus-mantia: the mag-astro-mancer* (1652). Authors of anti-astrological works were convinced that astrologers were responsible for the spread of irreligion and superstition and for the corruption of the Faith. Gaule vehemently ranted against the plague of astrologers in his preface to the reader, claiming that he was standing up for God and the common people:

> Only and indeed, I conceived my self called to stand up and speak for God, for Christ, for the Holy Ghost; for the word, the Church, the Saints; against such a press and pest of Magicall, Mag-astrologicall, Mago-manticall, Mag-ephemeriall, Mag-philosophicall, Mago-physicall, Mago-chymicall, Mago-mecuriall, Mag-hereticall, Mago schismaticall, Mag-hypocriticall, Mago-scripticall, Mag-atheisticall, Mago-comicall, Mago-jesuiticall, Mago-romanticall, Mago-quixaticall, Mago-sacerdotall, Mago-politicall, Mago fanaticall and Mago-diabolicall Books: of late crept, nay crowded in amongst us (some in their pamphletetizing edition, some in their voluminous translation) to the great dishonouring of God, denying of Christ, despiting of the Spirit, cauponizing of the word, disturbing of the Church, subverting of religion, distracting of the state, scandalling of weak Christians and seducing of the common people.[40]

These anti-astrological treatises argued that, as one of the divinatory sciences popularized by astrologers, dream divination was a particularly nefarious form of superstition, folly and witchcraft that was ultimately offensive to God. Melton addressed this message to his readers: "But in generall, Dreames are not to be beleeved: for they are most wicked and odious in the sight of God."[41] Authors such as Gaule and Melton believed that astrologers were ultimately responsible for much of the irreligion and schism of the period through their popularization of multiple techniques of divination. These critics saw themselves as champions of true religion and social order as well as defenders of the ignorant common people. According to them, knowledge of the future was "the sole property of a true God."[42] To claim otherwise was to presume divine prescience and contravene the dictates of providence.

A central aim of authors concerned with erroneous belief in predictive dreams was to convince their readers that dream divination was a superstitious and diabolical practice. In their demonological and anti-astrological works, John Gaule and William Perkins asserted that all forms of divination, including oneiromancy, were acts of witchcraft. Perkins explained in his treatise, *A discourse on the damned art of witchcraft* (1608): "The common observations of dreames in the world, whereby men imagine things to come to passe, & accordingly foretell them by those means, are vaine and superstitious and justly so condemned in the places before the damned."[43] John Gaule asserted that divination was diabolical and should be "censured ... not only because of a compact, either explicite or implicite, or of an invocation, adjuration, imprecation ... but also because of a superstitious assent, proud curiosity, presumptuous temptation."[44] According to Gaule, astrologers and witches conflated divination with prophecy and claimed for themselves a "gift" only given to true prophets: "Prophecy is from God, a gift inspired by the Holy Spirit: Divination is from the Devil, a delusion suggested by an evil spirit."[45] Above all, critics argued that to practice oneiromancy in order to seek signs of the future was to directly contravene the teachings of the Scriptures and the dictates of providence.

These writers believed astrologers were at the forefront of a growing problem of dream divination and held them directly responsible for the spread of irreligion, sedition and superstition, arguing that they corrupted the faith of the "common people." According to Sir John Melton, astrologers had misled the populace for their own "vain-glory" and "profit" through the sale of their almanacs, fortune-telling books and political prophecies. Melton elaborated in his anti-astrological tract, *The astrologaster, or, the figure-caster* (1620): "But the reason that many Astrologers and Prognosticators erre in their Opinion ... is because they doe not keepe themselves within the compasse of Astrologie, but thristie after Vaine-glory, goe beyond their limits."[46] In this statement, Melton espoused that astrologers claimed to know the outcome of every aspect of life, including the political fate of the nation, while such prescience belonged to God alone.

In works of demonology and anti-astrology, critics of dreams saw themselves rather patronizingly as champions of the "common" people, working

106 *"Nocturnal whispers of the Allmighty"*

to defend them from the "abuses" of astrologers. Because of a general lack of learning and a "natural inclination" towards superstition among common people, "swarms" of astrologers and "interpreters of dreams" had misled them. An exasperated John Brinley complained,

> Hence proceed those swarms of Fortune-Tellers, Geomancers, Diviners and Interpreters of Dreams, who possess the Common people with apprehensions, that they know all their Fate, the number of their Days, the Casualties of their Life; and by their natural inclinations and thoughts of their hearts: by this means Cheating the poor innocent Souls into the grossest Superstition imaginable.[47]

These writers thus saw astrologers as nefarious cheats who spread superstition amongst an ignorant populace out of a selfish desire for glory and profit.

In the view of most critics, to seek knowledge of God's secrets – to try and foretell the future – was a heretical, presumptuous vanity that also contradicted providence. Gaule chastised his readers: "Hath not the Scripture sufficiently forbidden to *tempt God*, by a curious scrutinie after all such things as pertain to his secret Will?"[48] Reginald Scot reprimanded practitioners of dream divination by referring to the Scriptures: "Doth not Daniel the Prophet say, even in this case. 'It is the Lord only that knoweth such secrets,' as in the exposition of Dreams is required? And doth not Joseph repeat those very words to Pharaohs officers, who consulted with him therein?"[49] For many writers, the Bible offered the clearest warning against dream divination and visions, even while it conversely offered practitioners and visionaries validation. Thomas Ady noted: "And whereas some may now question whether Dreames are now sent by God to forewarn, as in ancient times, so long as we have no Scripture to the contrary (but rather for it) wee may not deny it."[50]

Since the Scriptures offered contradictory views of dreams, describing them as both orthodox and unorthodox aspects of Christian belief, early modern people faced a difficult theological conundrum. Reginald Scot reminded readers of the scriptural admonishment, "not to follow nor hearken to the expositors of Dreams ... Eccles 24. Jerem. 27. Eccl. 5" for "such Divine power as onelie belongeth to God, as appeareth in Jeremie the Prophet."[51] Similarly, Thomas Ady noted that in the Bible, "dreams were proper to the Prophets only, Numb. 12. 6. and they that did falsely pretend such Dreams and Inspirations, to dissemble the Prophets, to seduce the people to Idolatry were Witches, or false Prophets, according to this second description of using lying Divinations and ought to be slain, Deut. 13.1.5."[52]

However, most demonologists were careful not to condemn outright the possibility of divine dreams, since, as William Perkins soberly mused, "by them the most worthie prophets of God have revealed Gods will in many things to his Church."[53] Following continental reformers' ideas, writers resolved this dilemma in one of two ways. First, Reginald Scot and John

Gaule argued that prophecy and divine dreams had ceased with the coming of Christ.[54]

> Whether Prophesie be now ceast? It was never intended to be perpetual. Even while it was, it was an act; not an habit: not permanent, but transient. The Spirit now in the illapse and again upon the recesse. It was a gift or grace, not so much personal, as vocational: pertaining not to ordinary duty so much, as extraordinary occasion ... It was therefore meet that the shadow should recede, now that the substance came in place; Prophecy was necessary for the Church of the Old Testament, because Christ was not yet come: but not so in this of the New; because Christ is come already. We have an Evangelical prophesie, abundantly recompencing.[55]

Second, writers such as Thomas Ady, more cautious about an outright denial of visions, suggested that divine dreams were, at best, rare possibilities.[56]

Another criticism of contemporary belief in supernatural dreams, which linked them with witchcraft, was that these were in fact demonic dreams sent by the Devil to lead the dreamer into sin and delusion. The danger of mistaking demonic dreams for divine was fundamentally based on the Apostle Paul's warning in 2 Cor. 11: 13: "for Satan himself is transformed into an angel of light."[57] William Perkins explained, "Concerning the third kinde of dreames, which are caused by the devill; It hath beene granted in all ages for a truth, that Satan can forme dreames in the brayne of men and by them reveall his divinations."[58] John Cotta also argued: "If these whispered revelations cannot bee of God, then are they necessarily of the Devil."[59] There was a very real danger, critics warned, that the "common people" could be misled by the Devil with false visions into superstition, illusion and schism. John Melton gave this warning to his readers: "To affirme with many old women that all dreames are true, for this is but a tricke of the devill to bring us into superstition."[60] Since divine dreams were either rare or had ceased altogether, dreams, according to demonologists, were much more likely to be demonic than divine.

Melancholy and the pathologization of dreams

To question the credibility of dreams as predictive oracles, critics utilized two other important counterarguments. First, they argued that ignorant folk mistook natural, "vain" dreams for divine visions. The majority of authors who denounced popular belief in predictive dreams drew on contemporary theories of natural dreams to combat what they saw as ignorant folly. Thomas Ady explained: "Natural dreames I deny not, which come from the multitude of business and from the natural disposition of the body, but none of these are any way concerning future events, but are only the objects of our Natural affections."[61] Thomas Nashe maintained: "A dream is nothing else

108   *"Nocturnal whispers of the Allmighty"*

but the Eccho of our conceits of the day. ... When all is said, melancholy is the mother of all dreames and of all the terrors of the night whatsoever."[62] Similarly, John Melton explained "dreames sometimes proceed from the fulnes of the belly, sometimes from the emptiness of the belly ... some hold that the cause of dreames ariseth from the business and affairs a man is most imployed in the day time."[63] By advocating natural theories of dreams, these writers drew from longstanding, less contested ideas about natural dreams and were fundamentally attempting to undermine "vulgar" beliefs in both dream divination and divine dreams.

Second, in response to the increase of sectarian visionaries and the spread of political prophecies in print, a more intellectually powerful counter-argument was launched in the 1650s when both Henry More and Meric Causabon drew from Robert Burton's ideas of "religious melancholy" to denounce the spread of sectarianism and prophetic visions as symptoms of "enthusiasm." These authors used Burton's theories to illustrate how visionaries and "enthusiasts" exhibited not divine inspiration but rather a form of religious madness resulting in false perceptions.[64] According to Burton, "religious melancholy" was caused by a "corrupt fantasie" and an excess of "fumes which arise from this corrupt blood."[65] The melancholic person, "if devout and religious, he is all for fasting, prayer, ceremonies, almes, interpretations, visions, prophecies, revelations, that he is inspired by the Holy Ghost, full of Spirit."[66] While the idea of religious madness was not necessarily new, Burton's appropriation of humoral medicine to explain the physiological and psychological causes of "religious enthusiasm" was a powerful explanatory tool that appealed to writers seeking to undermine the spread of sectarianism and prophetic visions.

Within the pathology of "religious enthusiasm," spiritual inspirations, dreams and visions were primary symptoms. In his important work, *Enthusiasmus triumphatus* (1656), Henry More clearly defined "enthusiasm" as "nothing else but a misconceit of being inspired."[67] "Enthusiasts" are so befuddled with melancholy that their "faculties ... can neither keep out nor distinguish betwixt her own fancies and reall truths."[68] That is to say, they took their delusions and natural dreams for a "misconceit" of receiving divine visions. According to More, a primary cause of these enthusiastic "flights of fancy" was the enormous force of the imagination, the ultimate cause of all madness and delusion.[69] Subsequently, all so-called prophets and visionaries were suffering from pathological delusions that were entirely natural in origin, making them more an object of pity and in need of "physic" rather than a threat to the social order and an object of awe.

More's powerful critique of visionaries, sectarians and contemporary beliefs in spiritual visions laid the foundations for eighteenth-century philosophers to develop these ideas to their logical conclusions. In response to the rise in "detestable Sects and heresies" and the "brainsicke fools" who claimed to be God's chosen prophets in the seventeenth century in England and Europe, eighteenth-century philosophers and writers began to undermine all beliefs in revealed religion. This ultimately led to further battles in print between advocates of revealed and rational religion.[70] At the heart of this debate was the problem of dreams as inspired messages from God.

Advocates of spiritual dreams

While critics lodged their counterattacks against popular belief in prophetic dreams, other writers such as the clerics Philip Goodwin and John Beale sought to present a middle ground, combatting what they saw as atheism and "sadducism." Drawing from both Scripture and Luther's commentaries on Genesis, Goodwin and Beale argued that divine dreams might indeed continue; however, the discerning Christian must distinguish these gifts from the illusions of the Devil. While these authors sought to temper an unhindered belief in divine dreams, they viewed the denial of the continuation of visions as atheistic and ultimately as a threat to undermine all Christian belief in revealed religion. Additionally, both Goodwin and Beale's defence of divine dreams represents the continuity of learned support for a supernatural understanding of dreams, notwithstanding the rise of "rational" religion.

Little is known about Goodwin and his life as a pastor of Watford during the Interregnum. What we do know paints a portrait of a well-educated cleric, genuinely interested in the pastoral care of his parishioners, whose income was enough to leave a legacy of 400 pounds and four properties to his five children and widow.[71] Goodwin matriculated at St. John's College, Cambridge, in 1623 and graduated B.A. in March 1627. It may be that at St. John's Goodwin developed his Calvinist sympathies and Puritan connections, since the college was renowned for its strong Puritan ideologies.[72] Immediately upon graduation Goodwin was ordained a deacon and priest at Peterborough and proceeded to the M.A. in 1630.[73] Some time after 1630, Goodwin married Sarah King of Watford. The couple had five children living in 1667, John, James, Philip, Joseph and a married daughter, Sarah Walker.[74] Around 1633 Goodwin was appointed the curate of All Saint's Church in Hertford; four years later he was appointed curate at Watford, becoming vicar in 1643. Goodwin's career as a minister finally ended in June 1661 when he was ejected for non-conformity and he died six years later in 1667.[75]

In his four published works of practical divinity, Goodwin espoused a program of further ecclesiastical reform, moderate sabbatarianism and a strict program of spiritual introspection for the individual and the family.[76] Each of his four publications was designed as a practical guide for correct religious worship. Moreover, each of Goodwin's works, including his treatise on dreams, appears to have been based on sermons given to his community. In 1649 Goodwin published his first work, *The evangelicall communicant in the eucharisticall sacrament, or, a treatise declaring who are to receive the supper of the Lord.* As the title indicates, this treatise was intended to instruct readers on the proper understanding of the sacrament of the Eucharist and the "duties preparatory to this present Supper."[77] Goodwin's second

110   *"Nocturnal whispers of the Allmighty"*

publication was an extension of his first and designed to provide a practical comprehensive guide for religious worship. *Dies dominicus redivivus, or, The Lords Day enlivened* (1654) attempted "to recover the spiritual part of that Pious Practice to its primitive life: Lamentably lost, in these last Declining times."[78] Goodwin's publication a year later, *Religio domestica rediviva: or, Family-religion revived* (1655), presented a complete handbook of religion for the spiritual edification of the entire family.[79] Addressed "especially unto all Householders" or heads of households, Goodwin outlined an extensive program for family worship that included individual and communal prayers, spiritual meditation and Bible reading.

Goodwin's last work, *The mystery of dreames, historically discoursed* (1658), in many ways was an extension of his earlier religious handbooks and aimed to provide a practical guide for using dreams to assist in the pastoral care of the soul. Published towards the end of his career as vicar of Watford, Goodwin's handbook of dreams is unusual when compared to other early modern English dream handbooks, such as Thomas Hill's *The moste pleasant arte of the interpretacion of dreames* (1576) and Thomas Tryon's *A treatise of dreams & visions* (1689).[80] As a treatise on dreams, Goodwin's work deviates from traditional oneirocritic and religious tracts, seeing dreams as more "profitably" understood as a mirror to the soul. That is to say, rather than see dreams as predictive or as divine revelations, Goodwin proposed a theory of dreams as products of individual spirituality combined with the influence of supernatural agents – most especially God and the Devil. Consequently, for Goodwin, dreams could best serve the dreamer as a means to cultivate Christian piety and edify the soul. He argues that knowledge of dreams is profitable, since "a right knowledg of these Dreames, may much incite to such pious practices and profit Gods people, both asleep and awake."[81] Throughout the treatise, Goodwin provides a guide for how to use dreams to gain insight into the soul of the dreamer, how to prevent demonic dreams and prepare oneself for receiving divine dreams and finally, how to distinguish divine from demonic dreams. Although Goodwin's work is innovative in the history of dream discourses, his handbook is a companion to the many devotional works of practical divinity circulating in the period, popular amongst the godly.

The mystery of dreames is an erudite Protestant manual of dreams. In his text, Goodwin adds credibility to his arguments and clearly demonstrates his learning by drawing on an eclectic and impressive range of classical and to a greater extent Protestant contemporary works. In support of his theory of dreams, Goodwin refers to authors such as Aristotle, Galen, Hippocrates, Plutarch, Plato, Pliny and Virgil, amongst lesser-known authors of antiquity. Similarly, he merges the ideas of the classics with works of the Church Fathers, Augustine, Tertullian and Ambrose and more contemporary Protestant authors such as Luther, Calvin, Melanchthon, Jerome Zanchi and Louis Lavater as well as referring to the sermons of contemporary English preachers. However, above all the Bible features as the most pervasive influence and source for Goodwin's ideas on dreams and his text is suffused with scriptural quotations and exegeses. One of Goodwin's main arguments for why dreams are so fundamental for Christians comes from a close reading of the Bible.

Unlike some writers, Goodwin was not overtly concerned with dreams as predictive oracles, nor did he subscribe to classical oneirocritic frameworks. Instead, he espoused a purely spiritual framework of dreams, advocating for them as useful tools for obtaining insight into the state of grace of the soul, cultivating a closer relationship with God and deepening piety. For Goodwin, dreams were a "mystery," a "close covered *Dish* brought in by *night* for the *Soul* to feed on."[82] Contrary to other early modern supernatural ideas of dreams as oracles or revelations, in Goodwin's schema dreams were in essence food for the soul, offering the godly spiritual nourishment. Yet, by their very nature dreams were also often "darke," "veiled" and "covered."[83] Thus, they required careful interpretation to reveal their true hidden meaning. As such, Goodwin's work *The mystery of dreames, historically discoursed* offered readers a spiritual handbook for interpreting dreams and revealing their inherent mysteries.

The need to clearly define dreams was timely when Philip Goodwin published his treatise in 1658. In part a response to the "vain and false" dreams of visionaries who were drawing away the faithful into sectarianism, sin and delusion, one of Goodwin's aims was to realign dreams firmly, safely and productively within a Puritan practice of intense spiritual introspection. By promoting dreams as part of the useful spiritual toolkit for Christians and by supporting the continuation of divine and demonic dreams, Goodwin also aimed to counter the arguments of critics of divine dreams such as Reginald Scot, John Gaule and Moïse Amyraut, who suggested that divine dreams had ceased and demonic dreams were entirely natural in origin.[84] In Goodwin's view, dreams were still meaningful and some were indeed supernatural in origin. Above all, his work endeavoured to provide a lasting practical handbook for Christians to better understand their dreams, not as visions in the tradition of revelations, but rather as instructive mirrors to the soul.

As I have been suggesting throughout this book, early modern English writings on dreams reveal the sense of the vulnerability of the dreamer to a range of external and internal natural and supernatural stimuli. Goodwin's treatise on dreams reveals another facet of the perceived vulnerability of the individual dreamer, in particular to a host of dangerous attacks by the Devil, who sought through demonic dreams to mislead the Christian into sin and delusion. According to Goodwin and based on the writings of Luther, in sleep we are particularly vulnerable to the assaults of the Devil, who seizes on our waking sinful thoughts to send "filthy dreams." Additionally, in sleep the Christian dreamer was also subject to "terrifying" dreams sent from God to scare sinners into repentance and remorse. Thus, in Goodwin's schema of dreams, in sleep we are vulnerable to both divine and demonic dreams, which arise without our consent. Since demonic

112 *"Nocturnal whispers of the Allmighty"*

dreams are sent to "defile" and divine dreams are designed to "instruct" the dreamer, Goodwin's handbook offered readers techniques for both protecting against and profiting from demonic dreams and, conversely, preparing for receiving divine "instructive" dreams. In a sense Goodwin's treatise conferred on readers a form of agency over their dreams.

A close reading of Philip Goodwin's treatise also provides useful insight into the way an English cleric promoted a spiritual understanding of dreams within a Puritan framework. While English historians have long debated who "Puritans" were and what constituted the Puritan worldview and religious praxis, scholars now view Puritanism as a "variety of Reformed Protestantism" and Puritans as a "fissiparous" group within the broad spectrum of English Protestantism, difficult to distinguish as individuals yet identifiable by the intensity of their spiritual praxis.[85] While Puritans were not a homogenous group and incorporated a spectrum of positions from moderate Puritanism to separatism, they were recognizable to each other in their own communities.[86] Although containing a diversity of religious views and practices, particularly during the Interregnum, overall the culture of Puritanism was one that emphasized individual salvation, preaching, expounding the Scriptures and intense spiritual introspection.[87]

Goodwin's work offers a detailed case study of the way Puritans sought to understand spiritual dreams during the Interregnum. As a cleric whose work and religious ideology sat firmly within the Puritan tradition of preaching, intense spiritual introspection and a deep concern with individual salvation, Goodwin's work on dreams provides us with important insight into the way that dreams were understood in the "fissiparous" culture of Interregnum Puritanism. As the only extant English Puritan discourse on dreams, his work is an important example of one of the "symbolic codes" or cultural frameworks through which dreams were understood.

A significant agenda of Goodwin's treatise is to show the problems of blindly believing in visions and dreams as revelations from God. In his section on "False and Deluding Dreams" Goodwin warns readers against "false dreams" as catalysts for disorder and schism in the church, in addition to their danger for the individual soul. Yet, despite this warning, like Luther, Goodwin asserted that heeding dreams is in fact a "duty" of the godly Christian. On the problem of dreams he wrote in his epistle,

> Dreames may be *ambigious* [sic] and to *deed* them may be *dangerous*; Or on the other side, proceeding from Dreames to deeds, maybe a duty. And therefore though Dream impressions may make strong propensions and cause Inclinations to act, yet a man wise and well instructed, will weigh all in Gods balance before, by suitable actings he seeks to fulfill the same.[88]

Since discerning demonic from divine dreams was a recurring problem for early modern writers, in his work Goodwin helpfully provided clear criteria.

He believed that there were two main kinds of dreams – natural and supernatural. Natural dreams were "such thoughts in sleep as the mind emits or sends out by its own intrinsecall power, the proper *Product* of mans own head and heart," while supernatural dreams were "such thoughts in sleep as are immitted or sent into the mind through some extrinsecall principle," that is to say, by supernatural agents.[89] In addition to the umbrella categories of natural and supernatural dreams, following Luther, Goodwin added divine and demonic dreams under the rubric of supernatural dreams. Divine dreams were those dreams "from God" whilst demonic dreams were those "wherein the *Devil* hath his industrious dealing for mens monstruous defiling and deluding."[90] Much of Goodwin's treatise is concerned with demonic dreams. Christians were particularly vulnerable to demonic or "evil dreams," since "by such Diabolicall delusions, have severall in daies past been seduced and drawn upon such actions, as have proved their destructions."[91] The knowledge of how to distinguish demonic from divine dreams was deemed fundamental for all Christians, since "the Soul is secret that conceives them, & Satan is subtill to conceal them."[92] Dream discernment for Goodwin was therefore necessary since "to discover and finde out false Dreames: This is indeed *difficult*, through *Satans* designs and Mans *heart* deceits ... *Sinne* and *Satan* much seek to hide their *foot-steps*."[93] To help resolve these difficulties, Goodwin presented criteria for discernment. Again drawing from the commentaries of Luther, he suggested that dreams from God were "deeply different" from those sent by the Devil and were "made up of things, *Highly eminent in the sight of God, & wholly consonant to the Word of God*." On the other hand, demonic dreams "be about matters of no such *eminency* in the one, nor any such *consonancy* to the other." They were "filled with foolish frivolous, vain and ridiculous things and at all times they are opposite and repugnant, either in whole or in part, to the pure and precious Word of *God*."[94]

Citing Luther's commentaries on Genesis, Goodwin also argued that divine dreams could be easily recognized by their moderateness and orderliness and the wonderful "effects" they had on the dreamer, such as revealing the sin of pride and cultivating piety. Demonic dreams, on the other hand, were disorderly and contained the "pills of poisonous errors" and were easily discerned by their violence, confusion and evil effects on the mind, body and soul of the dreamer:

> *Secondly*, the *Manner* after which they are wrought in, is also differing. Dreams from the *Devil* they come in a man. *As more Hasty, So more Hidden*. In these Dreamings the *Devils* drivings are like to the drivings of *Jehu*, furious and fierce, thoughts throng in and thrust out with violence and force, so that thereby reason is oft darkened, brain distempered and powers disturbed, foot-steps so frequently confused, that little is orderly discerned. Thoughts be in the minde like *Rebekahs* twins in her womb, strugling together: but they do not like them come forth, one holding

114 *"Nocturnal whispers of the Allmighty"*

the heel of another; but be full of inconsistencies, lubricities, slippery, severed and unsetled, rushings in and rollings about. Reason so roving from one thing to another, that the minde makes miserable non-sence.[95]

Luther's influence can be seen in Goodwin's emphasis on the dangers of demonic dreams. He believed that in sleep we are particularly vulnerable to demonic dreams, which threatened to lead the dreamer into sin, delusion and irreligion. Demonstrative of the complexity of Goodwin's schema of dreams, in addition to the categories of divine and demonic dreams, he elucidated numerous other subsets of dreams. These subsets formed the structure of his chapters in the treatise. First and foremost were "False and Deluding dreames," which included dreams mistaken for divine visions that were actually demonic. The second category created by Goodwin was "Filthy and Defiling dreames," those dreams sent by the Devil that drew on the inherent sinfulness of the dreamer and "defiled" the body, mind and soul of the individual. Third were "Vain and Idle Dreames," which were "worldly" dreams that corrupted the dreamer by infusing his or her thoughts with "vain" wishes and images. A fourth category was "Troublesome and Affrighting dreames" that were sent by God himself, in the tradition of Job, to test and scare the dreamer into piety and repentance. Finally, Goodwin delineates the category of "Profitable and Instructing Dreames" that included divine dreams sent by God for the spiritual instruction of the Christian dreamer. Each of these categories of dreams was given an entire chapter that first defined the kind of dream and then provided practical help on how to use the dream for the spiritual edification of the dreamer. Even demonic dreams might be useful, according to Goodwin, since they revealed the "secret" sinful state of the dreamer and allowed one to discover and expunge sins that might otherwise remain hidden.[96]

The Devil's "false and deluding" dreams were potentially more destructive, being able to mislead not only the individual dreamer but also potentially the entire community. "False" dreams, according to Goodwin, masqueraded as "true" but were in actuality "the sleights of *Satan*."[97] "False" dreams were especially dangerous because through them "since the Apostles died, in Dreams have divers been seduced."[98] According to Goodwin, the plethora of false visionaries and prophets on the Continent and in England were suffering not from divine revelations but rather from "dreaming delusions" whose author was the Devil.[99] The "sparks" of these dreams had fallen from the Continent onto English ground.[100] As a result, sectarian visionaries had flourished. Because of their "false dreams," sectarians had abandoned their parishes:

Dreames declaring how *God* did *advise* them, counsell them, command them what wayes to forbear and which wayes to bend themselves. So some have of late years deserted our *publicke Assemblies*, into separated companies, as being warned of *God* in Deames so to do. The last Instance

"Nocturnal whispers of the Allmighty" 115

I heard related, was of a *Woman* in a neighbouring *Town*, who dreamed that *God* one night said to her, *Come out from among them and be ye separate, & c.* She awaked, fell asleep again and heard the same from God; so that, said she, *the Dreame was doubled, to shew the certainty.* In obedience to which, she ever after forsook all publicke Ordinances, though many years after she did not live. Her own *Sister*, who received this same from her mouth, is yet alive to *witness* it.[101]

Here we can see the heart of the problem of "false" and "deluding" dreams for Goodwin. As a minister with the sincere desire to protect the spiritual welfare of his parish, Goodwin saw the spread of sectarianism and false claims to divine dreams as the deliberate work of the Devil, whose ultimate aim was to lead England into religious dissent and schism. The most effective method for combating "false" dreams, according to Goodwin, was to be able to correctly discern "true" from "false" dreams.[102] Although Goodwin certainly did not deny the possibility that God did continue to send divine dreams, he argued that this was a rare occurrence. In his view "false" dreams were like lumps of "sugar" – coated with sweet Scripture, yet hiding the poisonous errors within.[103]

Showing the impact of the events of the Münster Rebellion on English ideas of dreams, in the section on "False and Deluding dreames," Goodwin explicitly refers to the dreams of the "Anabaptists," whose erroneous beliefs and dreams "in times *remote*" spread from Münster, Germany, "as *Seed* sown by *Satans* hand on *English ground*."[104] As J.F. McGregor notes, the incidents at Münster remained for well over a century a potent example for contemporaries of the dangers of popular religious heresy.[105] On the problem of "false" dreams in England Goodwin elaborated further that,

In *later* times Men have had here at home many a mistaking *Dreame*: Dreames drawn in by the *Devil*, which they have taken as tendred to them by the hand of a *Holy God*. Concerning, *What God would do for them, & What they should do for God. Dreames* declaring how *God* would *advance* them, raise them, use them and make them high for his honour; promoting persons of the same *Principles*, to great possessions, transactions; setting them upon bold presumptions, proud predictions, as have appeared from some in their printed *Pamphlets*.[106]

In this passage Goodwin articulates his concern with the claims of contemporary English sectarians to divine dreams. He refers to their "proud predictions" and "printed *Pamphlets*" suggesting that he was responding to sectarians whose prophetic visions were publicized in print during the late 1640s and more so 1650s.[107] While it is difficult to know from Goodwin's brief reference which specific sectarian works he was responding to, his concern with Anabaptism was most likely triggered by the presence of Baptist and non-conformist conventicles in the vicinity of his parish of Watford

116   *"Nocturnal whispers of the Allmighty"*

during the 1640s and 1650s. Although Goodwin endeavoured to write a "historical" treatise on dreams, this excerpt suggests a more contemporaneous agenda. His inclusion of a lengthy discussion of "false and deluding dreams" shows how Goodwin sought to present an alternate explanation for contemporary claims to divine dreams. He argued that such dreams were not true revelations, rather they were demonic dreams disguised as divine. Thus, self-proclaimed visionaries were not suffering from "enthusiasm," neither were they mistaking natural for supernatural dreams, as other authors such as Thomas Hobbes and Henry More had suggested; rather, according to Goodwin's spiritual framework of dreams, they were victims of the Devil, who sought through "false" dreams to mislead individuals and their communities into sin, delusion and schism.[108]

Nehemiah Wallington's dreams

Evidence for a spiritual approach to dreams that emulates Goodwin's schema can be found in the notebooks and records of dreams of the London turner, Nehemiah Wallington (1598–1658). In his abundant collection of notebooks, of which seven survive, Wallington recorded his daily life, spiritual meditations and prayers, together with excerpts of sermons, newsbooks, letters and pamphlets. Due to their richness and sheer volume, Wallington's notebooks have attracted the attention of historians interested in the social and inner lives of Puritans. Paul Seaver presented the most extensive micro-history of "Wallington's world," while David Booy published a collection of excerpts of his notebooks.[109] Within his notebooks Wallington recorded numerous dreams, on which he meditated upon waking. Amongst these records are dreams that he interpreted in ways that resonate with Goodwin's schema of "instructive," "fearful" and "affrighting" dreams, showing how Puritans were already utilizing these ideas in the period before Goodwin's publication. As Goodwin would later assert, Wallington saw dreams as a useful source of spiritual edification and insight into the soul. For Wallington, dreams were a source of both spiritual comfort and anxiety, serving to reveal his inherent sinfulness as well as God's mercy and grace. Like Goodwin, Wallington believed the soul was vulnerable in sleep to the assaults of the Devil. Since he believed himself attacked by the Devil in dreams and apparitions, he saw the night as a particularly dangerous time. Above all, for Wallington, dreams were significant spiritual experiences, which conferred on him insight into his spiritual welfare, as well as being "instructive" messages from God meant either as warnings of his inherent sinfulness or as evidence of his election and God's merciful providence and grace.

In many ways Wallington was an exemplary student of Puritan spiritual regimens of daily prayer, Bible reading and introspection. Throughout his adult life Wallington engaged in a rigorous program of spiritual introspection, waking often between one and six am to pray, write his notebooks, read the Bible and meditate on his life. He also frequently attended sermons, on one occasion, heroically attending "ninteene sarmones in one weeke."[110] Having been raised in a godly household, Wallington learned early to practice a strict regimen of spiritual exercises that he assiduously incorporated into the centre of his family and private life as an adult. Perhaps due to his tendency to meditate on all aspects of his life, Wallington recorded numerous dreams that he clearly believed to be important clues to his spiritual welfare and election.

In the midst of the night hours, Wallington frequently awoke terrified by dreams or convinced he was being assaulted by the Devil. Like Goodwin, Wallington saw the night as a vulnerable time for Christians and wrote, "It is the terrour of the night which is so much the more terrible because it walketh in the darke and surpriseth a man before he is aware."[111] Wallington suffered from acute depression and spiritual anguish in his early years, being tempted by the Devil to commit suicide on numerous occasions. During this period and later in his life he records seeing the Devil in waking and sleeping visions. In his "Record of Gods Marcys, or Thankfull Remembrance" notebook, Wallington reflects on these experiences and wrote, "I being then troubled in my mind and Mellincollic I did thinke verily that the Divell did apeare unto me flying about the chamber like unto a blacke crooe."[112] As these appearances often occurred in the midst of the night, Wallington perhaps developed a deep-seated dread of the late hours. Here we can also see the way that individuals might draw from multiple ideas of dreams. Wallington viewed his visions of the Devil as both naturally and supernaturally inspired.

Wallington often experienced what he described as "fearfull dreames," which resonate with Goodwin's idea of "instructive" and "affrighting" dreams sent by God to terrify the faithful into repentance and piety. On January 1, 1629, Wallington experienced a "fearefull dreame" in which he had a vision of heaven and hell:

> For one night I dreamed I was dead and the day of judgment was come and I was raised and stoode betwixt heaven and hell, but wheither I should goe I knew not. Heaven I did see, was a glorious place and as it might be to my apprention a [very] spaces large rome and their sate in the mides of it our Saviour Jesus Christ very glorious I cannot expresse it and round about heaven sate all the saintes that ever was. And on the left hand: I saw hell a large deformed darke place: only a kind of fire burning there and the damned spirits taring one another. then thought I oh whither shall I goe and I thought I had one fote in heaven. One while I did thinke I should goe into heaven and another while I thought I should not and oh that I would I were one the earth againe, I would live better than ever I have done and oh that I had beleeved that theire was a heaven I would have had more care over my waies to have lived more uprightly and holy then every I have done. And thus strugeling

118   *"Nocturnal whispers of the Allmighty"*

> with my thoughts I did awake out of my sleepe in a masse and I tooke
> this dreame for a great warning of God to have a gratter regard of my
> life then ever I had.[113]

Wallington saw this dream not as a revelation but rather as a private
warning from God to live a more godly life. In essence this dream reflects
Wallington's acute anxieties about his election – whether he was among the
elect or the damned. In Goodwin's later schema this kind of dream was
deemed an "affrighting" divine dream, sent by God to warn the dreamer
of his or her potential damnation and to lead a more godly life. In his
notebooks, Wallington recorded numerous other "fearful" and "fritefull dremes," which he saw as warnings from God. On another occasion
in October 1654 he woke at 4 a.m. "out of some fritefull dreme" to "serch
my heart and find a stey of all filth." The dream caused a deep anxiety in
Wallington, yet he comforted himself with meditating on Christ's sacrifice
and thanked God for "keepeing me from gros sinns."[114]

Goodwin had also outlined what he defined as "vain dreames" – dreams
that revealed a preoccupation with worldly vanities. Wallington also recorded a number of dreams he described as "vain." In his notebook entitled "The groth of a Christian," in an entry dated November 22, 1642,
Wallington wrote, "And dreming this night many vaine dremes and so
wakeing with vaine worldly thoughts, It grived me sore that I could bit greet
my heart of the world and set on high with my God."[115] Wallington's "vaine
dreams" led him to strive harder to achieve godliness and he saw them as
a warning that he was dangerously preoccupied with worldly vanities. In
October 1654 Wallington recorded another "vaine worldly dreme," which
he saw as showing that "my imaginations of my heart are evill continually." The dream led him to rise, examine his conscience and meditate on
the story of Doctor Faustus. Being humbled by his own inherent sinfulness, Wallington comforted himself with the fact that "God presents his
deare and only sonn to me with all his merrits and free grace," for which he
thanked God.[116] Clearly for Wallington, in line with Goodwin's later idea
of "vain dreams," they were warnings from God to strive towards spiritual
excellence and a contemplation of spiritual above worldly matters. These
kinds of dreams, although being sources of anxiety, could be "instructive"
for the godly dreamer, who could utilize them as messages from God and
as indications of the deeper spiritual welfare of the soul. "Vain" dreams,
viewed through a Puritan framework of spiritual instruction, were viewed
as indications that the dreamer was falling into an ungodly preoccupation
with "worldly" thoughts, being ultimately a warning from a gracious God.

In addition to several "vain dreames," Wallington also recorded dreams
through which he derived great spiritual comfort. In 1643 on Easter Monday,
Wallington recorded a "heavenly drem" in which he was in his shop meditating on Psalms 125:1–2 that gave him great comfort. Wallington awoke
from the dream that assured him he "was the Lords" and that "I never

found the life of Grace so stering in my heart as now."[117] These spiritually reassuring dreams are reminiscent of the category of "instructive dreams," outlined by Goodwin, designed by God to edify and instruct the dreamer in a correct appreciation of God's mercy and grace. In June 1643, Wallington also recorded another dream in which Thomas Fairfax, the hero of the Parliamentary army, entered his shop. The dream left Wallington with a sense of deep spiritual joy so that on waking he meditated on the dream to understand its larger meaning. He saw the dream as a metaphor for God's entering "the house of my soule in private and publike" and wrote "these meditations tho with teeres filled my soule with joy in thinking what admiering at one anothers Joy that will be then."[118] Evidence for Goodwin's later schema of "instructive" dreams, which served to lead the dreamer into a deeper spiritual meditation and appreciation of God's grace and mercy, is therefore evident in Wallington's earlier records. This suggests that, for early to mid-seventeenth-century Puritans, dreams were an important source of spiritual edification.

Although Wallington never read Goodwin's treatise on dreams, (he died in August 1658), his views of dreams as a fundamental part of his spiritual experiences and as messages designed to warn, instruct and provide comfort from God, were most likely derived from his Puritan upbringing and extensive reading of godly handbooks as well as his private practice of intense spiritual introspection and meditation.[119] For Puritans such as Wallington, dreams were important tools for cultivating piety and could be scrutinized and meditated on as messages from God or as clues to their state of grace. As Goodwin had attempted to establish in his handbook, dreams were a "profitable" source of spiritual introspection and contained, for those who prepared themselves in the day, "instructive" messages from God that were meant to assist in the spiritual edification of the dreamer. In this schema even demonic dreams could be instructive and offer evidence of God's protection whilst serving to test the faithful. What links these authors together is undoubtedly that both Wallington and Goodwin shared a common spiritual worldview and religious praxis. Goodwin's handbook on dreams should therefore be seen not as emerging from the tradition of dreambooks or oneiromancy, or from the Christian tradition of revelations, but rather as part of a Puritan regimen of spiritual introspection and lived practice. Wallington's records and reflections on his dreams suggest how Goodwin's particular schema of dreams was not created in a vacuum but emerged from a Puritan practice of intense spiritual introspection.

John Beale on dreams

In addition to Philip Goodwin's defence and appropriation of dreams within a Puritan ethos, the more moderate Anglican cleric John Beale advocated for the continuation of divine dreams against contemporary criticism. Like Goodwin, Beale was a university-educated cleric whose writings on dreams

120 *"Nocturnal whispers of the Allmighty"*

echoed those of Luther and Calvin yet espoused a more theosophical and mystical understanding. While Goodwin's writings reflect the worldview of the "hotter sort of Protestants," Beale's religious views were aligned along a more moderate stance. However, due to his own personal experiences of prognostic dreams, both his own and those of others he knew, Beale was deeply convinced that God continued to send divine dreams as providential warnings and revelations while the Devil remained a more remote player.

Beale (b. 1608, d. 1683) was the son of a gentleman farmer and lawyer, Thomas Beale, who was educated at Eton and Cambridge. Like Goodwin, Beale matriculated from Cambridge in 1629, becoming a fellow in 1632. He graduated with a B.A. in 1633 and proceeded to an M.A. in 1636. Beale was gifted with a photographic memory, which enabled him to lecture without notes in King's College and he possessed a keen interest in hermetic and mechanical philosophy. During his early career he experimented with telescopes, thermometers and sundials. This learning would serve him well later in his correspondence with the Hartlib circle, whose appetite for natural philosophy and interest in prophetic dreams underlay his on-going correspondence with Samuel Hartlib and the inner circle. Beale became a tutor for his cousin Robert Pye and travelled around the Continent to Paris and Geneva seeking rare manuscripts. He resigned from Cambridge in 1640 due to an increasing hostility to his scientific ideas and soon after Beale had his assets sequestered. During the Civil War, Beale fled Hertfordshire to a Parliamentary camp and served as a chaplain to Humphrey Mackworth, a kinsman of his wife Jane Mackworth. Thereafter, Beale became master of St Catherine's Hospital, Ledbury, but in the early 1650s was dispossessed in favour of John Tombes, a Baptist. His connections with Sir Richard Hopton's wife, Elizabeth, earned him the position of vicar of Stretton Grandison in August 1654. Soon after, Beale became a member of the Herefordshire committee for ejecting scandalous ministers.[120] Given his similar career and proximity to Goodwin, who also served on this committee, it is possible that Goodwin knew Beale personally. He had certainly read Goodwin's treatise on dreams, since Samuel Hartlib had passed on the work after its initial publication.[121] Beale himself had become famous in 1653 after he published an innovative work on cider cultivation, *A Treatise on Fruit Trees* and he began a correspondence with Hartlib in 1656. Beale's published letters on cider production earned him the respect of Oliver Cromwell and resulted in an increase of English orchard revenues.

During his involvement with the Hartlib Circle, Beale corresponded with many of the contemporary leading lights of natural philosophy, including Robert Boyle and John Evelyn. The letters written by Beale, Hartlib and others in the circle reveal the importance of dreams and prophetic visions as part of their intellectual pursuits. Additionally, two of its members, including Beale and Lady Katherine Ranalagh, wrote unpublished treatises on dreams that were circulated amongst the intellectual community. Also demonstrative of their appetite for prophecies and consideration of dreams,

"Nocturnal whispers of the Allmighty" 121

the prophecies of Christina Poniatowska were disseminated in the circle, eliciting a vibrant discussion of dreams. Poniatowska was a Bohemian mystic whose visions experienced between 1627 and 1629 were featured in the Latin work *Lux in tenebis* (1657?) by John Amos Comenius (1592–1670), another correspondent of Samuel Hartlib. An English translation of this manuscript was distributed amongst the Hartlib circle and its members seriously believed Poniatowska's visions potentially revealed the divine will.[122] During her trances, Poniatowska experienced 24 visions of an "Elder" who showed her futurities between November 1627 and October 1629. These visions must be understood against the background of the plight of Bohemian Protestants, who were ejected in 1624 by an Act by the Holy Roman Emperor, Ferdinand. Poniatowska was the daughter of a Polish minister Julian Poniatowski who fled from Bohemia during the period of persecution. Her visions depicted and foretold the "miraculous liberation and glorious reflowering of the Church" and the divine wrath incurred against its persecutors. Inherently political and featuring the vibrant language of retribution, Poniatowska's visions brought hope to the displaced Bohemian Protestant community and a sense of divine purpose to their plight.

Indicative of the fact that learned interest and belief in prophetic dreams had not waned, Samuel Hartlib and his intellectual community keenly studied these visionary testimonies for glimpses of God's divine hand. After having been sent the manuscript copy of Poniatowska's visions, on the 20th January 1658/9 Benjamin Worsley (1618–1673), an English physician and the Surveyor-General of Ireland, wrote privately to Hartlib: "That the Gyft of Prophecy & all extraordinary & divine Revelation did so cease & determine in the Apostles times as [that] there was not ([or] or is not) to be any in the Church here after [That] [word deleted?] expected. / hath no sollid ground or colour in scripture that I know of."[123] He further commented:

> Yet when a dreame Prophecy vision Trance or extasy comes forth in the spirit of humblenesse, [?] of the head, beares wittnesse in all things of the scripture & Truth submitts it selfe to be iudged by the Prophecies of it. I say a vision thus coming forth having no other subiect that it speakes of, or pretends to, but \<the event of\> some Privat Acts of Providence in reference to the perticular dispensations of God \<in this world\> to this or that member or branch of this church or to this or that Countrey \<family\> or person. And challenging no other Authority then or beleefe from vs \<to it\> then what is warranted by the scripture and being willing to stand or fall as the truth of it shall be hereafter verified & manifested by God I say a Prophecy thus qualified and thus cloathed & disposed, I see no reason why we should quarrell at it, more then that I see a necessity it will and must be quarrelld at.[124]

As Luther had espoused, Worsley asserted that dreams might indeed be divine if they agreed with Scripture. Similarly, he counselled a prudent view of Poniatowska's dreams suggesting that some "seeme to be dreames rather then visions and the style & matter of some of them do rayse a doubt in me, whether they were any other then such dreames & Impressions in sleepe as are Ordinary <& naturall>."[125] Overall, Worlsey's commentaries to Hartlib demonstrate that in the later seventeenth century, despite the assertions of critics, members of the learned community continued to accredit dreams and visions as potentially inspired by God.

The Hartlib circle's interest in prophetic dreams and visions is further apparent from its many correspondences about another Continental visionary, Homme Theus, a 76-year-old Dutch schoolmaster based in Friesland who claimed to have received visions of angels warning of God's impending judgement. John Dury wrote to Hartlib in August 1661 with an account of the visionary, providing updates in subsequent letters.[126] Both he and John Comenius visited the visionary in The Hague seeking more information and a confirmation of the visions. These accounts were then circulated amongst the circle and John Beale and Samuel Hartlib were particularly interested in the case. According to Dury, Theus claimed:

> The Angell stood still till hee had recouered himself, & then told him *that* he was sent from God to Command him to goe to the Reformed Ministers of this Country, to bidde them exhort earnestly their hearers to Repent & abstaine from the profanes & sinfull excesses which abound in their courses, because God hath determined to visit this people with the Sword, with the plague and with famine, in the extremitie of all those plagues except they bee humbled & repent; that the Sword shall bee in all their quarters at once, *that* the plague shall bee such *that* the Liuing shall not bee able to Burie all the Dead, but *that* the Dogs shall eat the Carkases lying unburied, & *that* the famine shall bee such *that* a pound of bread shall bee worth a Ricksdollar.[127]

Hartlib sought the insight of his network and forwarded the account to both John Beale and John Worthington. Beale responded that although Hartlib knew that he was, "no despiser of the angelical visits of this last age" one must be wary due to "the notorious hypocrisy of professors and their revolts & sordid or selfish life in England, as well as in the Netherlands being too grossly apparent and common ignorance and falsehood being by some blessed rayes." Furthermore, Beale advised Hartlib to learn more about the morality of the visionary. If the visionary proved pious and a "lover of truth" his "angelic vision" might indeed be true since "God will not send a person, infamous amongst good men for falsehood, on his embassy."[128]

Due to his own personal experiences of prognostic dreams, apparitions and providential warnings, Beale himself firmly believed in the credibility of dreams as potentially divine and meaningful. In his correspondence with Hartlib and others he asserted that divine dreams continued and although one should be cautious of ascribing meaning to natural dreams, God continued to send these "nocturnal whispers of the Allmighty." According to Beale, dreams were "Visible acts of his glorious providence," which should be heeded with all due respect. In his discussion of Lady Katherine Jones, Viscountess Ranelagh's (22 March 1615–3 December 1691) unpublished treatise on dreams, Beale explained further:

> That Hee hath not forsaken his old methodes, but doth still continue to converse with them that feare his greate Name, & tremble at his Worde, by Visible acts of his glorious providence, which are drawne in such fayre characters, That they that run by may reade them, & wakeing, & with open eyes behold them & allso in the dead of *the* night when the outward organs of our earthly frame are chaind up & when the spirite alone is awakened to attend unto his Oracles. Reasons & furthr prooffes I doe now forbeare. Three things I would nowe briefely say. First, Tis a grosse sin & <very> agreeable to the Atheisme of this adulterated age, if wee shall neglect & despise thiese visits of the most high. Secondly, There may be more learnt[*altered from* learnd] in our reste & sleepe, & præ-parations of sanctity, [*word deleted*] perteining to the depths of true wisedome, charitable arts, & practicall knowledge, than by any other long studyes humane arts, or voluminous bookes. Thirdly, Wee may have <as> certaine & cleare discovery of <the difference> what is from God, & what is from Satan in thiese secrete Councells, as[*altered*] in any other affayres of our spirites or life, whilst wee are wakeing. yea the same rule, by which Abraham knewe, That it was God & not Satan, That comanded him to sacrifice the sonne of his promise, will suffice to discover, whether the dreame bee from God, or a Satanicall Temptation.[129]

Beale's own experiences had profoundly convinced him of God's continued use of dreams as prognostic warnings and divine messages. He explained to Lady Ranalagh in a letter that when he was a student at Eton he had dreamt that a black mastiff dog attacked his brother along the way to visit him. This transpired exactly as he had dreamt and he mused, "This stuc in my head then, That I might as well beleeve with the old Epicures, That the world was governd by the casuall dashes of atomes, as that 30 or 40 circumstances could agree together without the hand of God in it."[130] Such dreams were providential warnings sent by a benign maker to warn the faithful of future calamities. Beale's early prognostic dream instilled a deep fascination and conviction that dreams were divine messages. In his letters to the Hartlib circle, Beale narrated several other personal dreams that presented evidence of the credibility of dreams as "whispers of the Allmighty," including the following:

> When I was in Geneva in the house of Monsieur Sarrazin then Syndique, My spirite was much troubled with some of the writings of Socinians & of H Grot. most witty & learned men. In a dreame I had a Vision of one that lead mee to Dr Paschal, (whom at that time I had not seene) shewd mee

124 *"Nocturnal whispers of the Allmighty"*

> the Man, directed mee to enquyre Many bookes; I modestly seemd to aske their price. Some hee sold & the reste with many manuscripts of his owne hee gave. On the morrow morning I pursued the dreame. The figure of the man was the same, The words & deedes in all things the same.[131]

Beale's personal experiences with prophetic dreams as well as those of others he witnessed left him with a deep conviction that divine dreams continued and to neglect such dreams was to slight the hand of God. This lifelong fascination with dreams also led him to write his own lengthy manuscript on dreams, *A Treatise on the Art of Interpreting Dreams*, which he circulated amongst his intellectual peers in the Hartlib circle during the late 1650s.[132] Rather than becoming the object of mockery, Beale's writings on dreams earned him the respect of his intellectual community and others endorsed his ideas about the continuation of prophetic dreams in the correspondence network.

Beale's *A Treatise on the Art of Interpreting Dreams* was in part a response to the claims of contemporaries that divine dreams had ceased. This erudite work discussed dreams in accordance with Luther's system and Beale carefully critiqued Macrobius' schema of dreams and rejected this classical work in favour of a purely Christian and Scriptural exegesis. Like Luther and Goodwin, although Beale warns that false dreams can lead to superstition and folly, at the same time he acknowledged that true dreams are useful in revealing God's messages. According to his epistle, his main aim was to remedy the numerous mistakes made in distinguishing different kinds of dreams. Beale further explained,

> I doubt not, but I shall prove it a greate & necessary branch of Sanctity most heedefully to attend what God shall please to discover to us by this his owne holy Methode: & a grosse kind of profanenesse, too neerely agreeing with the Atheisticall[*altered*] sottishnesse of this degenerate age, To neglect the nocturnall whispers of the Allmighty. Fourthly, I recompt the interpretation of dreames to bee a very considerable branch of the <profound> learning of the Easte: a part of that true, old, & deepe philosophy, which fully agrees with the workes of God, & was first revealed by the Author & Governor of the world. In comparison of this The Græcian philosophy was but a kind of childish[*altered*] babling, a contest of words *that* bore noe effect, whilst this Orientall Learning did all the wonders.[133]

Like contemporary Protestant writers, including Philip Goodwin, whom Beale had read, divine dreams were "gifts" from God, which were ignored at one's peril. Moreover, Beale also rejected the classical works on dreams, in particular the commentary of Macrobius, who had declared nightmares and *insomnium* were meaningless and natural. According to Beale and as Goodwin had suggested, sometimes God sends *insomnium* and *somnium* to terrify, admonish or instruct Christians.

Conclusion

First emerging in the late sixteenth and becoming more prominent in the seventeenth century, theories and practices of dream divination and spiritual visions were subjected to an onslaught by a number of English authors concerned with the rise of irreligion, superstition and increasing challenges to the social and religious order. At the heart of debates about witchcraft, astrology and revealed religion was an apprehension about "erroneous" beliefs in dreams. In the views of these writers, the practice of dream divination and belief in visions or divine dreams were fundamentally suspect and dangerous catalysts of irreligion, disorder and the corruption of the Faith.

To combat these erroneous beliefs, writers promoted the idea of natural dreams over those of predictive and spiritual dreams. According to them, most dreams were either natural or demonic in origin and at best dreams might give physicians insight into the physical health of the dreamer. To resolve the contradictory views of predictive dreams in the Bible, writers such as Reginald Scot, John Gaule and Thomas Ady argued that divine dreams were either rare or had ceased to exist altogether after the time of Christ. Subsequently, they stated that any dreams that individuals claimed to be divine were most likely demonic in origin, a ploy of the Devil to mislead Christians into sin and illusion.

After 1650, in response to the emergence of radical visionaries during the Interregnum, writers such as Henry More, Meric Causabon and John Spencer argued that visionaries were suffering, not from divine inspiration, but rather from a form of "religious enthusiasm" or melancholic madness. This became a powerful argument in the campaign to undermine all aspects of revealed religion. As part of the newly promulgated pathology of religious madness, visions and dreams came to be understood as prime symptoms of the imagination's dangerous force and represented the mind's tendency to become deluded by the inner senses.[134] In the eighteenth century, ideas about "enthusiasm" and the "imagination" as dangerous catalysts of disorder were put forward to undermine all aspects of revealed religion. Enlightenment philosophers turned towards more "rational" views of religion, often controversially regarding all revealed religion, including examples in the Bible, as false. This outlook would led to accusations of atheism, "sadducism" and materialism against a number of intellectuals.[135]

However, despite the concerns of intellectuals, clerics and statesmen, the wider populace continued to buy almanacs, fortune-telling tracts and dream divination manuals (including debased versions of Artemidorus) well into the eighteenth and even the nineteenth century.[136] Additionally, the existence of visionaries and the spread of sectarianism and dissent in the Church continued: much to the chagrin of ministers, people continued to flock to support radicals, visionaries and sectarians, at least until the 1660s.

Yet, as I have also argued in this chapter, the contestation of dream divination and divine visions was nothing new. Debates about the significance and origin of dreams were a longstanding issue for intellectuals, theologians and writers, reaching back to antiquity and continuing throughout the medieval period, because it was deeply embedded in the Christian tradition. Concern with the social, spiritual and political power of visionaries and their claims to divine dreams, was therefore an ongoing issue in premodern culture, unique neither to the period nor to England. Similarly, the tendency of critics to utilize notions of natural dreams or Scriptural admonishments against false dreams was also a continuation of older counterarguments. At the heart of these debates was the issue of discernment and whether dreams originated from natural or supernatural, divine or demonic sources. The inherent problem was that most people were unable to distinguish divine from demonic dreams and thus mistook false dreams for true visions. However, although these debates were a legacy of earlier writings on dreams and discernment, the specific context of the English Civil Wars, the rise of astrology and growth of a popular appetite for fortune-telling tracts, as well as the increasing numbers of radical visionaries, combined to reignite the issue of dreams amongst writers concerned with irreligion, social disorder and superstition.

As I have also suggested, whilst dreams had their critics, they also had their defenders. Both John Beale and Philip Goodwin collectively sought to reinscribe the dream firmly within a Protestant ideology and Christian praxis. Reinterpreted within this framework, some authors suggested that dreams could be useful as "visible acts" of providence, spiritually edifying experiences that revealed man's inherent sin, or in some cases as divine revelations. Above all, such writings illustrate that numerous understandings of supernatural and spiritual dreams pervaded the early modern world. This thoroughly Protestant understanding of dreams was one that permeated broader understandings of dreams so that individuals such as Nehemiah Wallington would carefully scrutinize his dreams for signs of providential warnings and also his election.

Finally, the legacy of the Protestant Reformation was to fundamentally reinscribe the dream within a thoroughly Protestant discourse. Reformers' rejection of classical models of dream codification and their insistence on a model of dreams and dream interpretation that was solely reliant on Scripture subtly shifted ideas of supernatural dreams. The result was that the supernatural dream was imbued with an even more problematic status. In direct response to the rise of radical visionaries in fringe Protestant groups, the dream became the subject of a heated debate about access to the divine and ultimately the need for clearer distinctions between orthodox and unorthodox religious praxis and the lines dividing the natural, preternatural and supernatural worlds. Underlying these discourses was simultaneously the issue of demonic dreams. While the struggle to delineate divine from demonic, natural from supernatural dreams continued, giving rise to an increasingly pathological view of the dream, nightmares continued to plague the populace and received equal attention.

Notes

1 Anna Trapnel, *Strange and wonderful newes from White-Hall* (London, 1654), 4.
2 Stevie Davies, "Trapnel, Anna (*fl.* 1642–1660)," in *Oxford Dictionary of National Biography*, online edn., edited by Lawrence Goldman, (Oxford: OUP 2004), (accessed 6 June 2008), http://www.oxforddnb.com.myaccess.library.utoronto.ca/view/article/38075; James Holstun, *Ehud's dagger: class struggle in the English Revolution* (London; New York: Verso, 2002), 257–304.
3 Henry More, *Enthusiasmus triumphatus, or, a discourse of the nature, causes, kinds and cure, of enthusiasme* (London, 1656); Meric Casaubon, *A treatise concerning enthusiasme, as it is an effect of nature: but is mistaken by many for either divine inspiration, or diabolical possession* (London, 1654); John Spencer, *A discourse concerning vulgar prophecies* (London, 1665).
4 For excellent historical studies of the issues of discernment see: Rosalynn Voaden, *God's Words, Women's Voices: The Discernment of Spirits in the Writing of Late-medieval Women Visionaries* (Rochester: York Medieval Press, 1999); Alison Weber, "Spiritual Administration: Gender and Discernment in the Carmelite Reform," *Sixteenth Century Journal* 31, no. 1 (2000): 123–46; Dyan Elliot, "Seeing Double: John Gerson, the Discernment of Spirits and Joan of Arc," *The American Historical Review* 107, no. 1 (2002): 26–54; Nancy Caciola, *Discerning Spirits: Divine and Demonic Possession in the Middle Ages* (Ithaca: Cornell University Press, 2003); Moshe Sluhovsky, *Believe Not Every Spirit: Possession, Mysticism, & Discernment in Early Modern Catholicism* (Chicago; London: University of Chicago Press, 2007); Gábor Klaniczay and Éva Pócs eds., *Communicating with the Spirits* (Budapest: CEU Press, 2005).
5 Elliot, "Seeing Double: John Gerson, the Discernment of Spirits and Joan of Arc."
6 See for example: Elizabeth Poole, *A vision: wherein is manifested the disease and cure of the kingdome* (London, 1649); Elizabeth Poole, *An alarum of war, given to the army and to their high court of justice* (London, 1649); Nicholas Smith, *A warning to the world, being sundry strange prophecies revealed to Nicholas Smith* (London, 1653); Anna Trapnel, *Strange and wonderful newes from White-Hall* (London, 1654); Arise Evans, *The bloudy vision of John Farly, interpreted by Arise Evans* (London, 1653); Arise Evans, *The voice of Michael the archangel, to his Highness the Lord Protector* (London, 1653); Arise Evans, *Mr. Evans and Mr. Penningtons prophesie: concerning seven yeers of plenty and seven yeers of famine and pestilence* (London, 1655).
7 Elinor Channel, *A message from God, by a dumb woman to his Highness the Lord Protector* (London, 1653); Arise Evans, *An eccho to the book called, A voyce from heaven* (London, 1653).
8 Thomas Tryon, *A treatise of dreams & visions* (London, 1689), 8.
9 Henry Howard, *A defensative against the poyson of supposed prophecies* (London, 1583), 11.
10 Alexandra Walsham, "'Frantick Hacket': Prophecy, Sorcery, Insanity and the Elizabethan Puritan Movement," *The Historical Journal* 41, no. 1 (1998): 27–66.
11 Peter Marshall, *Reformation England 1480–1642* (London: Hodder Arnold, 2003), 49–50.
12 Richard L. Kagan, *Lucretia's Dreams: Politics and Prophecy in Sixteenth-Century Spain* (London: University of California Press, 1990).
13 Nathan A. Finn, "Curb Your Enthusiasm: Martin Luther's Critique of Anabaptism," *Southwestern Journal of Theology* 56, no. 2 (Spring 2014): 179; Kirchhoff, Karl-Heinz and Hans J. Hillerbrand. "Münster," in *The Oxford Encyclopedia of the Reformation* (Oxford University Press, 1996), (accessed 25 June 2016),

128   *"Nocturnal whispers of the Allmighty"*

http://www.oxfordreference.com.myaccess.library.utoronto.ca/view/10.1093/acref/9780195064933.001.0001/acref-9780195064933-e-0969.

14 Jan N. Bremmer, "Prophets, Seers and Politics in Greece, Israel and Early Modern Europe," *Numen* 40, no. 2 (1993): 170.

15 Martin Luther, *Luther's Works, Volume 3, Lectures on Genesis Chapters 15–20*, edited by Jaroslav Pelikan (Saint Louis: Concordia, 1961), 10.

16 Martin Luther, *Luther's Works, Volume 7, Lectures on Genesis, Chapters 38–44*, edited by Jaroslav Pelikan and Walter A. Hansen (Saint Louis: Concordia, 1965), 121–22.

17 Guy G. Stroumsa, "Dreams and Visions in Early Christian Discourse," in *Dream Cultures: Explorations in the Comparative History of Dreaming*, edited by David Shulman and Guy G. Stroumsa (New York; Oxford: Oxford University Press, 1999), 196.

18 Claire Gantet, "Dreams, Standards of Knowledge and Orthodoxy in Germany in the Sixteenth Century," in *Orthodoxies and Heterodoxies in Early Modern German Culture Order and Creativity, 1500–1750*, edited by Randolph Head and Daniel Eric Christensen (Leiden: Brill, 2007), 74–75; S.F. Kruger, *Dreaming in the Middle Ages* (Cambridge: Cambridge University Press, 1992), 37–39.

19 Martin Luther, *Luther's Works, Volume 6, Lectures on Genesis, Chapters 31–37*, edited by Jaroslav Pelikan and Hilton C. Oswald (Saint Louis: Concordia, 1970), 329.

20 *Ibid.*, 333.

21 Luther, *Works, Volume 7*, 119–20.

22 Luther, *Works, Volume 6*, 329.

23 *Ibid.*, 330.

24 Luther, *Works, Volume 3*, 10.

25 Luther, *Works, Volume 6*, 334.

26 Luther, *Works, Volume 3*, 10.

27 Luther, *Works, Volume 6*, 332.

28 Luther, *Works, Volume 3*, 330.

29 Martin Luther, *Luther's Works, Volume 5, Lectures on Genesis, Chapters 26–30*, edited by Jaroslav Pelikan (Saint Louis: Concordia, 1968), 239.

30 Philip Goodwin, *The mystery of dreames, historically discoursed* (London, 1658), epistle.

31 Luther, *Works, Volume 3*, 166.

32 John Calvin, *Commentaries on the prophet Daniel, Vol. 1*, translated by Thomas Myers (Edinburgh: Calvin Translation Society, 1852), 117.

33 *Ibid.*

34 *Ibid.*, 119.

35 *Ibid.*, 124.

36 Thomas Ady, *A candle in the dark* (London, 1655); Reginald Scot, *The discoverie of witchcraft* (London, 1584); William Perkins, *A discourse of the damned art of witchcraft* (Cambridge, 1608); John Cotta, *The infallible true and assured witch, or, the second edition of the tryall of witch-craft* (London, 1625); John Brinley, *A discovery of the impostures of witches and astrologers* (London, 1680).

37 Ady, *Candle in the Dark*, 18.

38 Perkins, 99 -100.

39 *Ibid.*; John Gaule, *Pus-mantia the mag-astro-mancer, or, The magicall-astrologicall-diviner posed and puzzled* (London, 1652), A3r, 182–183; Scot, 99; Brinley, A4v; John Melton, *The Astrologaster, or, The figure-caster* (London, 1620), 47; Henry Howard, *A defensative against the poyson of supposed prophesies* (London, 1583), 22.

40 Gaule, A5r.

"*Nocturnal whispers of the Allmighty*" 129

41 Melton, 69.
42 Gaule, 27.
43 Perkins, 96.
44 Gaule, 60.
45 *Ibid.*, 193.
46 Melton, 34.
47 Brinley, A4r.
48 Gaule, 51.
49 Scot, 181–82.
50 Ady, 19.
51 Scot, 177.
52 Ady, 19.
53 Perkins, 94.
54 Scot, 177–81; Gaule, 204–205.
55 Gaule, 204.
56 Ady, 19.
57 Perkins warned: "The devill in these [dreams], as well as in other things can transforme himselfe into an Angel of light. But howsoever the case be hard and the devil politick, yet by the light of direction from the word of God, there may some true differences be met downe between them" [Perkins, 99].
58 *Ibid.*, 97.
59 Cotta, 54.
60 Melton, 67.
61 Ady, 20–21.
62 Thomas Nashe, *The terrors of the night or, A discourse of apparitions* (London, 1594), Ciiii(r)–Ciiii(v).
63 Melton, 66–67.
64 Robert Burton, *The anatomy of melancholy,* edited by Holbrook Jackson (New York: New York Review of Books, 2001), 311–432.
65 Robert Burton, *The anatomy of melancholy* (Oxford, 1621), 260.
66 *Ibid.*, 250.
67 More, 2.
68 *Ibid.*
69 *Ibid.*, 6.
70 See for example: Charles Chauncy, *Enthusiasm describ'd and caution'd against: a sermon* (Boston, 1742); Blacksmith, *A defence of Christianity against the power of enthusiasm* (Bristol, 1764); Thomas Chubb, *A discourse concerning reason, with regard to religion and divine revelation* (London, 1731); Theophilus Evans, *The history of modern enthusiasm, from the Reformation to the present times* (London, 1752); Joseph Eyre, *A dispassionate inquiry into the probably causes and consequences of enthusiasm: a sermon, preached July 30, 1798, in the parish church of St. Mary's, Reading* (Reading, London and Oxford, 1798); Bishop Gibson, *The Bishop of London's pastoral letter to the people of his diocese; … by Way of Caution, Against lukewarmness on one hand and enthusiasm on the other* (London, 1739); Thomas Mortimer, *Die and be damned. Or an antidote against every species of Methodism; and enthusiasm* (London, 1758); Anthony Ashley Cooper Shaftesbury, *A letter concerning enthusiasm, to My Lord ****** (London, 1708); John Wilder, *The trial of the spirits: or a caution against enthusiasm, or religious delusion. In a sermon preached before the University of Oxford, August 5th. 1739* (Oxford, 1739).
71 PROB 11/324/453, Will of Philip Goodwin, 29th August 1667; Edmund Calamy and Samuel Palmer, *The Nonconformists Memorial; Being an Account of the Lives and Sufferings and Printed Works of the Two Thousand Ministers Ejected*

130   *"Nocturnal whispers of the Allmighty"*

    from the Church of England ..., Vol. II, 2nd ed. (London, 1802), 314; Gordon Goodwin, "Goodwin, Philip (d. 1699), Divine," in *Dictionary of National Biography* (Oxford: Oxford University Press, 1890), (accessed 12 June 2013), http://www.oxforddnb.com.myaccess.library.utoronto.ca/view/olddnb/10995.

72 John Spurr, *English Puritanism 1603 - 1689* (New York: St. Martin's Press, 1998), 68.

73 H.R. French, "Goodwin, Philip (*d.* 1667)," in *Oxford Dictionary of National Biography,* online edn., edited by Lawrence Goldman (Oxford: OUP, 2004), (accessed 2 March 2011), http://www.oxforddnb.com/view/article/10995.

74 PROB 11/324/453.

75 Calamy, *Nonconformists Memorial,* 314.

76 Goodwin, *Evangelicall communicant;* Philip Goodwin, *Dies dominicus redivivus; or, The Lords Day enlivened or a treatise, as to discover the practical part of the evangelical Sabbath: so to recover the spiritual part of that pious practice to its primitive life: lamentably lost, in these last declining times* (London, 1654); Philip Goodwin, *Religio domestica rediviva: or, Family-religion revived* (London, 1655); Goodwin, *Mystery of dreames.*

77 Goodwin, *Evangelicall communicant,* 18.

78 Goodwin, *Dies dominicus redivivus,* frontspage.

79 Manuals of family religion were popular in the period and were part of the Puritan agenda to promote intense religious devotion. For an informative article on manuals of family religion by nonconformists in the period see, Andrew Chambers and Michelle Wolfe, "Reading, Family Religion and Evangelical Identity in Late Stuart England," *The Historical Journal* 47, no. 4 (2004): 875–96.

80 Thomas Hill, *The moste pleasuante arte of the interpretacion of dreames ...* (London, 1576); Thomas Tryon, *A treatise of dreams & visions ...* (London, 1689).

81 Goodwin, *Mystery of dreames,* B6r - B6v.

82 *Ibid.*

83 *Ibid.*

84 In his discussion of dream divination and claims to divine dreams, Reginald Scot had made this argument in his *The discoverie of witchcraft* (1584). Similarly, John Gaule had also suggested divine dreams had ceased in his antiastrological work *Pus-mantia* (1652). Reginald Scot, *The discoverie of witchcraft* (London, 1584), 177–81; John Gaule, *Pus-mantia the mag-astro-mancer, or, The magicall-astrologicall-diviner posed and puzzled* (London, 1652), 204–205. Moïse Amyraut, the French Protestant theologian, much admired in England, also argued for the cessation of divine dreams in his work, *A discourse concerning the divine dreams mention'd in Scripture* (1676). [Moïse Amyraut, *A discourse concerning the divine dreams mention'd in Scripture ...* (London, 1676), 40–41].

85 John Coffey and Paul C.H. Lim, eds., *The Cambridge Companion to Puritanism* (Cambridge: Cambridge University Press, 2008), 2–4.

86 *Ibid.*

87 Christopher Durston and Jacqueline Eales, eds., *The Culture of English Puritanism, 1560 - 1700* (Houndmills: St. Martin's Press, 1996), 1–31.

88 Goodwin, *Mystery of dreames,* A10r.

89 *Ibid.,* 13.

90 *Ibid.,* A11v.

91 *Ibid.*

92 *Ibid.,* 24.

93 *Ibid.,* 39.

94 *Ibid.,* 41.

95 *Ibid.,* 42–43.

96 *Ibid.,* A12r-A13r.

97   *Ibid.*, 28.
98   *Ibid.*, 32.
99   *Ibid.*
100 *Ibid.*, 36.
101 *Ibid.*, 37.
102 *Ibid.*, 40.
103 *Ibid.*, 42.
104 *Ibid.*, 36.
105 J.F. McGregor, "The Baptists: Fount of All Heresy," in *Radical Religion in the English Revolution,* edited by J.F. McGregor and B. Reay (Oxford: Oxford University Press, 1984), 25–26.
106 Goodwin, *Mystery of dreames*, 36–37.
107 Examples include the printed works of the Fifth Monarchists Anna Trapnel and Arise Evans, as well as the Independent clerics, John Rogers, Vavasor Powell and Henry Jessey, amongst others. Anna Trapnel, *Strange and wonderful newes from White-Hall* (London, 1654); Arise Evans, *An eccho to the book called A voyce from heaven* (London, 1653), 8–9, 25, 78, 82; Arise Evans, *The bloudy vision of John Farly* (London, 1653); Vavasor Powell, *Spirituall experiences, of sundry beleevers Held forth by them at severall solemne meetings and conferences to that end* (London, 1653), 234, 278, 357, 369; John Rogers, *Ohel or Beth-shemesh A tabernacle for the sun* (London, 1653), 424–25, 430–31, 434–35; Henry Jessey, *The exceeding riches of grace advanced by the spirit of grace, in an empty nothing creature viz. Mris. Sarah Wight* (London, 1647), 58, 86, 89, 148–50.
108 Hobbes, *Leviathan*, 175, 344, 429; More, *Enthusiasmus triumphatus*, 2–6, 24–31.
109 Paul S. Seaver, *Wallington's World: A Puritan Artisan in Seventeenth-Century London* (Stanford, CA: Stanford University Press, 1985); Nehemiah Wallington, *The Notebooks of Nehemiah Wallington, 1618–1654: A Selection*, edited by David Booy (Aldershot: Ashgate, 2007).
110 Nehemiah Wallington, "A Record of Gods Marcys, or a Thankfull Remembrance," Guildhall Library, MS 204, fols. 49–50.
111 *Ibid.*, fol. 380.
112 *Ibid.*, fol. 8.
113 *Ibid.*, fol. 47–48.
114 Nehemiah Wallington, "An Extract of the passages of my life," Folger Shakespeare Library, MS V.a. 436, 407.
115 Nehemiah Wallington, "The groth of a Christian," British Library, MS Add. 40 883, fol. 49v.
116 Wallington, "An Extract," 407.
117 Wallington, "Groth of a Christian," fol. 83v.
118 *Ibid.*, fol. 104.
119 Booy, "Introduction," in *Notebooks of Nehemiah Wallington*, 20.
120 Patrick Woodland, 'Beale, John (*bap.* 1608, *d.* 1683)', in *Oxford Dictionary of National Biography* (Oxford: Oxford University Press, 2004); online edn., Jan 2008, (accessed 21 May 2015), http://www.oxforddnb.com.myaccess.library.utoronto.ca/view/article/1802.
121 Richard Scott, "Dreams and the Passions in Revolutionary England" (PhD, University of Sheffield, 2014), 111, (accessed 18 June 2014), http://etheses.whiterose.ac.uk/5917/.
122 "Scribal Copy, Christina Poniatowska'S Revelationes Divinae," English Translation Of the Latin Original, translated by W.J. Hitchens, Ref: 35/7/1A-37B; 1B-2B, 3B & 37A-B BLANK, *The Hartlib Papers,* edited by M. Greengrass, M. Leslie and M. Hannon (Sheffield: HRI Online Publications, 2013), (accessed 27 April 2016), http://www.hrionline.ac.uk/hartlib.

132 *"Nocturnal whispers of the Allmighty"*

123 "Letter, Benjamin Worsley To Hartlib, 20 January 1658/9," Ref: 33/2/11A-12B, *The Hartlib Papers*, edited by M. Greengrass, M. Leslie and M. Hannon (Sheffield: HRI Online Publications, 2013), (accessed 27 April 2016), http://www.hrionline.ac.uk/hartlib.

124 *Ibid.*

125 *Ibid.*

126 "Letter, John Dury to Hartlib, 12 August 1661," Ref: 4/4/30A, *The Hartlib Papers*, edited by M. Greengrass, M. Leslie and M. Hannon, (Sheffield: HRI Online Publications, 2013), (accessed 27 April 2016), http://www.hrionline. ac.uk/hartlib.

127 *Ibid.*

128 *The Diary and Correspondence of Dr. John Worthington*, edited by J. Crossley, Vol. I (Chetham Society Vol. XIII: Manchester, 1847), 356–65.

129 "Letter, [John Beale] To [Hartlib], 28 May 1657," Ref: 25/5/1A-12B, *The Hartlib Papers* edited by M. Greengrass, M. Leslie and M. Hannon (Sheffield: HRI Online Publications, 2013), (accessed 27 April 2016), http://www.hrionline. ac.uk/hartlib.

130 *Ibid.*

131 *Ibid.*

132 John Beale, "Treatise on the Art of Interpreting Dreams," Undated, 25/19/1-28, in *The Hartlib Papers: A Complete Text and Image Database of the Papers of Samuel Hartlib (C.1600–1660),* 2nd edition, edited by Mark Greengrass, Michael Leslie and Michael Hannon (Sheffield: Sheffield University Library, 2002).

133 *Ibid.*

134 Lucia Dacome, "'To What Purpose Does It Think': Dreams, Sick Bodies and Confused Minds in the Age of Reason," *History of Psychiatry* 15, no. 4 (2004): 395–416.

135 John Spurr, "'Rational Religion' in Restoration England," *Journal of the History of Ideas* 49, no. 4 (1988): 563–85; John Redwood, *Reason, Ridicule and Religion* (London: Thames & Hudson, 1976); Jane Shaw, *Miracles in Enlightenment England* (Cambridge: Cambridge University Press, 2008).

136 Maureen Perkins, "The Meaning of Dream Books," *History Workshop Journal* 48 (Autumn 1999): 103–14; Anon, *The entertaining fortune book, as to what relates to good or bad fortune in either sex* (London, 1755); Anon., *Wit's cabinet a companion for gentlemen and ladies* (London, 1710); Anon., *Dreams and moles, with their interpretation and signification* (London, 1780); Andrew Bell, *Nocturnal revels: or, a general history of dreams in two parts* (London, 1707); William Lilly, *The book of knowledge; treating of the wisdom of the ancients* (London, 1753); Mother (Ursula) Shipton, *Mother Shipton's legacy. Or, a favorite fortune-book in which is given a pleasing interpretation of dreams* (York, 1797).

4 "The terrors of the night"
Nightmares and sleep disorders

Introduction

The terrors of the night – dreams, nightmares and sleep disorders – plagued men, women and children throughout the early modern period. As the writings of the most famous English diarist Samuel Pepys (1633–1703) illustrate, early modern sleep was often a source of extreme anxiety and discomfort. On the 3rd of December 1661, Samuel Pepys recorded the following dream:

> And so to bed, but had a very bad night by dreams of my wife's riding with me and her horse throwing her and breaking her leg and then I dreamed that I ... [was] in such pain that I waked with it and had a great deal of pain there a very great while till I fell asleep again and such apprehension I had of it that when I rose and trussed up myself thinking that it had been no dream.[1]

This was one of several such nightmares Pepys experienced, which left him deeply disturbed upon waking. While Chapter 1 explored ideas and experiences of sleep as a significant facet of the history of dreams, this chapter considers nightmares and sleep disorders as a closely related yet distinct category of nocturnal life. A central aim is to elucidate the darker side of dreams and reveal the dream as an acute source of terror and anxiety. Linked to the growth of nocturnalization and as part of the nocturnal experience, sleep disorders and nightmares are an understudied facet of early modern history that reveals the night, sleep and dreams as sources of inherent anxiety. Through a study of a wide range of texts – medical, religious, philosophical and literary – as well as accounts from private writings this chapter will bring the study of dreams into the eighteenth century and discuss its implications in relation to the historiographical issue of the "disenchantment of the world," believed to occur in the long eighteenth century. Since a complex spectrum of ideas about the nature and origins of the nightmare or "incubus" (sleep paralysis) and nightmares continued into the eighteenth century, this chapter helps to further complicate our understanding of post-enlightenment culture.

Figure 4.1 "Stripes of Conscience or the Midnight Hour." Etching by: H. Brocas. Wellcome Library, London.

Ideas about the causes of nightmares can be loosely categorized into natural, preternatural and supernatural etiologies. As I explored in the previous chapter, writers such as Philip Goodwin argued that dreams could be authored by the Devil or demons and were injected into the mind to "defile" the soul or mislead the sleeper into sin, delusion and heresy. Goodwin also explained that "Troublesome and affrighting dreams" might derive from God himself to scare the dreamer into piety and repentance for sins committed in waking life. The Devil might also send "false and deluding dreams," which masqueraded as divine in an attempt to trick the dreamer into believing him-/herself gifted with prophetic dreams. These dreams might fall into the category of the preternatural, since the Devil's knowledge of futurities was obtained through centuries of observation and not through true knowledge of the future. Parallel to these ideas were natural theories of dreams, explored in Chapter 1, which suggested that such dreams affected sleep as a result of natural processes, such as indigestion or humoral imbalances.

"The terrors of the night" 135

These ideas were not necessarily opposing and co-existed from the sixteenth through the eighteenth century. Thus, a variety of ideas circulated about "fearful dreams" that incorporated several genres, including (but not limited to) natural, demonic and divine dreams.

Historians have marked the eighteenth century as one of seismic changes to cultural attitudes towards sleep. According to Sasha Handley, English writers became increasingly interested in sleep and sleep disorders in the long eighteenth century.[2] However, as I will demonstrate, these concerns were apparent much earlier in the period of the sixteenth and early seventeenth century. Similarly, the evidence of sleep remedies in family recipe books and the medical records of English physicians in the sixteenth and seventeenth centuries contest the assertions of Roger Schmidt, who argued that the eighteenth century was plagued by bouts of insomnia, the ultimate modern sleep disorder.[3] Handley also posits that the eighteenth century was a transitional period that marked significant changes to contemporary sleeping habits, most notably those of the social elite. Due to socio-economic and urban developments, Handley suggests that it became increasingly modish for the social elite to cultivate disrupted sleep patterns and late hours as part of the newly fashionable "code of civility."[4] Other historians have also marked the period as one of significant transitions to cultural conceptualizations and experiences of night, a subject closely related to histories of nightmares and sleep disorders. Craig Koslofsky's ideas about the growth of "nocturnalization" suggest that the night became increasingly legitimized as a period of respectable piety and less terrifying as a result.[5] This marked a change to cultural views of the night that was, according to Koslofsky, an unexpected consequence of the European Reformations.

Yet, I would suggest that early modern people clung to ideas of night as a liminal, sometimes dangerous period. While certainly the reformations forced men and women to reconsider the night as a period that "intensified the light," one might also consider that the use of evenings as a period of orthodox intense spiritual meditation and reflection was in fact a stalwart legacy of the Catholic Church itself and practiced for millennia by its multitude of monks, nuns, saints and other spiritual soldiers. Night as a period of prayer, introspection and piety was long held as a liminal period of both salvation and damnation. Although the Devil lurked in the shadows, the light of the soul through prayer and piety was illuminated as a result. In sleep and other alternate states of consciousness the pious were blessed (or cursed) with dreams and visions of both God and the Devil.

Additionally, angels as well as demons visited men and women in the nocturnal hours making the discernment of spirits an ongoing issue for early modern visionaries.[6] As Chapter 3 demonstrated, reformers such as Martin Luther also viewed the night as the dangerous province of the Devil, who under the cover of darkness waged war on humans by infiltrating their sleeping minds and deceiving them with demonic dreams disguised as

136 *"The terrors of the night"*

divine. So too, Nehemiah Wallington's frequent skirmishes with the Devil during his nocturnal private spiritual meditations suggest a more complex psychological experience and cultural attitude towards the midnight hours. Night, in other words, both before and during the period of religious reformation was often associated with piety and salvation, even while underlying it was the threat of moral darkness, demonic agents and evil.

As Owen Davies, Willem de Blécourt and other historians have shown, belief in supernatural agents, witches, ghosts and other hobgoblins continued into the nineteenth century.[7] This reveals a reluctance of the wider populace to let go of cultural notions of the night as the province of the otherworld. The invention of artificial lighting may have inadvertently served to deepen and lengthen the shadows. Consequently, the colonization of the night that Koslofsky portrays was perhaps a much longer, messier process and the history of night is, like histories of dreams and sleep, often deeply ambiguous, reflecting more continuities than stark changes. However, Alexandra Walsham's suggestion that the Reformation may have served to "expand the category of the preternatural and to collapse the miraculous into the natural" also holds weight.[8] Ideas about the nightmare, a supernatural encounter and demonic dreams were also explained increasingly in terms of the natural disorders of the body, while some dreams, deemed demonic, were alternatively explained as preternatural acts of sleight of hand ministered by the Devil. This is not to suggest, however, that the supernatural disappeared altogether from the world or that the collective understandings of the cosmos became starkly polarized and rationalized. Rather, as Moshe Sluhovsky and Nancy Caciola suggested, these categories were ambiguous and often entangled, being neither mutually exclusive nor necessarily in contestation with each other.[9]

Evidence for experiences and understandings of sleep disorders and terrible dreams in premodern England is abundant. In addition to printed medical, philosophical, literary and religious works, unpublished medical casebooks and recipe books form another important body of evidence that demonstrates widespread attitudes towards the prognosis and cure of common sleep disorders and terrifying dreams. The medical notebooks of the English astrologer-physicians Simon Forman (1552–1611) and his *protégé* Richard Napier (1559–1634), as Lauren Kassell demonstrated, offer us a rich repository of information about early modern relations between physicians and their patients, as well as the practice of medicine in the broader community. As Kassell suggests, such works both shaped and were simultaneously shaped by medical knowledge.[10] Napier and Forman's casebooks convey vital details about the common role that sleep disorders and terrifying dreams played in men, women and children's lives. In the thousands of records of patient's illnesses are frequent references to individual sleep disturbances and dreams that left persons bereft of sleep and imbued with a lingering sense of terror. These records thus help to reveal the very real physiological, psychological and emotional impact that sleep disorders and

"The terrors of the night" 137

dreams had on individual lives and to show how, as early as the sixteenth and seventeenth centuries, sleep disorders were a common complaint.

In addition to medical casebooks, the records of household recipe books, containing both medical and cookery recipes, also confer important insight into the lived experience and common problems of sleep disorders. As Elaine Leong has shown, recipe books were part of a complex process of authorship in which family members, both male and female, compiled recipes from members of the household, external family members, physicians and friends into a single volume that was passed down through generations and added to by subsequent family members. These works therefore acted as both family archives and significant practical manuals of medical knowledge.[11] Such family heirlooms were an important facet of medical knowledge and practice at the household level and often contained core medical and cookery recipes that included stock treatments and remedies for common illnesses and complaints, including sleep disorders. For this reason, medical recipe books offer us an important resource for additional insight into the history of sleep at the level of the household.

Sleep disorders: Causes and remedies

The inability to sleep and chronic terrifying dreams were noted symptoms of illness in early modern England, much earlier than the period outlined by Roger Schmidt. While Sasha Handley suggests that sleep disorders were deliberately cultivated as "modish" marks of genius amongst the social elite in the eighteenth century, sixteenth- and seventeenth-century records suggest that the broader populace saw such disorders as undesirable, frustrating and indicative of ill health. For this reason, many men and women sought treatment from physicians and used remedies from household recipe books.[12] Medical writers were clearly aware of several common sleep disorders that affected people of all ages. In manuals of health, writers defined sleep disorders with a list of their symptoms and recommended cures. Perhaps the most common sleep disturbance was excessive "waking" or "vigilance" – the inability to sleep.

The commonality of sleeping problems can be proven by the numerous complaints of insomnia found in the medical notebooks of Richard Napier and his associates. According to Michael MacDonald's figures based on an extensive survey of Napier's medical notebooks, 20 percent of all cases of men and women who saw Napier reported trouble sleeping. Of these, 2.7 percent complained of having "fearful dreams."[13] The recent digitalization of Napier and Simon Foreman's medical notebooks overseen by Lauren Kassel and funded by the Wellcome Trust has allowed for much greater access to this important medical archive from which much of the following case studies were drawn.[14] Of the 115 cases of sleep problems found in Napier's and his associates' records, patients' ages ranged from 15 months to 80 years old and encompassed both males and females from a wide social spectrum, including members of the gentry and lower classes. These

138 *"The terrors of the night"*

cases were recorded between 21 November 1597 and 9 March 1620 and add further evidence that the problem of sleep disorders was paramount much earlier in the late sixteenth and early seventeenth century.[15]

A closer inspection of Napier and Foreman's casebook entries reveals more detail about the frequency and detail of his patients' sleeping problems. Goodwife Charity Ashbourne (*b.* 1561–1563) came twice to see Napier about sleeping problems. In May 1599 she visited Napier complaining she was "very sorely pained in her head light headed & swelled in her face very red. can take no sleepe nor rest."[16] The problem persisted and in March 1602 Ashbourne returned to Napier suffering from the same condition.[17] Thomas Potter, a local vicar (*b.* 1538), also consulted Napier twice seeking assistance for chronic bouts of insomnia. In May 1599, Potter saw Napier for the first time; Napier wrote in his casebook, "Mr Potter of Willing of 60. complayneth of a payne at his harte & the winde lyeth there. may the 12. die Saturni. h. 8. 30. am. 1599. cannot sleepe nor rest."[18] Potter's wife saw Napier in 1600 on behalf of her husband saying he "cannot sleepe his water betwixt yellow & red thick leeke puddle."[19] Bouts of sleeplessness also afflicted the Widow Nichols who, according to the casebook, "sleepeth very ill."[20] The fact that Napier and his colleagues recorded these references to disrupted sleep patterns suggests that both patients and physicians understood cases of insomnia or "vigilance" as serious symptoms of ill health. While some patients consulted Napier and his associates solely about acute or chronic insomnia, others included the inability to sleep as part of a list of other conditions. These patients were often kept awake due to the intense bodily pains and discomforts caused by the presenting symptom or chief complaint.

The inability to sleep might also be accredited to acts of witchcraft and supernatural agents in the period, showing how both patients and physicians might simultaneously subscribe to both natural and supernatural causes for sleep disorders. On the 7th December 1598, Goody Joan Malins (aged 26 to 36) brought in her infant child John [Joan] Malins (aged 15 months), complaining that for "a yere & a quarter lacking a fortnight as it were pined in all her lims & bodye hed a poer bare creature. cannot sleepe not at any time in a moneth or fortnight but crye and Drinke." Napier wrote in Latin in the margins that the mother believed her child afflicted with witchcraft.[21] Similarly, Lettice Balle of Nash (aged 17) came to Napier's practice complaining of insomnia, which was also suspected to be the result of witchcraft. Napier's associate, Mr Gerence James, recorded in the casebook, "whether any evill tongue have power over her. Cannot sleepe is light headed & sometymes talkes Idly."[22] Indicating that physicians might also consider supernatural agents as causes for sleeplessness, James believed a local witch might have cursed Balle. Other patients also sought the help of Napier and his associates due to problems sleeping, believing themselves cursed or bewitched. Bridget Tomkyns (aged 63) of Newnton reported to Napier in 1608 that she "feareth that shee is under an ill tongue [and] feareth the loosing of her sences for lack of slepe."[23] These cases suggest that although medical authors often

"The terrors of the night" 139

ascribed sleep disorders to natural causes, physicians and the broader populace may have embraced alternate supernatural explanations. Napier himself was an astrologer-physician and his practice was based on a firm belief in the supernatural power of the planets to influence human health.

Indicative of the fact that terrible dreams were part of the prognosis of disease that required treatment in the late sixteenth and seventeenth centuries, Napier's patients also reported nightmares as part of their list of complaints. Ann Roor of Filgrath (aged 37) came to see Napier on the 29th of January 1629, complaining of "fearfull dreams and a bad stomach." The same year, on 7th September, Amy Amoson of Monmouth (aged 40 years) reported having "17 nights very fearfull dreams, head ill."[24] Similarly, Mrs. Doggil of Storm, Stratford (aged 26) came to Napier because she was one night "fright in her sleep ... head ill," while Joseph Sparo (aged 11) "was fryghtfull in the night" and couldn't sleep.[25] Even more terrifying, recurring nightmares of children drove Thomas Bently of Turvey, Bedfordshire (aged 33) to seek the assistance of Napier in March 1603.[26] For these men and women, dreams were deep sources of anxiety and terror that disrupted their nocturnal regimens of sleep and disturbed their diurnal lives, driving them to seek medical help.

Other patients reported sleeping too much. Susan Blundell was an 11-year-old girl whose mother took her to Napier since she was "now given mutch to sleeping" and slept "the space of 24 hours but that her sleepe was interrupted with her usual fites & that very often her mother came to tell me of it."[27] Another concerned parent, Anthony Smith, sought Napier's help in 1598 as his 4-year-old daughter was "very exceeding sleepy can eat nothing and keepeth her bed, looketh pale."[28] Children's sleep disorders appear prominently in Napier's records with parents deeply concerned if their children slept either too little or too much. Hugh Tomson brought his 11-year-old son William to Napier in 1598 with chest pains saying, "he could not sleep all this night."[29] Adults and older persons also reported sleep disorders and problems sleeping and there is no clear pattern of patients' age or gender. Statistics gathered from *The Casebooks Project* suggest that most patients with sleep disorders were aged between 20 and 60.[30] These records suggest that the inability to sleep and other sleep disorders were apparent in a period much earlier than historians have previously asserted. As early as the late sixteenth century, physicians such as Napier were consulted for remedies to treat sleep disorders. Unfortunately, Napier's records do not include the patients' prescribed treatments or cures, merely their astrological chart and brief notes about their ailments.

According to published medical and philosophical tracts, insomnia or "vigilance" was conceived of as a serious illness caused by the excessive "hot and dry brains" of individuals whose humoral complexions were fundamentally imbalanced. The result was a wasting away of the body and a deterioration of the overall complexion of the insomniac. Robert Burton explained, "It causeth dryness of the brain, frenzy, dotage and makes the body dry, lean, hard and ugly to behold ... the temperature of the brain

140   *"The terrors of the night"*

is corrupted by it, the humors adjust, the eyes made to sink into the head, choler increased and the whole body inflamed."[31] Other causes, according to Andrew Boorde, were "a weknes of the brayne, or els thorow sicknes, anger, or fasting, or els thorowe solicitudenes of repletion or extreme heate, or extreme colde in the feete or such like."[32]

Physicians prescribed remedies that were designed to restore the balance of the humours and remoisten the brain so that natural sleep could ensue. Diets that included moist foods such as lettuce were frequently prescribed. Levine Lemnie wrote, "sleep must be provoked with Lettice and other salter herbes, that doe humect [sic] and refresh the braine and all parts of the body."[33] In addition to moist foods, other substances used to procure sleep were endorsed, such as women's breast milk and opiates. Boorde gave a remedy for insomnia as follows, "Take of the oyle of violettes an unce, of Opium halfe an unce, incorporate this together with womans milke and with a fine linnen cloth lay it to the temples."[34] When these natural remedies failed, early modern writers also suggested that insomniacs use the preternatural properties of gems to induce sleep. Nicholas Culpeper (1616–1654), an extremely popular medical writer, wrote in his medical handbook *Culpeper's school of physick* (1659) that the gem jacinth assisted in procuring sleep whilst others such as granite, worn about the body, took away sleep.[35]

The evidence of unpublished recipe books, which included stock remedies for procuring sleep, also suggests that insomnia was a common sleep disorder in the seventeenth and eighteenth centuries. These works were valuable household compendiums of medical and culinary knowledge that were passed down generation to generation. In each volume were typically stock recipes for the most common illnesses and ailments including ague, scurvy, colds, cuts and sores, broken bones, plague, dropsy and palsy, amongst others. Stock treatments or "polychrests" – universal cures – were meticulously listed, often including such family favourites as "Hungary water" or "aqua mirabolus."[36] Incorporated amongst these medical recipes were remedies to procure sleep. Elizabeth Jacob's recipe book dating roughly between 1654 and 1685 included four recipes "to procure sleep." One recipe advised the following: "Take of landinum halfe a grain and mix it with methirdale and make it into a pill and give it and it will give rest, Take noe more without good Advice."[37] Other recipes in her book included the stock ingredients for sleep aids, including nutmeg, ale, cowslips and poppy.[38] Some sleep remedies were imbibed as a liquid or consumed as a pill while others were placed in clothes and wrapped around the head at bedtime. A recipe from around the mid-seventeenth century prescribed the following treatment: "Take a spoonfull of wine vinegar as much rosewater two spoonfulls of oyloliver: & runne into it some leaven wheat bread & a handfull of red rose leaves dryed & powderd & mix them & lay them on a linnen cloth & soe spread it on his temples let him lay quietly."[39] Elizabeth Jacob included the following recipe that could be modified depending on the age of the insomniac:

> Take the red poppy and cut the black from them, then sift them, then beate them in a morter, with some sack, then straine it and to a pint

of sirup, put one pound of suger then boile it up while it ropes, with a quantity of sack for an Old body and for the middle Age with White wine and for younger people with beare.[40]

Jacob's recipes were typical of many appearing in family recipe books in the period and these sometimes reveal insight into collective ideas about the cause of the sleep disorder. Joanna Saint John's recipe for procuring sleep listed the following recipe: "For those that are neare distraction with vapours & cannot sleep boyle as much Hemp seed brused as oatmeal in water grad & take it an night it causeth sleep & is also losening."[41] Lady Cowper wrote somewhat disdainfully of the Duchess of Buckingham's habit of taking laudanum to help her sleep: "I am told the Duch[ess] of Buck[ingham] every night takes an 150 Drops of Laudenum to quiet the anguish she yet lives in. I need somewhat to make me sleep after these vexable things but neither Cares nor Fears have yet reduced me to such Remedys. I trust to God in whose Care I repose my Confidence and quiet my Mind."[42] For the uber pious and those disdainful of kitchen physic, prayer and faith in God were equally powerful alleviants for sleeplessness.

The frequency with which recipes to procure sleep appears in seventeenth- and eighteenth-century unpublished recipe books suggests that insomnia or disruptions to sleep were commonly experienced in the period. Perhaps due

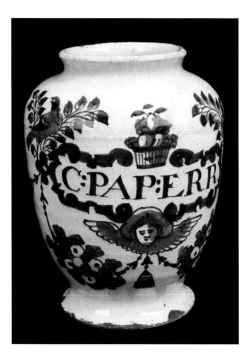

Figure 4.2 Drug Jar. Unknown maker. England, United Kingdom, 1670–1740. Science Museum, London, Wellcome Images.

142　*"The terrors of the night"*

to the considerable expense incurred by consulting professional physicians in the period, men, women and children were often treated at home with household remedies, which were passed down generation to generation. This evidence, in addition to that of casebooks and other medical writings, suggests that the problem of sleep disorders, particularly insomnia, was common long before the eighteenth century and the advent of public street lighting.

In addition to insomnia or "vigilance," another common sleep disorder was "starting out of sleep" or abrupt waking. The English physician Andrew Boorde saw this disease as caused by "a melancholy humour or els of an angery or a feareful heart, or els of a pencifull mynde, or a fearfull dreame."[43] As a remedy, he advised listening to pleasant music, avoiding lying "upright" or going to bed with a full stomach.[44] Those sensitive to waking abruptly, according to Levine Lemnie, were believed to suffer from too much study and excessive moist brains: "But they that have the nookes and cells of their braine slenderly moist, are ready to awake at every little stirring or wagging, for that the thin vapour and small fume which possetheth the heat, being nothing thicke, doth quickly vanish and passe away."[45]

Nightmares or "fearful dreams"

In addition to sleep disorders like insomnia and "starting out of sleep," nightmares or "fearful dreams" were a source of vexation and sleep deprivation in the period. Mentioned at the beginning of this chapter, James Beattie often suffered from terrifying dreams and recounted how, "Once, after riding thirty miles in a high wind, I remember to have passed part of a night in dreams, that were beyond description terrible: insomuch that I at last found it expedient to keep myself awake."[46] Similarly, Nehemiah Wallington's precious few hours of sleep were plagued with "fearfull dreames," and he recounted in his notebook, "And as for my sleepe that I could not quietly: for my distempered thoughts keept mee waking and when I did sleep oh the fearefull dreames and sites that I had then."[47] Lady Cowper viewed sleep with trepidation and she wrote in her diary on June 30th, 1709, "My Whimsy: Day is now past from fearfull Dreams, from terrifying Imaginations; and from the power of Evil Spirits, Good Lord Deliver me."[48] These accounts demonstrate how night-time dreams could be a source of deep terror and anxiety for men and women in the period.

An examination of the narratives of early modern men and women's nightmares, much like modern-day ones, indicates that death and illness were prominent themes. Early modern diarists recorded certain nightmares that unquestionably lingered in their conscious minds after waking. On the 12th July 1647, Elias Ashmole, the astrologer and collector of antiquities, had a horrifying dream of a woman who was eaten by crows. That morning he cast a horary question to see if the nightmare would "prove any hurt to me/or London/ or thereabout."[49] Thomas Vaughan dreamt frequently of his dead wife and saw one particular dream as presaging his own death.[50] In an entry dated 1658 he noted, "On Friday the 16 of July I my self sickinid att napping and that night dreamed, I was pursued by a stone horse, as my heare wife dreamed, before shee sickened and I was griviously troubled all night with a suffocation att the Heart, which continued all next day most violently and still it remaines, but with some little remission."[51] This dream deeply affected Vaughan, who grieved intensely for his dead wife and feared for his own death.

Alice Thornton's acutely terrifying dream in 1660 of blood on her delivery bed helps to show that women experienced nightmares that can be interpreted as a deep-rooted fear of death in childbirth. In her autobiography she wrote,

> My Dream, 1660
> Upon my removall to St. Nickolas and Mr. Thornton was gon to London, about the suits of my brother Sir Christopher Wandesforde, I, being great with child, dreamed one night that I was laid in childe-bed, had the white sheete spread and all over it was sprinkled with smale drops of pure blood, as if it had bin dashed with one's hand, which so frighted me that I tould my aunt of it in the morning; but she putt it of as well as she could and said dreams was not to be regarded; but I kept it in my mind till my child died.[52]

Although her aunt tried to placate her and convince her otherwise, Thornton believed this nightmare prewarned her of the imminent death of her child. Sadly the dream proved true and Thornton lost her child.

The prolific diarist Samuel Pepys had a particularly bad night's sleep after a long day at the office on the 3rd of December 1661 due to nightmares as follows:

> [I] had a very bad night by dreams of my wife's riding with me and her horse throwing her and breaking her leg and then I dreamed that I ... [was] in such pain that I waked with it and had a great deal of pain there a very great while till I fell asleep again and such apprehension I had of it that when I rose and trussed up myself thinking that it had been no dream. Till in the daytime I found myself very well at ease and remembered that I did dream so and that Mr. Creed was with me and that I did complain to him of it and he said he had the same pain in his left that I had in my right ... which pleased me much to remember.[53]

Like Thornton's prenatal nightmare, Pepys' dream lingered well into his waking day and he was placated by the fact that his associate had a similar experience. Perhaps more terrifying was the nightmare experienced by John Dee on the 24th November 1582: "Saturday night I dreamed that I was dead and afterwards my bowels were taken out and I walked and talked

144 *"The terrors of the night"*

with diverse and among other with the Lord Treasurer who was come to my house to burn my books when I was dead and thought he looked sourly on me."[54] Grotesque bodily harm was perhaps the least of Dee's unconscious fears manifesting in this narrative; he also fretted over the loss of his prized book collection. With their nightmarish graphic visual and emotional landscapes, such records of dreams starkly reveal the deep sense of terror and anxiety men and women experienced both during their dreams and upon waking. They also help to reveal the fact that the night and nocturnal hours were often a time of inherent fear.

Within the humoral schema of the body and health, terrible dreams were understood to be the result of an excess of melancholy and a symptom of ill health. According to Sir William Vaughan (1575–1641), the inward cause of terrible, natural dreams are "evill humors, specially melancholicke, which through blacknesse thereof, doth darken the light of understanding" and "imprints," fearful images on the brain.[55] Thomas Nashe argued that "melancholy was the mother of dreames and of all the terrours of the night whatsoever."[56] Similarly, Robert Burton, the seventeenth-century expert on melancholy, explained that this humour stirred up in the imagination "many monstrous and prodigious things, especially if it be stirred up by some terrible object, presented to it by the common sense or memory."[57] He thus advised, "Against fearful and troublesome dreams, *incubus* and such inconveniences, wherewith melancholy men are molested, the best remedy is to eat a light supper and of such meats as are easy of digestion."[58]

Terrifying dreams were believed to be caused by a spectrum of supernatural, preternatural and natural stimuli, which shows the opaque fluidity of the cosmology of dreaming. Against terrifying dreams "injected" by God or the Devil, writers on dreams suggested prayer and private meditation before sleep. A prayer book written by Richard Day in 1578 included the following prayer to be said, "when we be redy to sleep:"

> O Lord our governour, & defender, both to shield us now lying unable to help our selves from the craftines & assaults of our cruell enemy: & also to call us then unto thee, when we shalbe yet more unable at the finishing of the race of this life, not for our own deserts, but for thy own mercy sake ... And now let us so fall a sleep in thee, as thou only, & those exceding, great, & incredible good thinges may in such wise be present alway before us by the insight of our minds, as we may not be absent from thee, no not even in sleep: that such dreames may doth keep our beds and bodies pure & undefiled and also chere our harts with that blessed joy of thine.[59]

Philip Goodwin also recommended private meditations before sleep to defend against the threat of demonic dreams.[60] The Devil may have his dread fortresses and demonic legions, but "Good men when they sleep from sinne and hold close to the service of God, they supplant Satans throne, their prayers are as great guns and batter the devils buildings."[61]

A debilitating fear of supernatural and natural assaults during sleep is apparent in the writings of more moderate writers. The physician and philosopher Sir Thomas Browne (1605–1682) said his prayers before sleep and wrote, "I dare not trust it without my prayers and an half adieu to the world." A nocturnal prayer from his work the *Religio Medici* (1635) reads as follows:

> The night is come, like to the day,
> Depart not Thou, great God, away.
> Let not my sins, black as the night,
> Eclipse the lustre of Thy light: ...
> Thou, Whose nature cannot sleep,
> On my temples Centry keep:
> Guard me 'gainst those watchful foes,
> Whose eyes are open while mine close.
> Let no dreams my head infest,
> But such as Jacob's temples blest.
> While I do rest, my Soul advance;
> Make my sleep a holy trance.[62]

A profound fear of the nocturnal hours and the attacks of the Devil are also clear in seventeenth-century sectarian writings. The Fifth Monarchist John Rogers admitted in his spiritual handbook that as a child "before I durst sleep" he made sure to "say my prayers and my Our Father and I believe in God & c and the Ten Commandments" for fear of malevolent supernatural assaults as he slept.[63] Renowned for her piety and religious regimen of worship, Lady Cowper also prayed fastidiously at night to ask God to protect her from terrifying dreams:

> At night I pray Almighty God to keep mee [sic] from ye power of Evil Spirits and of evil men; from fearfull Dreams and terrifying Imaginations; from Fire and all sad Accidents; and to give me Hope and Trust in His Infinite Never' failing Mercies and in the Merits of my Savior Jesus. I believe my prayer is heard, Else I cannot account, how I escape so many Mischeifs [sic], I know of, Doubtless more that's know not of. O Lord: To All thy Creatures Thou art kind o're all thy tender Mercies are; He Bless Thee Dayly Now 'Twill be my work Eternally Above.[64]

The practice of prayers before bed may be part of the "sacralization of household piety" that Sasha Handley explored in her studies of sleep practices and religious devotion in the late seventeenth century.[65] As she suggests, the seventeenth century witnessed the "intensification of sacralized sleep-regimens" or "sleep-piety," including night-time prayers, that was the

146 *"The terrors of the night"*

result of pastoral attempts to reform household piety and instil religious practices firmly into household life.[66] Yet while Handley suggests these attempts were in force after the Restoration, the evidence of earlier prayer books and diaries suggest the practice of night-time prayers before bed had been common as early as the sixteenth century and possibly earlier. These accounts further add weight to the idea that both the dream and the night were sources of acute anxiety and fear for early modern men, women and children long before the eighteenth century and also problematize the process of nocturnalization.

When prayers did not work writers advised avoiding certain foods. Robert Burton suggested, "To procure pleasant dreams and quiet rest" his readers should avoid eating "beans, pease, garlic, onions, cabbage, vension, hare, [using] black wines, or any meat hard of digestion at supper, or [lying] on their backs."[67] The ideal sleep for health was therefore either quiet or filled with pleasant dreams. Above all, the way to perfect sleep was believed to be facilitated by moderating the diet, exercise, sleep and passions of the individual. The dangers of excess threatened to lead the body, mind and soul into sloth, distemper, disease and even death. Although too much "watch" was debilitating for the body, so was "immoderate sleep," which "maketh the body apt unto palsies, apoplexies, falling sicknesse, rheumes and impostumes."[68]

According to the moral economy of the body, Thomas Cogan warned that afternoon naps and immoderate sleep made "a man slothfull … causeth head ach" and "breedeth rhumes."[69] Consequently, the proper time for sleep was only at night and its duration should be typically "7, 8 or 9 hours."[70] As an indication of how little these ideas changed throughout the period, by the late eighteenth century similar advice was recommended in prescriptive manuals. The author of the tract, *Directions and observations relative to food, exercise and sleep* (1772), recommended no "less than six nor more than nine Hours in a Day."[71] A popular work by William Buchan, *Domestic medicine* (1772), also urged moderation in sleep, promoting what historian Lucia Dacome described as a form of "bodily domestication."[72] Buchan gave this advice to readers, "Sleep, as well as diet, ought to be duly regulated. Too little sleep weakens the nerves, exhausts the spirits and occasions diseases; and too much renders the mind dull, the body gross and disposes it to apoplexies, lethargies and such like."[73] The custom of "indolent and slothful" people who indulged in "lolling a-bed" for more than nine hours was therefore deemed to be conducive to a weak and disease-prone constitution.[74]

Interestingly, this idea of the appropriate length of sleep recommended for healthy adults differs little from advice given by modern sleep research. Although scientists acknowledge that the ideal length of sleep differs between individuals and is dependent on age, health and lifestyle, according to research conducted by the National Sleep Foundation, "for teenagers, 8 to 10 hours was considered appropriate, 7 to 9 hours for young adults and adults and 7 to 8 hours of sleep for older adults."[75] What is also notable is that, although A. Roger Ekirch suggests premodern people typically

"The terrors of the night"   147

experienced a pattern of segmented sleep, this is not discussed in manuals of health or discussions of the proper regimens of sleep.

The time of sleep was also important for one's overall constitution and helped prevent disturbed sleep. Robert Burton recommended, "the fittest time is two or three hours after supper, whenas [sic] the meat is now settled at the bottom of the stomach."[76] Francis de Valangin argued that "night was the most proper time for Sleep" and that ideally the best sleep was "enjoyed before Midnight."[77] Showing the "sociable sleeping" habits of people in the eighteenth century, which historians Handley, Ekirch and Peter Stearnes have outlined as increasingly late and disruptive, Valangin complained that modern city life had led people to unnatural long hours of wakefulness:[78]

> We need not look far to find many striking Instances of the Necessity of Sleeping in the Night and of reserving the Day for Labour and Action; for we see, that Country People who go to Bed betimes and frequently soon after Sun-set, although they rise again with the Sun, after but a few Hours Rest, are generally healthy and strong, whilst most of our London and Towns-People, who keep awake till Midnight and pass a proportional Part of the next Day in Sleep, are wan, pale and always ailing.[79]

The way to ideal health was therefore to sleep at night and wake at dawn. To deviate from this advised regimen of sleep was to risk a variety of sleep disorders and diseases. Above all, the ideal type of sleep was ultimately quiet and filled with pleasant dreams.

The *Incubus* or the nightmare: Sleep paralysis in early modern England

Perhaps the most terrifying early modern nocturnal sleep disorder was the "*incubus*" or "nightmare." In early modern England, the nightmare was understood as a specific sleep disorder in which the victim was "oppressed," "invaded" or laid upon by a malevolent being in sleep. While sleep researchers today define this experience as a disorder known as sleep paralysis, premodern English ideas saw it as either a disease of the body, manifesting in terrible dreams, or as the real assaults of demonic beings, witches or spirits. In the eighteenth century John Bond, a physician who trained in Edinburgh, explained the key symptoms associated with the phenomenon in his work, *An essay on the incubus, or night-mare* (1753):

> The Night-mare generally seizes people sleeping on their backs and often begins with frightful dreams, which are soon succeeded by a difficult respiration, a violent oppression on the breast and a total privation of voluntary motion. In this agony they sigh, groan, utter indistinct sounds and remain in the jaws of death, till, by the utmost efforts of nature, or some external assistance, they escape out of that dreadful torpid state.[80]

"The terrors of the night"

One of the nightmare's most horrifying aspects was the victim's encounter with a demonic being who attacked while the dreamer was in a paralytic state and lay on his or her chest preventing movement or breath. While early modern English medical authors like Bond saw this as a terrifying dream instigated by disorders in the body's natural physiology, this encounter led many victims to conclude that they had been subjected to the real assaults of demons, witches or spirits. Subsequently, there are two schools of thought concerning the nightmare in early modern England: those who saw it as a disease of the body manifesting in terrible dreams and those who saw it as the real assaults of witches, demons or spirits, which I will define as the "hag-riding" tradition. Thus, at the heart of debates about the nightmare experience was the problem of discerning between supernatural and natural causes, dreams and reality, as well as doubts concerning the reliability of the senses.

In medical writings the nightmare itself was traditionally conceptualized as a disease symptomatic of humoral excess and the strange effects of the body on the mind and faculty of the imagination. Although today we use the term "nightmare" to encompass all kinds of bad dreams, early modern

Figure 4.3 "The Nightmare." By: Henry Fuseli after Thomas Holloway. Appearing in *The poetical works of Erasmus Darwin.* ... By: Erasmus Darwin. Wellcome Library, London.

writers understood the nightmare as an experience involving a specific set of symptoms, caused by supernatural or natural forces. As I will demonstrate, writings on the nightmare reveal a complex spectrum of theories that incorporate fragments of classical lore, traditional beliefs and contemporary medical understandings of the body and mind. Throughout this chapter I use the terms "nightmare," "*incubus*" or "mare" to refer specifically to premodern understandings.

Both natural and supernatural ideas of the nightmare continued and co-existed throughout the early modern period, at least until the nineteenth century. A survey of medical ideas about the causes of the nightmare over the period 1550 to 1760 shows how slowly these notions evolved and indicates that most writers drew their conclusions from longstanding medical theories. The majority of English medical texts argued that the *incubus* was caused by indigestion, the supine position of the body in sleep or humoral imbalances. Similarly, cures for the *incubus* changed little from the sixteenth to the eighteenth century, with physicians and medical writers continuing to counsel a strict regimen of a moderate diet, bloodletting and purging and an avoidance of the supine position in sleep.

However, this is not to suggest there were no changes in medical theories about the nightmare. Eighteenth-century writers such as John Bond sought to establish more empirical models for the nightmare by appropriating William Harvey's theories about the circulation of the blood. Similarly, other eighteenth-century medical writers posited that this disease was a symptom of the nervous condition of the "spleen" or "hypochondria" and "hysteria."[81] As the emphasis on the *incubus* shifted from the humours to the circulatory and nervous systems in the eighteenth century, the primary site for the "mare's" origin also shifted from the stomach to the brain.

Although both lay manuals of health and learned medical treatises described the *incubus* as a natural disease of the body, there is evidence that the supernatural theory of the nightmare persisted well into the nineteenth century. Seventeenth- and eighteenth-century medical writers frequently complained about their patients' belief of the nightmare as a supernatural assault by demonic beings. Moreover, incidents of being "hag-ridden" and "witch-ridden" continued in English records of witchcraft. Owen Davies has found evidence in the areas of Somerset and Dorset as late as 1875 of men and women accusing persons of "hag-riding" or sending the "mare" to them.[82] Therefore, the development of premodern ideas about the nightmare in England reveals a degree of complexity and continuity, rather than the emergence of progressive, medical and rational models. Moreover, the co-existence and continuity of natural theories of the mare also complicates a simple model of the rise of rational, medical thought.

The etymology of terms associated with the nightmare in the English language shows that its origins were firmly situated in beliefs that saw it as a supernatural assault by nocturnal demons or spirits. While the precise origins of the term "nightmare" are still something of a mystery, "mare" most

150 *"The terrors of the night"*

likely derived from the Anglo-Saxon root word "mara" meaning "crusher."
Another alternative, as Owen Davies suggests, is that "mare" derives from
the Germanic "mahr," or the Old Norse "mara," both referring to "a supernatural being, usually female who lay upon people's chests at night, thereby
suffocating them."[83] According to the *Oxford English Dictionary*, "nightmare" itself derives from the genitive of "night n." and "mare n.," which
most likely originated from the Low German derivative of *Nachtmahr* or
Nachmaar.[84] The linguistic root words from which the English term "nightmare" originates reveal the earlier associations of the experience with assaults by nocturnal demons. Additionally, these clues also highlight the key
feature of the terrifying encounter as being centred on the experience of a
malevolent being suffocating, crushing and physically oppressing the victim. As Owen Davies argued, European derivatives of the "nightmare" also
reflect this important facet of "pressure:"

> The sense of pressure of weight is integral to the nightmare both as a
> concept and as an experience and so it is not surprising that it is also
> prominent in the linguistics. The first element of French *cauchemar*
> derives from *caucher* ("to tread on"). The second element of Icelandic
> *martröd* comes from *troda*, meaning "to squeeze, press, ride." The idea
> of pressure is also present in other terms for the nightmare experience
> that do not share the mare element. In German we find *alpdrücken*
> ("elf-pressing") and *hexendrücken* ("witch-pressing"). The term for
> the nightmare in medieval French *appesart,* Italian *pesuarole*, Spanish
> *pesadilla* and Portuguese *pesadela* all derive from the verb *peser*, mean-
> ing "to press down upon." ... Hungarian *boszorkany-nyomas* means
> "witches pressure."[85]

The sense of being pressured or strangled by a supernatural being is also
prominent in early modern accounts of the nightmare, as well as in modern
descriptions of sleep paralysis, so that researchers today view it as a central
feature of the disorder.[86] One of the first known English uses of "nyghtesmare" appeared in Chaucer's *Miller's Tale* in 1410 in reference to protecting
a house against "every evyl wyght ffor the nyghtesmare."[87] Later early modern English authors referred to the experience as the "nyghte mare," "nightmare," "night-mare," "mare," *ephialtes, incubus* and the "hag," whilst the
verbs being "hag-ridden," "witch-ridden," "wizard-pressed" or "hagged"
were used colloquially.[88]

English references to the nightmare in medical writings also use the Ancient Greek term, *ephialtes* or the Latin *incubus* to refer to the same experience as a disease of the body. In classical Latin *incubus* was used to refer to a
male nocturnal demon, while *succubus* referred to the female species. *Incubus*
derives from the Latin *incubare* meaning "to lie upon" and was used in medieval and early modern works of theology and demonology, alongside *succubus,* to refer to night demons who assaulted their victims either physically or

"The terrors of the night" 151

sexually. This tradition appears to be linked to the later early modern English "hag-riding" phenomenon. *Ephialtes* in Greek is probably etymologically related to a verb meaning "to leap upon" and was also used in medical texts alongside *incubus* to refer to the nightmare as a natural disease.[89] Thus, from at least the sixteenth century onwards, medical authors appropriated the terms originally associated with supernatural beings, *incubus* and *ephialtes*, to refer to the nightmare as a disease or disorder of the body. This might serve to illustrate the observation of Alexandra Walsham that the early modern period saw the compression of the supernatural into natural and preternatural categories.[90] However, all derivatives of the original terms used to refer to the nightmare suggest a supernatural being who comes at night when dreamers are sleeping and creeps or lies on their chests, inducing in their victims a state of heightened fear. Due to the intense feelings of acute terror and helplessness associated with the encounter, "nightmare" became later used in English around the nineteenth century to describe any terrifying dream, losing its earlier specificity as referring to a particular kind of dream experience.[91] The etymology of the term "nightmare" serves as a revealing testimony to the underlying cultural beliefs and attitudes towards the phenomena.

In early modern medical tracts and dictionaries, definitions of the nightmare also reveal further details of the etymology as well as the close relationship between the supernatural and natural etiologies. Philip Barrough (*fl.* 1560–1590), a licensed physician at Canterbury, wrote in his medical tract, *The methode of physicke* (1583), "*Ephialtes* in Greeke, in latin *Incubus* and *Incubo*. It is a disease, where as one thinketh him selfe in the night to be oppressed with a great waight and beleeveth that some thing commeth upon him and the pacient thinketh him selfe strangled in this disease. It is called in English the Mare."[92] The English physician Andrew Boorde discussed at length the different views of the nightmare and explained,

> *Ephialtes* is the greke word. *Ephialtes* is the barbarus word. In latin it is named *Incubus* and *Succubus*. In English it is named the Mare. And some say that it is a kinde of spirite the which doth infest and trouble men when they be in their beddes sleeping, as Saint Augustine sayth. *De civitate dei.* Cap. rr. and Saint Thomas of Alquine [sic] sayth in his first parte of his divinitie, *Incubus* doth infest and trouble women and *Succubus* doth infest men. Some holdeth opinion that Marlin was begotten of his mother, of the spirite named *Incubus*, Esdras doth speake of this spirit and I have red much of this spirite in *Speculum exemplorum* and in my time at saint Albones here in England, was infested an Ancresse of such a spirite as she shewed me and also to credible persons, but this in my op[in]ion that this *Ephialtes* otherwise named the Mare, the which doth come to man or woman when they be sleeping, doth come of some evil humour, considering that they the which be thus troubled sleeping, shal thinke that they doe see, heere and feele, the thing that is not true. And in such troubles sleeping, a man skarse draweth his breath.[93]

152 *"The terrors of the night"*

From Boorde's discussion it is evident that the nightmare was the site of two co-existing ideologies, one that saw it as the real supernatural assaults of demonic beings and the other that saw it as a natural disease, resulting in terrifying dreams. Later in the seventeenth century Robert Burton also discussed the nightmare as a symptom of melancholy and explained in his most famous work, *The anatomy of melancholy* (1621), "in such as are troubled with *incubus*, or witch-ridden (as we call it); if they lie on their backs, they suppose an old woman rides and sits so hard upon them that they are almost stifled for want of breath; when there is nothing offends but a concourse of bad humours, which trouble the phantasy."[94]

These descriptions changed little into the eighteenth century, so that in Steven Blankaart's *The physical dictionary* (1702) we find, "*Ephialtes*, or *Incubus*, the Night-Mare, is a depraved Imagination, whereby People asleep fancie that their Wind-pipe is oppressed by some superincumbent Body, that their Breath is stop'd." A decade or so later, in Ephraim Chambers' *Cyclopedia* (1728) the nightmare is defined as, "*Incubus*, or the Night-Mare, is the Name of a Disease consisting in an Oppression of the Breast, so very violent, that the Patient cannot speak, or even Breathe."[95] While descriptions of the symptoms of the disease are remarkably similar, medical theories saw the nightmare as caused by a mixture of physiological and psychological factors that combined produced the horrifying dream of a creeping being suffocating the dreamer.

The majority of actual accounts of the "mare" come from witchcraft trials and are part of the "hag-riding" tradition. In these records, witches and their demonic familiars were believed to assault their victims while they slept by creeping onto their paralyzed bodies to suffocate and "ride" them. As Owen Davies and Willem de Blécourt demonstrated, these incidents appear in trial records both in England and Europe.[96] In an English witchcraft trial at York in 1595, Dorothy Jackson accused her neighbour of witchcraft, claiming that she was "ridden with a witch three times of one night, being thereby greatly astonished and upon her astonishment awakened her husband." In a Northumberland trial, Nicolas Raynes accused Elizabeth Fenwick of "hag-riding" his wife, who "after being threatened, has been continually tormented by Elizabeth, a reputed witch, who rides on her and attempts to pull her on to the floor."[97] Indicative of the persistent belief into the eighteenth century that witches sent the "mare," a letter to *The Spectator* in 1711 gave the account of Old Moll White, a reputed witch, whose crimes included "giving Maids the Night-Mare."[98] Davies studied the trial records of Somerset and Dorset in the late nineteenth century and found six court cases between 1852 and 1875 that involved witches being accused of "hag-riding."[99]

Premodern English experiences of the nightmare could also incorporate tales of being assaulted by demonic animals and are associated with cases of possession. In the account of witchcraft written by Edward Fairfax concerning the bewitchment of his daughter, Helen Fairfax, is an incident in which she was "laid" upon by a demonic cat. On November 3, 1621, Helen

"The terrors of the night" 153

complained to her parents sleeping beside her that "a white catt hath laid longe upon mee and drawne my breath and hath left in my mouth and Throate so filthy a smell that it doth poyson mee."[100] Similarly, in the trial records of the possession of Richard Dugdale, a Lancashire gardener who became bewitched in July 1695, one of the witnesses testifying to his possession, John Fletcher, a husbandman of Harwood, reported to the jury how he was one night "in bed with the said Dugdale and I felt something come up towards my knee; then I felt it creep up till it came towards my heart and it was about the bigness of a little dog or cat."[101] The descriptions of being laid upon by demonic beings, here in the form of animals, which "creep" and steal the breath of their victims, suggests another form of the nightmare.

Evidence for the persistence of supernatural etiologies of the nightmare can be found in a range of printed works outside of witchcraft records. Authors of medical works and dream treatises repeatedly complained that the "vulgar" masses still believed that the nightmare was in fact a supernatural phenomenon. Edmund Gardiner, a seventeenth-century medical writer, wrote in his tract, *Phisicall and Approved Medicines* (1611), "this dreadfull griefe which some being much deceived, thinking that it must onely proceede of witchcraft."[102] Thomas Willis (1621–1675) a well-respected English physician, wrote in his chapter on the nightmare in his work *De anima brutorum* (1672), "The common people superstitiously believe, that this passion is indeed caused by the Devil and that the evil spirits lying on them, procures that weight and oppression upon their heart. Though indeed we do grant, such a thing may be, but we suppose that this symptom proceeds oftenest from mere natural causes."[103] Similarly, Thomas Tryon declared in *A treatise of dreams and visions* (1689), "And tho the Vulgar, when they are thus affected, conceit it some external thing comes and lies upon them, which they fancy to be some Ghost, or Hob-Goblin, yet the truth is, it proceeds from inward causes."[104] These comments indicate persistence in the belief that the nightmare was a supernatural physical or psychic assault.

In early modern England medical theories of the nightmare co-existed with supernatural ones, both drawing from ideas that went as far back as Antiquity. Galenic lore suggested that humoral imbalances were the root cause of the disease. Most writers of sixteenth- and seventeenth-century English medical books asserted that the *incubus* was caused by an excess of melancholy, phlegm or "vital spirits," which arose as a result of indigestion, eating "hard meats" and drinking liquors.[105] Consequently, it was believed that the body's excess humours caused "vapours" to ascend to the brain, triggering the imagination to produce horrible visions in the mind. Richard Haydock explained the causes of the nightmare in his manuscript on dreams, the *Oneirologia* (1605):

> In the Incubus, or Night-mare, the vitall and Animall spirits are soe oppressed with the multitude of grosse vapours, that men thinke themselves overlaine by some hagge, or oppressed with some ponderous

154   *"The terrors of the night"*

> burthen. By which examples it is evident, that the actions of the minde close prisoned in the body, in time of Sleepe (it selfe never sleepinge) are distorted and missed by similitude of the cheife swayeinge humours, nowe become exorbitant by inequality of temperature. Where a carefull difference is to bee put beetweene this first naturall kinde of Dreame and the seconde: insoemuch as these vapours stirre the Phantasie to make and forme images answerable to theire owne nature without the helpe of preinherent formes in the Phantasie: whereas in the other the Phantasie workes only uppon the late imprinted formes and Ideas of the matters last thought of, or earnestly intreated of, the senses beeinge nowe kindely bounde by a temperate and milde ascendinge vapour. And this is the cause, why they are formall, rationall and coherent: when these are only materially significative, from the Elementary part of the man, beeinge forerunners of a subsequent disease, as smoake is of fier.[106]

According to Haydock, the humours oppressed the animal or vital spirits, so that the imagination produced dreams of being "oppressed" by "some hagge" or "some ponderous burthen." The mind was therefore misled by the senses into believing what was dreamt was in fact real. Thus, the difficulty here was discerning between reality and fantasy, dreaming and waking states.

Similarly, Samuel Collins (*bap.* 1618–1710), a well-respected English anatomist and physician, wrote in his medical treatise, *Of the nightmare* that the disease was "chiefly" made "by a gross vapour comming from thence to the braine." These "grose vapours" obstructed the "passages of the brayne" so that the "nerves" were affected as well as the "phancy." The result was difficulty breathing and dreams of "horrible" objects.[107] The mind was therefore deceived by the senses into believing what was dreamt was in fact real.

Drawing on longstanding ideas, seventeenth-century writers also argued that the "supine" position of the body in sleep frequently gave rise to the nightmare. Samuel Collins explained, "The nightmare is ... a more dangerous malady of the braine. Because the kinder passages of the brayne are truely obstructed, from which the body being layed in a supine posture do Chiefely labour with this disease."[108] Physicians generally believed that this position encouraged the noxious vapours of hard meats to ascend to the brain. Indeed, a typical cure for the *incubus*, according to most manuals of health, was to avoid the supine position and instead to lie on one's side during sleep. Consequently, sixteenth- and seventeenth-century medical writers argued that the nightmare was a disease caused by imbalances in the body's natural processes and their dangerous effects on the imaginative faculty. The terrifying dreams associated with the nightmare were therefore understood as disturbed mental images that were products of a disordered body.

As with other sleep disorders, the dangers of excess were used to explain the moral and physiological causes of the nightmare. In 1651 Thomas Hobbes dismissed as mere superstition the belief that the nightmare was a demonic assault. To Hobbes, the real cause of the *incubus* sprang from "gluttony, it makes men believe they are invaded, opprest and stifled with a great weight."[109] The dangers included the sins of excessive drinking, eating, sex and even sleep. According to Samuel Collins, the chief causes of the disease were "overmuch drinking" and a "gross vaporous diet."[110] This schema is indicative of the way that diseases in this period were considered part of the moral economy of the body and conceived of as divine retribution for immoderate excesses of all forms. The body itself was a potential vehicle of punishment for those who indulged too much in their appetites.

Excessive indulgence also led to a dangerous overabundance of the body's natural fluids. Thomas Tryon noted that the *incubus* caused an abundance of "Phlegm" that impeded the animal spirits resulting in a temporary paralysis of the body's natural functions.[111] The dangers of excess could lead to a deadly commingling of humoral fluids in the stomach that rose to the brain, causing the terrifying dreams associated with the nightmare of being physically oppressed by a malevolent being. Samuel Collins explained, "the cause is to be grose flegme or Melancholy (not lodged in the braine but about the midriffe) from which growing turgide by immoderate drinking and crudity of ill concocted ailmente the diaphrame and lunges are oppressed and from a grosse vapours, conveyed into the fauces & braine."[112]

Moderation was seen to be the key to good health in premodern English physic: restraint of the body's excessive appetites was viewed as essential for the overall well being of the individual. Robert Bayfield, an English physician who wrote both medical and religious works, suggested that the best prophylactic for the *incubus* was "a slender diet," in addition to an avoidance of the supine position.[113] Thomas Tryon's *A treatise of dreams and visions* (1689) also counselled moderation:

> The Cure is to be effected by a regular diet and such as may generate good spirits; and prevent the increase of *Melancholy* and *Phlegm*; avoid full *Suppers* and excess in *Liquors*, which oft occasion the Disease; use convenient purging and sometimes breathing a Vein may be expedient, especially in *Women*, in certain Obstructions peculiar to that Sex: the Black Seeds of the Male *Piony* are much commended in this Distemper.[114]

Francis Bacon also recommended using a powder of the "peony" seed as a cure for the nightmare as did Nicholas Culpepper in his work *The English Physician* (1652).[115]

The general consensus among physicians about prophylactic treatments for the *incubus* was therefore to counsel moderation or a "slender diet," especially for supper. They also advised patients to avoid drinking liquors, restrain excessive alcohol consumption and temper "gluttony." Phillip Barrough explained, "This vice is caused of excesse of drinking and continuall rawnes of the stomake, from whence do ascend vapours grosse and

156 *"The terrors of the night"*

cold, filling the ventricles of the brain, letting the faculties of the braine to be dispersed by the senewes."[116] Through excess, physicians believed bouts of the nightmare could become chronic and lead to more serious illnesses such as "epilepsie," "palsy" or "apoplexy." According to Barrough, "It is good to remedie this evill at the first: for if it continewe, it induceth and sheweth before some grevous disease, as the *Apoplexie,* the falling sicknes, or madnesse."[117]

Early eighteenth-century medical works typically recycled identical notions of causes and remedies for the nightmare, as expounded by their seventeenth-century predecessors. Theories about the influence of the humours were slow to disappear from early modern medicine. However, during the mid-eighteenth century physicians began to shift away from humoral theories. Instead, they began to assert that the nightmare was instigated by disorders of the circulatory and nervous systems; this indicated a shift away from Galenic medicine. Furthermore, the primary site of the *incubus* shifted from the stomach to the brain. New ideas about the circulatory system, brain and nerves were incorporated into explanations of the *incubus*. John Radcliffe wrote in his *Pharmacopoeia Radcliffeanna* (1718), "In an *Incubus,* the plentiful Repast at Bed-time distends the Bowels and the supine Posture in Sleep, causes the Victuals to press upon the descending Artery, so that nothing can circulate freely to the lower Extremities: and the whole Blood oppresses the Brain." This obstruction of the arteries caused the "nerves" to be compressed "so that we find a Sense of some Weight upon us" during attacks of the *incubus*.[118]

However, this does not necessarily mean that all embraced these medical models. Andrew Baxter (1687–1750), a significant eighteenth-century philosopher, argued that a natural theory of the nightmare, which ascribed it as a "distemper of the brain," was nothing less than "absurd." In his important work, *An Enquiry into the Nature of the Human Soul* (1733), he posited that the true cause of this phenomenon was a form of demonic possession.[119] In sleep, according to Baxter, the body and mind were vulnerable to the assaults of intelligent beings who "wait for and catch the opportunity of the indisposition of the body, to represent at the same time something terrifying also to the mind." In Baxter's view it was absurd to consider that the rational soul would produce terrifying dreams and instil such disorder into the mind. He argued that the disorder of the body associated with the nightmare and "the disagreeable vision made to accompany it, are two different things."[120] In his view, dreams were products not of the individual sleeper's body or mind, but rather of supernatural beings who "represent" or inject dreams in what was essentially a form of possession in sleep. Although Baxter's ideas were critiqued, particularly by Thomas Branch, the fact that he was able to put forward such theories in the eighteenth century shows that not all intellectuals were exclusively committed to a natural theory of the nightmare.[121] However, most later medical writers including John Bond scoffed at these theories as "wild opinions" smacking of superstition and an ignorance of natural medicine.[122]

In the eighteenth century John Bond's *Essay on the incubus or nightmare* (1753) published in London was one of the first printed English medical works to focus solely on explaining the causes, nature and cure of the nightmare. His work endorsed the growing medical view that the nightmare was the result of the stagnation of blood.[123] Little is known about Bond, other than that he was a physician who submitted a Latin version of his work on the *incubus* for his doctorate at the University of Edinburgh in 1751.[124] Bond's English treatise is an accessible, though learned, medical treatise on the *incubus* as a natural disease. The brief chapters discuss Bond's own theory of the nightmare, including case studies, cures and prophylactics.

Bond himself was a chronic sufferer of the nightmare. In his preface he explained the reason for his interest in the *incubus*:

> Being much afflicted with the Night-mare, self-preservation made me particularly inquisitive about it. In consulting the ancient Physicians, I found little information concerning it, except dreadful prognostics; nor could a rational account of it be expected from them, as they were unacquainted with the circulation of the blood.[125]

Bond was critical of most previous ideas of the nightmare. In his treatise Bond suggested that "the Night-Mare is commonly, and, I believe, justly, attributed to a stagnation of the Blood; but how this stagnation is produc'd has not been explain'd, so far as I know, in a satisfactory manner."[126] In his medical opinion, the real cause of the nightmare lay in the inhibition of blood, caused by the supine sleeping position.[127] Bond's emphasis on the cause of the *incubus* as lying deep within the vessels and circulatory system, reduced the visions associated with this experience to the mere reflections of a suffocated brain. In his theory the heart was responsible for instigating a stagnation of the blood, due to its weight resting on the vertebrae in sleep. The pressure of the heart on the veins caused the blood to stop circulating through the lungs whilst simultaneously preventing the blood from returning to the head. Yet, despite the ingenuity of his theory, as later authors such as Robert Whytt would declare, according to Bond's logic: "If they were true, some degree of the night-mare ought to happen to every person that lies on his back, especially after eating a full meal."[128]

In Bond's view initial symptoms of the *incubus* were "frightful dreams." Since the body and mind were united with a special "harmony and connection, the Diseases of the one always affect the other in a very sensible manner."[129] The "hideous association of ideas" that formed "frightful spectres" in the imagination during attacks of the nightmare were products of this relationship. Bond even suggested that these dreams were perhaps "intended as a stimulus to rouse the sentient principle in us" so that the sleeper would shift his or her position and "by that means avoid the approaching danger."[130] The most "perfect sleep," according to Bond, was a dreamless one, since dreams themselves were conceivably, "a Disorder of the Body"

158 *"The terrors of the night"*

that prevented "perfect rest."[131] Bond's idea of dreams as disorders of the body supports Lucia Dacome's idea of the pathologization of dreams in the eighteenth century. Yet, as I have suggested, ideas about dreams as linked to madness and disease were indeed also present in medical writings and theories of the sixteenth and seventeenth centuries.[132]

The case studies of the nightmare Bond includes to illustrate his theories are dramatic.[133] While Bond himself subscribed to a purely medical theory of the nightmare, he included accounts from individuals who believed themselves assaulted by the Devil or night demons. For example, Bond included the case of a clergyman who suffered from the *incubus* and believed he had been attacked by the Devil.

> A corpulent Clergyman, about fifty years old, who is very fond of strong beer and flesh suppers, but so subject to the Night-mare, that he is obliged to stint himself to a certain quantity every night; whenever he happens to take an over-dose, he groans so loudly that he often wakens all the People in the house. He has assur'd me, that, in these fits, he imagin'd the Devil came to his bedside, seiz'd him by the Throat and endeavoured to choack him. Next day he observ'd the black impressions on his hard Fingers on his Neck.[134]

Although Bond viewed this case as an example of the dangers of excess, the clergyman himself believed that he had been a victim of the Devil. In this instance, the Devil left physical proof of his manifestation in the "black impressions" made on the clergyman's neck.

At the beginning of his work, Bond made sure to distance himself from "superstitious" beliefs and wrote, "I have not introduc'd any thing in this Essay that did not appear serious or probable. I have therefore omitted an inquiry into the origin of old epithets and quaint names commonly given to this Disorder; such as *Hag-riding, Wizard-pressing, Mare-riding, Witch-dancing* &c. nor did I think it requisite to mention particularly the *curious Charms* adapted to each superstitious name."[135] Bond elaborated further that the word "nightmare" itself, a "strange term," most likely derived from "superstitious notions which the British had and perhaps still have, of it."[136] While supernatural ideas of the causes of the nightmare still circulated, Bond as a physician laboured rather to present a serious medical treatise on the natural causes of the *incubus* as a naturally occurring yet dangerous disease of the body.

Ideas about the natural causes of the *incubus* evolved slowly. Medical theories circulated from the sixteenth to eighteenth century with the majority of medical works reiterating the longstanding ideas that the nightmare was a terrifying dream that resulted from humoral imbalances and sleeping in the supine position. Some authors also adhered to notions that the *incubus* was a product of the senses deceived by the "chimeras" of the imagination, a symptom of a disordered brain. Rather than a process of "medicalization," the history of the nightmare reveals a continuation of medical theories, with subtle shifts in explanations for the primary causes of the disease.

However, this is not to suggest that there were no significant developments in ideas of the nightmare. Although the majority of authors recycled older ideas, in the eighteenth century medical writers such as John Bond attempted to present more empirical theories of the nightmare based on new developments in knowledge of the body and disease. They postulated that the *incubus* was ultimately a symptom of the stagnation of the blood. Yet, these new models largely failed to impress the medical professions and the wider populace, both tending to cling to more traditional views of the natural and supernatural causes of the nightmare. Showing how continuity rather than change characterizes the history of the nightmare as the dark other of the dream, beliefs that it was the supernatural assaults of demons, witches and spirits also persisted amongst the broader populace, despite the longstanding co-existence of natural theories. Whilst physicians may have thought their patients suffered from the *incubus* as a natural disease, patients themselves, due to their own perceptions of the experience as a terrifying assault by a demonic being, often believed otherwise. This suggests that supernatural and natural theories of the nightmare were neither contradictory nor mutually exclusive in premodern culture and helps to complicate historical ideas of the rise of rational thought and post-enlightenment culture.

Notes

1 Samuel Pepys, *Diary: for the first time fully transcribed from the shorthand manuscript in the Pepysian Library, Magdalene College, Cambridge.* Vol. 3 (Boston: F.A. Niccolls, 1892–1899), 139.
2 Sasha Handley, "From the Sacral to the Moral: Sleeping Practices, Household Worship and Confessional Cultures in Late Seventeenth-Century England," *Cultural and Social History* 9, no. 1 (2012): 27–46, "Sleepwalking, Subjectivity and the Nervous Body in Eighteenth-Century Britain: The Nervous Body in Eighteenth-Century Britain," *Journal for Eighteenth-Century Studies* 35, no. 3 (September 2012): 305–23, "Sociable Sleeping in Early Modern England, 1660–1760," *History* 98, no. 329 (January 2013): 79–104.
3 Roger Schmidt, "Caffeine and the Coming of the Enlightenment," *Raritan* 23, no. 1 (Summer 2003): 129–49.
4 Handley, "Sociable Sleeping," 79–80.
5 Craig Koslofsky, *Evening's Empire: A History of the Night in Early Modern Europe* (Cambridge: Cambridge University Press, 2011), 1–18, 91–127.
6 See for example: Moshe Sluhovsky, *Believe Not Every Spirit: Possession, Mysticism, & Discernment in Early Modern Catholicism* (University of Chicago Press, 2007); Gábor Klaniczay and Eva Pócs, eds., *Communicating with the Spirits* (Budapest: CEU Press, 2005); Gábor Klaniczay, "The Process of Trance: Heavenly and Diabolic Apparitions in Johannes Nider's 'Formicarius,'" in *Procession, Performance, Liturgy and Ritual: Essays in Honor of Bryan R. Gillingham* (Ottawa: The Institute of Medieval Music, 2007), 203–58; Moshe Sluhovsky, "The Devil in the Convent," *The American Historical Review* 107, no. 5 (2002): 1379–1411; Susan Juster, "Mystical Pregnancy and Holy Bleeding: Visionary Experience in Early Modern Britain and America," *The William and*

160 *"The terrors of the night"*

Mary Quarterly 57, no. 2 (2000): 249–88; Barbara Newman, "Possessed by the Spirit: Devout Women, Demoniacs and the Apostolic Life in the Thirteenth Century," *Speculum* 73, no. 3 (1998): 733–70.

7 Willem de Blècourt and Owen Davies eds. *Witchcraft Continued: Popular Magic in Modern Europe* (Manchester; New York: Manchester University Press, 2004); Davies, *The Haunted: A Social History of Ghosts* (Houndsmills: Palgrave, 2007); Davies, *Witchcraft, Magic and Culture, 1736–1951* (Manchester: Manchester University Press, 1999); Wouter J. Hanegraaff, "How magic survived the disenchantment of the world" Religion 33 (2003): 357–80; Michael Hunter, *The occult laboratory: magic, science and second sight in late seventeenth-century Scotland* (Woodbridge: Boydell Press, 2001).

8 Alexandra Walsham, "The Reformation and 'the Disenchantment of the World' Reassessed," *The Historical Journal* 51, no. 2 (2008): 509.

9 Nancy Caciola and Moshe Sluhovsky, "Spiritual Physiologies: The Discernment of Spirits in Medieval and Early Modern Europe," *Preternature: Critical and Historical Studies on the Preternatural* 1, no. 1 (2012): 3.

10 Lauren Kassell, "Casebooks in Early Modern England: Medicine, Astrology and Written Records," *Bulletin of the History of Medicine* 88, no. 4 (2014): 595–625.

11 Elaine Leong, "Collecting Knowledge for the Family: Recipes, Gender and Practical Knowledge in the Early Modern English Household," *Centaurus; International Magazine of the History of Science and Medicine* 55, no. 2 (May 2013): 81–103; "Making Medicines in the Early Modern Household," *Bulletin of the History of Medicine* 82, no. 1 (2008): 145–68.

12 Handley, "Sociable Sleeping," 91. For Handley's recent discussion on remedies for sleep loss see, *Sleep in early modern England* (New Haven; London: Yale University Press, 2016), 61–68.

13 Michael MacDonald, *Mystical Bedlam: Madness, Anxiety and Healing in Seventeenth-Century England* (Cambridge: Cambridge University Press, 1985), Table D. 1.

14 Lauren Kassell et al. ed., "Welcome | Casebooks Project," *Casebooks Project*, (accessed 29 June 2015), http://www.magicandmedicine.hps.cam.ac.uk.

15 Kassell, "Search results summary (Subtopic: Sleep problems)," *Casebooks Project*, (accessed 15 November 2014), http://www.magicandmedicine.hps.cam.ac.uk/the-casebooks/search/cases/results/summarise?t=211&to=1&tm=7.

16 "CASE12376 (Normalised Version)," *Casebooks Project*, (accessed 7 July 2016), http://www.magicandmedicine.hps.cam.ac.uk/view/case/normalised/CASE12376?sort=date&order=asc.

17 "CASE16631 (Normalised Version)," *Casebooks Project*, (accessed 7 July 2016), http://www.magicandmedicine.hps.cam.ac.uk/view/case/normalised/CASE16631?sort=date&order=asc.

18 "CASE12439 (Normalised Version)," *Casebooks Project*, (accessed 7 July 2016), http://www.magicandmedicine.hps.cam.ac.uk/view/case/normalised/CASE12439?sort=date&order=asc.

19 "CASE12959 (Normalised Version)," *Casebooks Project*, (accessed 7 July 2016), http://www.magicandmedicine.hps.cam.ac.uk/view/case/normalised/CASE12959?sort=date&order=asc.

20 "CASE11940 (Normalised Version)," *Casebooks Project*, (accessed 8 July 2016), http://www.magicandmedicine.hps.cam.ac.uk/view/case/normalised/CASE11940?sort=date&order=asc&t=211&tm=7&nt1=1.

21 "CASE11853 (Normalised Version)," *Casebooks Project*, (accessed 7 July 2016), http://www.magicandmedicine.hps.cam.ac.uk/view/case/normalised/CASE11853?sort=date&order=asc&t=35&t=26&t=86&tm=3&tl=211&tm1=7&nt1=1. Note: the sex of the child was undetermined.

"*The terrors of the night*" 161

22 "CASE14852 (Normalised Version)," *Casebooks Project*, (accessed 7 July 2016), http://www.magicandmedicine.hps.cam.ac.uk/view/case/normalised/CASE 14852?sort=date&order=asc&t=35&t=26&t=86&tm=3&tl=211&tm1=7&ntl=1.
23 "CASE32880 (Normalised Version)," *Casebooks Project,* (accessed 8 July 2016), http://www.magicandmedicine.hps.cam.ac.uk/view/case/normalised/CASE 32880?sort=date&order=asc&t=211&tm=7&ntl=1.
24 Richard Napier, "Medical Notebooks," Bodleian Library, MS Ashmole 407, fols. 36, 125.
25 Richard Napier, "Medical Notebooks," Bodleian Library, MS Ashmole 221, fols. 60, 223.
26 "CASE14719 (Normalised Version)," *Casebooks Project*, (accessed 8 August 2016), http://www.magicandmedicine.hps.cam.ac.uk/view/case/normalised/CASE 14719?sort=date&order=asc&t=211&tm=7&ntl=1.
27 "CASE13518 (Normalised Version)," *Casebooks Project,* (accessed 29 June 2015), http://www.magicandmedicine.hps.cam.ac.uk/view/case/normalised/CASE 13518?sort=date&order=asc&cj1=2&tl=211&tol=1&tm1=7.
28 "CASE11741 (Normalised Version)," *Casebooks Project*, (accessed 29 June 2015), http://www.magicandmedicine.hps.cam.ac.uk/view/case/normalised/CASE 11741?sort=date&order=asc&cj1=2&tl=211&tol=1&tm1=7.
29 "CASE11787 (Normalised Version)," *Casebooks Project*, (accessed 29 June 2015), http://www.magicandmedicine.hps.cam.ac.uk/view/case/normalised/CASE 11787?sort=date&order=asc&cj1=2&tl=211&tol=1&tm1=7.
30 Lauren Kassell, "Search results summary (Subtopic: Sleep problems)," *Casebooks Project,* (accessed 15 November 2014), http://www.magicandmedicine.hps.cam.ac.uk/the-casebooks/search/cases/results/summarise?t=211&to=1&tm=7.
31 Robert Burton, *The anatomy of melancholy*, Part. I, ed. Holbrook Jackson (New York: NYRB Press, 2001), 249–250. Note: here Burton is quoting Levine Lemnie.
32 Andrew Boorde, *The breviarie of health* (London, 1587), 117v.
33 Levine Lemnie, *The touchstone of complexions* (London, 1633), 212.
34 Boorde, *Breviarie of health,* 117v–18r.
35 Nicholas Culpeper, *Culpeper's school of physick, or, The experimental practice of the whole art wherein are contained all inward diseases from the head to the foot* … (London, 1659), 263, 266.
36 Leong, "Making Medicines in the Early Modern Household," 153.
37 Elizabeth Jacob, *Recipe Book*, Wellcome Library, MS.3009, 57.
38 *Ibid.*, 63, 96, 135.
39 "A book of receites," Wellcome Library, MS. 144, (1650–1739?), fol. 53r.
40 Jacob, 96.
41 Joanna Saint John, "Recipe Book," Wellcome Library MS. 4338, (1680), 81v.
42 Lady Sarah Cowper, "Diary," Volume 2, 1703–1705, Hertfordshire Archives and Local Studies, D/EP F30, *Perdita Manuscripts*, (accessed 12 February 2015), fol. 146r. http://www.perditamanuscripts.amdigital.co.uk.myaccess.library.utoronto.ca/collections/doc-detail.aspx?documentid=20804&list=Alphabetical&id=3.
43 Boorde, *Breviarie of health,* 48r.
44 *Ibid.*
45 Lemnie, *Touchstone of complexions,* 92.
46 Beattie, *Dissertations moral and critical,* 228.
47 Nehemiah Wallington, *The Notebooks of Nehemiah Wallington, 1618–1654: A Selection*, edited by David Booy (Aldershot: Ashgate, 2007), 50.
48 Lady Sarah Cowper, "Diary," Volume 4, 1706–1709, Hertfordshire Archives and Local Studies, D/EP F32, *Perdita Manuscripts*, (accessed 13 February 2015), fol. 188r. http://www.perditamanuscripts.amdigital.co.uk.myaccess.library.utoronto.ca/collections/doc-detail.aspx?documentid=20830&list=Alphabetical&id=3.

162 *"The terrors of the night"*

49 Elias Ashmole, *Elias Ashmole, his autobiographical and historical notes, his correspondences and other contemporary sources relating to his life and work*, Vol. 2, edited by C.H. Josten (Oxford: Clarendon Press, 1966), 454.
50 Pepys, *Diary*, Vol. 1, 284–85; Vaughan, British Library MS Sloane 1741, fols. 10, 90, 91, 103, 104.
51 Vaughan, MS Sloane 1741, fol.107.
52 Alice Thornton, *The Autobiography of Mrs Alice Thornton of East Newton, Co. York*, Vol. 62, Surtees Society Durham Publications (Durham: Andrews and Co., 1875), 123.
53 Samuel Pepys, *The Diary of Samuel Pepys: A New and Complete Transcription*, edited by Robert. Latham and William. Matthews, Vol. 3 (Berkeley, CA: University of California Press, 1970), 139.
54 John Dee, *The Private Diary of Dr. John Dee and the Catalogue of His Library of Manuscripts* (London: Camden Society, 1842), 10.
55 William Vaughan, *Approved directions for health* (London, 1612), 63.
56 Nashe, *Terrors of the night*, Ciiii(v).
57 Burton, *Anatomy of melancholy*, Part. I, 159.
58 *Ibid.*, Part. II, 101.
59 Richard Day, *A booke of Christian prayers, collected out of the auncie[n]t writers and best learned in our tyme, worthy to be read with an earnest mynde of all Christians, in these daungerous and troublesome dayes, that God for Christes sake will yet still be mercyfull unto us* (London, 1578), 9v-10r.
60 Philip Goodwin, *The mystery of dreames, historically discoursed* (London, 1658), 75.
61 *Ibid.*, 124.
62 Thomas Browne, *The Religio Medici and Other Writings* (London: J.M. Dent, 1962), 85.
63 John Rogers, *Ohel or Beth-shemesh A tabernacle for the sun …* (London, 1653), 419–20.
64 Lady Sarah Cowper, "Diary," Volume 5, 1709–1711, Hertfordshire Archives and Local Studies, D/EP F33, *Perdita Manuscripts*, (accessed 10 February 2015), fol. 5v. http://www.perditamanuscripts.amdigital.co.uk.myaccess.library.utoronto.ca/collections/doc-detail.aspx?documentid=20860&list=Alphabetical&id=3.
65 Handley, "From the Sacral to the Moral."
66 *Ibid.*, 28. See also: Handley, *Sleep in early modern England*, 69–107.
67 Burton, *Anatomy of Melancholy*, Part. II, 252.
68 Thomas Elyot, *The castle of health* (London, 1610), 71.
69 Thomas Cogan, *The haven of health* (London, 1636), 271.
70 *Ibid.*, 275.
71 *Ibid.*; *Directions and observations*, 22.
72 William Buchan, *Domestic medicine: or, a treatise on the prevention and cure of diseases by regimen and simple medicines* (London, 1772), 108; Lucia Dacome, "'To What Purpose Does It Think': Dreams, Sick Bodies and Confused Minds in the Age of Reason," *History of Psychiatry* 15, no. 4 (2004): 395.
73 Buchan, *Domestic medicine*, 108.
74 *Directions and observations*, 23.
75 Max Hirshkowitz et al., "National Sleep Foundation's Sleep Time Duration Recommendations: Methodology and Results Summary," *Sleep Health: Journal of the National Sleep Foundation* 1, no. 1 (March 1, 2015): 40–43.
76 Burton, *Anatomy of Melancholy*, Part. II, 100.
77 Francis De Valangin, *A treatise on diet, or the management of human life* (London, 1768), 272–73.
78 Sasha Handley, Peter Stearnes, Perrin Rowland, Lori Giarnella and A. Roger Ekirch have charted a shift in the sleeping habits of people in the eighteenth

and nineteenth centuries towards more extended periods of wakefullness. Peter Stearnes, Perrin Rowland and Lori Giarnella, "Children's Sleep: Sketching Historical Change," *Journal of Social History* 30, no. 2 (Winter 1996): 345–366. Ekirch, "Sleep We Have Lost," 383.

79 De Valangin, *A treatise on diet,* 277–78.
80 John Bond, *An essay on the incubus or night-mare* (London, 1753), 2.
81 Richard Blackmore, *A treatise of the spleen and vapours* (London, 1725), 16–24.
82 Owen Davies, "Hag-riding in Nineteenth-century West Country England and Modern Newfoundland: An Examination of An Experience-centred Witchcraft Tradition," *Folk-Life* 35, no. 1 (1997): 36–53.
83 Owen Davies, "The nightmare experience, sleep paralysis and witchcraft accusations," *Folklore* 114 (2003): 183.
84 "nightmare n. and adj.," "mare, n.2," and "*Incubus*, n.," *Oxford English Dictionary Online.* 2012.
85 Davies, "The nightmare experience," 184.
86 J.A. Cheyne, "The Ominous Numinous: Sensed Presence and 'other' hallucinations," *Journal of Consciousness Studies* 8, no. 5 (2001): 1–18.
87 "nightmare n. and adj.," OED.
88 *Ibid.*
89 My thanks are due here to Professor Emeritus R. B. Todd for his views regarding the etymology of *Ephialtes.*
90 Walsham, "The Reformation and 'the Disenchantment of the World' Reassessed," 509.
91 "nightmare n. and adj.," OED.
92 Philip Barrough, *The methode of phisicke conteyning the causes, signes and cures of inward diseases in mans body from the head to the foote* (London, 1583), 3.
93 Boorde, *Breviarie of Health,* 44. Note, in addition to Merlin, according to legend, Martin Luther was also the offspring of an *Incubus* and a nun.
94 Burton 2001, 253.
95 Steven Blankaart, *The physical dictionary* (London, 1702), 124; Ephraim Chambers, *Cyclopaedia: or, an universal dictionary of arts and sciences* (London, 1728), 382.
96 Davies, "The nightmare experience," 181–203; de Blécourt, "Bedding the nightmare," 227–45.
97 Davies, "The nightmare experience," 286.
98 *The Spectator* (London, 1723), 128.
99 Davies, "Hag-riding in Nineteenth-Century West England," 36.
100 Fairfax, BL MS Add. 32495, fol. 2.
101 Anon, *Evidences of the Kingdom of Darkness* ... (London, 1770), 225.
102 Edmund Gardiner, *Phisicall and approved medicines* ... (London, 1611), 55.
103 This work was translated into English in 1683 by S. Pordage. Thomas Willis, *Two discourses concerning the soul of brutes...* (London, 1683), 142.
104 Boorde, *Breviarie of Health,* 44.
105 Note, this work was reprinted in 1695 and 1700. Thomas Tryon, *A treatise of dreams & visions* (London, 1695), 24–25.
106 Richard Haydock, "Oneirologia, or, a Brief Discourse of the Nature of Dreames," Dramatic and poetical miscellany, Folger Shakespeare Library, MS j.a.1 Vol. 5, f.7v.
107 Samuel Collins, "Of the nightmare," British Library, MS Sloane 1821, fols. 95–96. Note, this excerpt, running at 24 pages, is part of a larger collection of medical writings bound as one manuscript volume that includes eight medical treatises, which discuss subjects such as "Of the crampe" and "Of the plague." The section "Of the nightmare" (fols. 90 - 114) is also reproduced in the same

164 *"The terrors of the night"*

volume in Latin as "De incubo" (fols. 127–40). According to the British Library catalogue, all eight treatises were written by Samuel Collins.

108 Collins, fol. 95.
109 Thomas Hobbes, *Philosophicall rudiments concerning government and society* (London, 1651), 184.
110 Collins, fol. 97.
111 Tryon, 24–25.
112 Collins, fol. 94. Note, according to the *Oxford English Dictionary*, "fauces" refers to, "The cavity at the back of the mouth, from which the larynx and pharynx open out." *Oxford English Dictionary Online*, s.v. "fauces," (accessed 30 October 2012), http://datacentre.chass.utoronto.ca.myaccess.library. utoronto.ca/cgi-bin/oed/new/oed-idx?fmt=entry&type=entry&byte=136994175.
113 Robert Bayfield, *Tes iatrikes kartos, or, A treatise de morborum capitis essentiis & pronosticis adorned with above three hundred choice and rare observations* (London, 1663), 65.
114 Tryon, 25–26.
115 Francis Bacon, *Sylva sylvarum: or a naturall historie in ten centuries* (London, 1627), 259; Nicholas Culpeper, *Mr. Culpepper's Treatise of aurum potabile …* (London, 1652), 193.
116 Barrough, 34.
117 *Ibid.*
118 John Radcliffe, *Pharmacopoeia Radcliffeana,* 3rd ed. (London, 1718), 111.
119 Andrew Baxter, *An enquiry into the nature of the human soul; wherein the immateriality of the soul is evinced from the principles of reason and philosophy* (London, 1733), 203.
120 *Ibid.*
121 Thomas Branch, *Thoughts on Dreaming* (London, 1738).
122 Bond, 5.
123 Blackmore, *Treatise of the Spleen*, 16.
124 John Bond (M.D.), *Dissertatio medica inauguralis, de incubo: quam … pro gradu doctoratus … eruditorum examini subjicit Joannes Bond …* (Edinburgh, 1751).
125 Bond, Preface.
126 *Ibid.*
127 *Ibid.*, 19–20.
128 Robert Whytt, *Observations on the nature, causes and cure of those disorders which have been commonly called nervous hypochondriac, or hysteric* (Edinburgh, 1765), 317–18.
129 Bond, 22.
130 *Ibid.*, 23.
131 *Ibid.*, 23–24.
132 Lucia Dacome, "'To What Purpose Does It Think,'" 395–416.
133 *Ibid.*, 407.
134 Bond, 55.
135 *Ibid.*, Preface.
136 *Ibid.*, 2.

Conclusion

In his private alchemical notebook, the Anglican minister Thomas Vaughan (1622–1660) recorded the following dream, which is worth recounting in full.

> The month and the day I have forgot: but having prayed constantly for remission of sinnes, I went to bed: and dreamed, that I lay full of sores in my feet and cloathed in certain Rags, under the shelter of the great Oake, which growes before the Courtyard of my fathers house and it rained round about me. My feet that were sore with Boyles and corrupt matter, troubled mee extremely, soe that being not able to stand up, I was layd all along. I dreamed that my father & my Brother W. who were both dead, came unto mee and my father sucked the corruption out of my feete, soe that I was presently well and stood up with great joy and looking on my feete, they appeared very white and cleare and the sores were quite gone. Blessed bee my good God! Amen![1]

As this rather horrific account illustrates, early modern dream narratives are rich in details of the hidden inner lives of men, women and children. For historians, they offer unique insight into the unconscious emotional landscapes of past people that few other records can provide. Vaughan's dream is, at first glance, grotesque, nightmarish and steeped in the emotive language of suffering, illness, joy and anguish. Persons close to him, lost to death and disease, also populate his dream, showing how dreams might link to the realms of the dead and were a liminal space in the individual and cultural psyche. With its narrative of decay, sickness and the miraculous cure provided by his father, Vaughan's dream might, in the hands of psycho-analysts, become a narrative of unconscious desire and anxiety – the censored remnants of a disguised homoerotic wish. Yet, understood within the context of predominant early modern beliefs in dreams, Vaughan's dream begins to tell a different story, of sin, piety and redemption, of the power of prayer and of a deep anxiety about one's physiological and spiritual health.

As I've attempted to demonstrate, the history of the dream in the early modern world was complex and marked by subtle shifts and notable conti-nuities. Classical medical ideas about natural dreams reflecting imbalances

166   *Conclusion*

in the humours were slow to erode. Similarly, the notion that dreams reflect psychological material originated in the writings of Plato and Aristotle and early modern English writers were well aware that our dreams contain stark insight into unconscious individual anxieties, preoccupations and desires. The tensions surrounding supernatural or divine dreams were an age-old problem closely tied to the discernment of spirits. Throughout the medieval period, in times of social and political crisis, visionaries claiming divine dreams sparked heated debates about the continuity of prophecy and revealed religion, as well as the means to distinguish divine from demonic, natural from supernatural dreams. These debates resurfaced during the period of the Reformation due to the emergence of radical visionaries who attached themselves to fringe Protestant groups in particular.

As Lyndal Roper and Daniel Pick observed in their earlier work, the history of the dream is marked by a series of pendulum swings and oscillations.[2] While I am suggesting its history is marked by notable continuities, which stretch from the classical to the eve of the modern era, there were also subtle shifts within the system of beliefs surrounding dreams. As Chapter 3 outlined, the Protestant Reformation and subsequent Radical Reformation catalyzed a shift in religious approaches to dreams. The horrifying events of the Anabaptist siege of Münster and Jan van Leiden's claims to divine visions, amongst other radical visionaries at large during the period, led many European reformers to reject outright the continuity of divine dreams. While Martin Luther did not completely refute the continuity of divine dreams, he strongly cautioned against an unhindered belief in dreams. Similarly, Luther's rejection of the classics as a source of authority on dreams in favour of a purely Protestant, Scripture-based theory of dreams and dreaming was equally influential in shifting contemporary understandings of spiritual dreams. These ideas filtered into English understandings of dreams through the writings of Philip Goodwin and John Beale, amongst others, who further reshaped ideas of spiritual dreams within a Protestant and Providentialist framework.

However, scepticism about divine dreams and their continuity as prophetic oracles to the future was a longstanding legacy of the ancient Greeks and the classical world. In Homer's epics dreams might pass through the gates of ivory (truth) or horn (falsity), demonstrating how the ancient Greeks understood some dreams as true or divine and others as false and meaningless. This paradox was never fully resolved in later centuries and became enmeshed in Christian dialogues about the discernment of spirits. The twelfth-century reaction against claims to visions, as a result of the rise of female visionaries, was echoed and mirrored in those of the sixteenth and seventeenth centuries in England and Europe. The dream, in other words, was long associated with false prophecy and visionaries themselves were a constant source of suspicion, caught between the realms of the natural and supernatural, divine and demonic. As historians have shown, the line between a demonic and divinely inspired vision was thin indeed.[3]

An early modern English history of the dream also complicates ideas about the rise of rational worldviews. A natural theory of dreams and dreaming did not rise to supplant the supernatural. Rather, both these categories had co-existed since the classical world and continued their complex relationship. Between these broad poles was an infinite shade of the preternatural – things outside of the normal yet neither purely natural nor supernatural in origin. As Darren Oldridge suggests in his recent study, rather than "seeking a transition from a supernatural to a 'scientific' understanding of the world, historians of early modern England ... can more fruitfully examine the shifts that occurred within a system of beliefs" in which the occult or supernatural was ever-present.[4] We might instead view the history of the dream as a cycle, which oscillated and supported a spectrum of beliefs, rather than a clear-cut linear and dichotomous process neatly categorized into natural and supernatural beliefs that marched teleologically towards more rational, scientific and modern views. In reality, historical processes are much more messy, ambiguous and inconsistent. Belief in the supernatural or preternatural properties and origins of dreams was slow to wane. Likewise, natural and medical views of dreams originally espoused by the ancient Greeks and Romans were a recurrent theory of dreaming that proved resilient to change.

Collective writings on dreams, sleep and nightmares also reveal the inherent sense of vulnerability of the body, mind and soul in sleep. In the unconscious state of sleep, the dreamer was at the mercy of a host of internal and external supernatural, preternatural and natural forces. Men, women and children might, against their will, have demonic or divine dreams "injected" into their sleeping minds and be subject to the supernatural whims of invisible agents. In nightmares, experiences of sleep disorders or the dramatic accounts of the "mare" or *incubus*, the dreamer suffered acute and often chronic bouts of terror and anxiety that was deeply vicarious and debilitating. Dreams, the night and the realms of sleep therefore continued to be a source of primal fear, despite the luminescence of the new material world of artificial lighting and the century that saw the birth of "reason." Perhaps, in the dead of night it is a basic human response that all rationalism flees in the face of a vivid nightmare. The dream remained a liminal, vital force in the shadows and an elusive, nebulous facet of nocturnal life and experience.

At the same time, while inherently vulnerable, early modern people could exercise agency over their dreams. Through the use of dreambooks, the oblique, hidden "mysteries" of dreams could be decoded and revealed. Likewise, while prey to a deluge of divine and demonic dreams, supernatural and preternaturally "injected" into the sleeping mind, pious Christians might seize agency over their dreams according to the work of Philip Goodwin. Within his Protestant schema of dreams as spiritual toolkits for the soul, even demonic dreams might be useful in revealing one's inherent sinfulness and weakness. Against the tide of sleep disorders and terrifying natural dreams, men, women and children might resort to home remedies

168   *Conclusion*

and prescribed recipes as alleviants. Thus, while vulnerable, early modern people were able to seize agency over the dream in a variety of ways.

Throughout the book, I have suggested that collective understandings of dreams were defined within three broad cultural lenses: (1) health, (2) prediction and (3) spirituality. However, this is not to suggest that these frameworks were absolute or that to subscribe to one belief was to refute another. Many writers of handbooks of dreams and those who recorded personal dream narratives were equally comfortable subscribing to natural, predictive or spiritual views of the dream. After all, according to early modern dream theories there was an infinite variety of dreams. The decision to relegate the origin of the dream to natural, supernatural or even preternatural causes was the prerogative of the individual dreamer, who might ascribe one particular dream as natural – caused by indigestion – and another as divine – a message from his or her maker - with little thought.

A variety of different kinds of texts also reveal a complex mosaic of early modern thought about the dream. Discussions of dreams and dreaming were significant facets of discourses hitherto unexplored, including but not limited to: lay and learned works of medicine, literature, oneiromancy, popular divination books, almanacs, natural philosophy, demonology, theology and the occult. In addition to these discourses, writings on dreams featured in numerous private records, in particular diaries, letters and memoirs. However, the most extensive discussions of dreams in early modern England occurred in lengthy dream discourses, most notably those of Thomas Hill, Philip Goodwin, John Beale and Thomas Tryon.

Dream discourses were, however, far outpaced in print by the numerous dreambooks and fortune-telling books appearing in greater numbers in the seventeenth century. Since no other historical studies of dreams have examined the contents of early modern dreambooks, the study of English dreambooks is an important addition to our knowledge of the dream in early modern English culture. Yet, while I have been mainly concerned with outlining the history of theories of dreams through these diverse writings, I have also sought to link these ideas to actual experiences of dreams.

As I have also demonstrated, private narratives and reflections on dreams do support a general knowledge of the three major frameworks, or lenses, through which dreams were understood. In these writings dreams were linked to a person's temperament, or physiology, as well as to psychological fears and wishes. As I showed in Chapter 2, individuals such as Alice Thornton, Katherine Austen and Ralph Josselin, amongst others, also understood dreams to be sometimes predictive. They related dreams that accurately foretold the deaths, illnesses and fortunes of not only the dreamer, but also members of the family and community. Evidence of a broad acceptance of spiritual dreams and divine dreams in particular, can be found in the persistence of support for and continuing experience of prophetic visions. Moreover, evidence for a spiritual approach to dreams that anticipates Philip Goodwin's schema can be substantiated by the records and reflections of dreams in the notebooks of Nehemiah Wallington.

Conclusion 169

What is also clear from this study is that while modern western notions of dreams are largely limited to psychological models, early modern English writers saw dreams as caused by a wider variety of natural and supernatural, internal and external factors. Premodern ideas of dreams, unlike modern conceptualizations, saw them as providing insight, not only into our past history, but also into our present and future. According to early modern English theories, dreams were useful in offering insight into the health of the dreamer's body, mind and soul. Consequently, dreams were in fact considered in a way perhaps more holistic than modern western approaches to dreams. Dreams were viewed as useful as part of the diagnosis of disease and health of the body as well as the mind. Additionally, dreams were important spiritual experiences that, according to Philip Goodwin, revealed spiritual insight into the dreamer's sin and piety. They might also bring one closer to God and more terrifyingly the Devil. Regardless of how dreams were interpreted or understood, what is pervasive is the sense that dreams were important individual and collective experiences that deserved to be recorded and contemplated, interpreted and decoded.

Notes

1 Thomas Vaughan, "Notebook," BL MS Sloane 1741, fol. 105.
2 Lyndal Roper and Daniel Pick, eds., *Dreams and History: The Interpretation of Dreams from Ancient Greece to Modern Psychoanalysis* (London: Routledge, 2004), 7.
3 Gábor Klaniczay and Eva Pócs, eds., *Communicating with the Spirits* (Budapest: CEU Press, 2005); Moshe Sluhovsky, *Believe Not Every Spirit: Possession, Mysticism, & Discernment in Early Modern Catholicism* (Chicago; London: University of Chicago Press, 2007); Moshe Sluhovsky, "The Devil in the Convent," *The American Historical Review* 107, no. 5 (2002): 1379–1411; Nancy Caciola and Moshe Sluhovsky, "Spiritual Physiologies: The Discernment of Spirits in Medieval and Early Modern Europe," *Preternature: Critical and Historical Studies on the Preternatural* 1, no. 1 (2012): 1–48.
4 Darren Oldridge, *The Supernatural in Tudor and Stuart England*, Reprint edition (London: Routledge, 2016), 154.

Bibliography

Archival Sources

Anonymous. "A book of receites." Wellcome Library, MS. 144.

Austen. Katherine. "Book M." British Library, MS Add. 4454.

Beale, John. "Treatise on the Art of Interpreting Dreams." Undated, 25/19/1–28. In *The Hartlib Papers: A Complete Text and Image Database of the Papers of Samuel Hartlib (C.1600–1660)*. 2nd edition. Edited by Mark Greengrass, Michael Leslie and Michael Hannon. Sheffield: Sheffield University Library, 2002.

Collins, Samuel. "Of the nightmare." British Library, MS Sloane 1821. fols. 90–114.

Cowper, Lady Sarah. "Sarah Cowper's Diary." Volume 1, 1700–1702. Hertfordshire Archives and Local Studies. D/EP F29. Available online through: Adam Matthew, Marlborough. *Defining Gender*, fol. 141v. Accessed 11 February 2015. http://www.gender.amdigital.co.uk.myaccess.library.utoronto.ca/Documents/Details/Sarah%20Cowpers%20Diary%20Volume%201%2017001702.

———. "Diary." Volume 2, 1703–1705. Hertfordshire Archives and Local Studies. D/EP F30. *Perdita Manuscripts*. Accessed 12 February 2015. http://www.perditamanuscripts.amdigital.co.uk.myaccess.library.utoronto.ca/collections/doc-detail.aspx?documentid=20804&list=Alphabetical&id=3.

———. "Diary." Volume 3, 1705–1706. Hertfordshire Archives and Local Studies. D/EP F31. *Perdita Manuscripts*. Accessed 12 February 2015. http://www.perditamanuscripts.amdigital.co.uk.myaccess.library.utoronto.ca/collections/doc-detailsearch.aspx?documentid=20823&searchmode=true&previous=0&dt=10140711280637808&aid=Women&id=2.

———. "Diary." Volume 4, 1706–1709. Hertfordshire Archives and Local Studies. D/EP F32. *Perdita Manuscripts*. Accessed 13 February 2015. http://www.perditamanuscripts.amdigital.co.uk.myaccess.library.utoronto.ca/collections/doc-detail.aspx?documentid=20830&list=Alphabetical&id=3.

———. "Diary." Volume 5, 1709–1711. Hertfordshire Archives and Local Studies. D/EP F33. *Perdita Manuscripts*. Accessed 10 February 2015. http://www.perditamanuscripts.amdigital.co.uk.myaccess.library.utoronto.ca/collections/doc-detail.aspx?documentid=20860&list=Alphabetical&id=3.

The Diary and Correspondence of Dr. John Worthington. Edited by J. Crossley, Vol. I. Chetham Society Vol. XIII: Manchester, 1847.

Fairfax. Edward. "A discourse on witchcraft." British Library, MS Add. 32495.

172 *Bibliography*

Foreman, Simon. "Notebooks." Bodleian Library, MS Ashmole 1472.

Haydock, Richard. "An extract from Richard Haydock's *Oneirologia.*" British Library, MS Lansdowne 489. fol. 138 b.

———. "Oneirologia, or, a Brief Discourse of the Nature of Dreames." *Dramatic and poetical miscellany.* Folger Shakespeare Library, MS j.a.1 Vol. 5.

Isham, Elizabeth. "My Booke of Remembrance." Edited by Elizabeth Clarke and Erica Longfellow, *Perdita Manuscripts.* Accessed 29 April 2016. http://web.warwick.ac.uk/english/perdita/Isham/index_bor.htm.

Jacob, Elizabeth. "Recipe Book." Wellcome Library, MS 3009.

John, Joanna Saint. "Recipe Book." Wellcome Library, MS 4338, 1680.

Kassell, Lauren. "Search results summary (Subtopic: Sleep problems)." *Casebooks Project.* Accessed 15 November 2014. http://www.magicandmedicine.hps.cam.ac.uk/the-casebooks/search/cases/results/summarise?t=211&to=1&tm=7.

Kassell, Lauren (ed.) et al." CASE537 (Normalised Version)." *Casebooks Project.* Accessed 7 July 2016. http://www.magicandmedicine.hps.cam.ac.uk/view/case/normalised/CASE537?sort=date&order=asc&t=26&tm=3&ntl=1.

———. "CASE11741 (Normalised Version)." *Casebooks Project.* Accessed 29 June 2015. http://www.magicandmedicine.hps.cam.ac.uk/view/case/normalised/CASE11741?sort=date&order=asc&cjl=2&tl=211&tol=1&tml=7.

———. CASE11787 (Normalised Version)." *Casebooks Project.* Accessed 29 June 2015. http://www.magicandmedicine.hps.cam.ac.uk/view/case/normalised/CASE11787?sort=date&order=asc&cjl=2&tl=211&tol=1&tml=7.

———. "CASE11853 (Normalised Version)." *Casebooks Project.* Accessed 7 July 2016. http://www.magicandmedicine.hps.cam.ac.uk/view/case/normalised/CASE11853?sort=date&order=asc&t=35&t=26&t=86&tm=3&tl=211&tml=7&ntl=1.

———. "CASE11940 (Normalised Version)." *Casebooks Project.* Accessed 8 July 2016. http://www.magicandmedicine.hps.cam.ac.uk/view/case/normalised/CASE11940?sort=date&order=asc&t=211&tm=7&ntl=1.

———. "CASE12376 (Normalised Version)." *Casebooks Project.* Accessed 7 July 2016. http://www.magicandmedicine.hps.cam.ac.uk/view/case/normalised/CASE12376?sort=date&order=asc.

———. "CASE12439 (Normalised Version)." *Casebooks Project.* Accessed 7 July 2016. http://www.magicandmedicine.hps.cam.ac.uk/view/case/normalised/CASE12439?sort=date&order=asc.

———. "CASE12959 (Normalised Version)." *Casebooks Project.* Accessed 7 July 2016. http://www.magicandmedicine.hps.cam.ac.uk/view/case/normalised/CASE12959?sort=date&order=asc.

———. "CASE1299 (Normalised Version)." *Casebooks Project.* Accessed 7 July 2016. http://www.magicandmedicine.hps.cam.ac.uk/view/case/normalised/CASE1299?sort=date&order=asc&t=26&tm=3&ntl=1.

———. "CASE13518 (Normalised Version)." *Casebooks Project.* Accessed 29 June 2015. http://www.magicandmedicine.hps.cam.ac.uk/view/case/normalised/CASE13518?sort=date&order=asc&cjl=2&tl=211&tol=1&tml=7.

———. "CASE1407 (Normalised Version)." *Casebooks Project.* Accessed 7 July 2016. http://www.magicandmedicine.hps.cam.ac.uk/view/case/normalised/CASE1407?sort=date&order=asc&t=26&tm=3&ntl=1.

———. "CASE14719 (Normalised Version)." *Casebooks Project.* Accessed 8 August 2016. http://www.magicandmedicine.hps.cam.ac.uk/view/case/normalised/CASE14719?sort=date&order=asc&t=211&tm=7&ntl=1.

Bibliography 173

————. "CASE14852 (Normalised Version)." *Casebooks Project.* Accessed 7 July 2016. http://www.magicandmedicine.hps.cam.ac.uk/view/case/normalised/CASE 14852?sort=date&order=asc&t=35&t=26&t=86&tm=3&tl=211&tml=7&ntl=1.

————. "CASE16631 (Normalised Version)." *Casebooks Project.* Accessed 7 July 2016. http://www.magicandmedicine.hps.cam.ac.uk/view/case/normalised/CASE 16631?sort=date&order=asc.

————. "CASE32880 (Normalised Version)." *Casebooks Project.* Accessed 8 July 2016. http://www.magicandmedicine.hps.cam.ac.uk/view/case/normalised/CASE 32880?sort=date&order=asc&t=211&tm=7&ntl=1.

"Letter, Benjamin Worsley To Hartlib, 20 January 1658/9." Ref: 33/2/11A-12B. In *The Hartlib Papers.* Edited by M. Greengrass, M. Leslie and M. Hannon. Sheffield: Published by HRI Online Publications, 2013. Accessed 27 April 2016. http://www.hrionline.ac.uk/hartlib.

"Letter, [John Beale] To [Hartlib], 28 May 1657." Ref: 25/5/1A-12B. In *The Hartlib Papers.* Edited by M. Greengrass, M. Leslie and M. Hannon. Sheffield: Published by HRI Online Publications, 2013. Accessed 27 April 2016. http://www.hrionline.ac.uk/hartlib.

"Letter, John Dury to Hartlib, 12 August 1661." Ref: 4/4/30A. In *The Hartlib Papers.* Edited by M. Greengrass, M. Leslie and M. Hannon. Sheffield: Published by HRI Online Publications, Sheffield, 2013. Accessed 27 April 2016. http://www.hrionline.ac.uk/hartlib.

Napier, Richard. "Medical Notebooks." Bodleian Library, MS Ashmole 221.

————. "Medical Notebooks." Bodleian Library, MS Ashmole 407.

North, Roger. "On Dreams." British Library, MS Add. 32526.

"Scribal Copy, Christina Poniatowska'S Revelationes Divinae." English Translation Of Latin Original. Translated by W.J. Hitchens. Ref: 35/7/1A-37B; 1B-2B, 3B & 37A-B BLANK. In *The Hartlib Papers.* Edited by M. Greengrass, M. Leslie and M. Hannon. Sheffield: Published by HRI Online Publications, 2013. Accessed 27 April 2016. http://www.hrionline.ac.uk/hartlib.

Vaughan, Thomas. "Notebook." British Library, MS Sloane 1741. fols. 1–108.

Wallington, Nehemiah. "An extract of the passages of my life." Folger Shakespeare Library, MS V. a. 436.

————. "A Record of Gods Marcys, or a Thankfull Remembrance." Guildhall Library, MS 204.

————. "The groth of a Christian." British Library, MS Add. 40883.

"Will of Philip Goodwin 29th August 1667." National Archives, England, PROB 11/324/453.

"Will of Philip Goodwin, Clerk of Liston, Essex, 1st June 1699." National Archives, England, PROB 11/451/8.

Printed Primary Sources

Ady, Thomas. *A candle in the dark.* London, 1655.

Ambrose, Isaac. *Ultima, = the last things in reference to the first and middle things: or certain meditations on life, death, judgement, hell, right purgatory, and heaven.* London, 1650.

Amyraut, Moïse. *A discourse concerning the divine dreams mention'd in Scripture together with the marks and characters by which they might be distinguish'd from vain delusions.* London, 1676.

174 Bibliography

Anonymous Works

———. *Aristotle's legacy: or, his golden cabinet of secrets opened. In five treatices.* London, 1699.

———. *The art of courtship, or, The School of delight containing amorous dialogues, complemental expressions, poems, letters and discourses upon sundry occasions relating to love and business.* London, 1686.

———. *A collection of miscellany letters, selected out of Mist's Weekly Journal.* Vol. 1. London, 1722.

———. *The compleat book of knowledge: treating of the wisdom of the antients and shewing the various and wonderful operations of the signs and planets, and other celestial constellations, on the bodies of men, women and children.* London, 1698.

———. *Daniels Dreames.* London, 1556.

———. *Directions and observations relative to food exercise and sleep.* London, 1772.

———. *Dr. Flamstead's and Mr. Patridge's New Fortune-Book.* London, 1729.

———. *Dreams and moles, with their interpretation and signification.* London, 1780.

———. *The entertaining fortune book, as to what relates to good or bad fortune in either sex.* London, 1755.

———. *Evidences of the kingdom of darkness: being a collection of authentic and entertaining narratives of the real existence and appearance of ghosts, demons, and spectres.* London, 1770.

———. *The High Dutch fortune-teller wherein all those questions relating to the several states, conditions and occasions of humane life, are fully resolv'd and answer'd.* London, 1700.

———. *Interpretiatiiones seu somnia Danielis prophete revelata ab angelo missus [sic] a deo primo de diebus Lune.* Rome, 1479.

———. *Nocturnal revels: or, a general history of dreams. In two parts.* Vols. 1 & 2. London, 1706.

———. *Nocturnal revels; or, an universal dream-book. In two parts complete.* London, 1749.

———. *Nocturnal revels; or, a universal dream-book.* London, 1750.

———. *Nocturnal revels; or, a universal dream-book.* London, 1767.

———. *Nocturnal revels: or, universal interpretor of dreams and visions.* London, 1789.

———. *The old Egyptian fortune-teller's last legacy: containing, I. The wheel of fortune by pricking with a pin. … VII. Omens of good and bad luck.* London, 1775.

———. *Oniropolus, or dreams interpreter.* London, 1680.

———. *The problemes of Aristotle with other philosophers and phisitions.* Edinburgh, 1595.

———. *The problemes of Aristotle with other philosophers and phisitions.* London, 1597.

———. *Somnia Salomonis David regis fili una cum Danielis prophete somniorum interpretatione: novissime ex amussim recognita oîbus mendis expurgata.* Venetiis, 1516.

———. *The Spectator.* Vol. 2. 6th ed. London, 1723.

———. *A treatise of diseases of the head, brain & nerves … By a physician.* London, 1714.

———. *The true fortune teller.* London, 1698.

———. *Wits cabinet or A companion for young men and ladies.* London, 1684.

———. *Wits cabinet or, A companion for young men and ladies them.* London, 1698.

Aristotle. *The Complete Works of Aristotle.* Edited by Jonathan Barnes. Vol. 1. Princeton: Princeton University Press, 1984.

Artemidorus. *Artemidori De Somniorum Interpretatione Libri Quinq[ue]. De Insomniis, Quod Synesii Cuiusdam Nomine Circu[m]fertur.* Venetiis, 1518.

Bibliography   175

———. *Artemidori Daldiani … De somniorum interpretatione, libri quinq[ue], iam primum à Iano Cornario medico physico Francofordensi, Latina lingua conscripti.* Translated by Janus Cornarius. Basileae, 1539.

———. *Artemidori Daldiani … De somniorum interpretatione, libri quinq[ue]/ iam primum à Iano Cornario medico physico Francofordensi, Latina lingua conscripti.* Translated by Janus Cornarius. Basileae, 1544.

———. *Artemidori Daldiani … De somniorum interpretatione, libri quinq[ue],/ iam primum à Iano Cornario medico physico Francofordensi, Latina lingua conscripti.* Lugduni, 1546.

———. *Artemidorus' Oneirocritica: Text, Translation, and Commentary.* Translated by Daniel E. Harris-McCoy. Oxford: Oxford University Press, 2012.

———. *The interpretation of dreames, digested into five books by that ancient and excellent philosopher, Artimedorus.* London, 1644.

———. *The interpretation of dreams digested into five books by that ancient and excellent philosopher, Artimedorus.* London, 1656.

———. *The interpretation of dreams digested into five books by that ancient and excellent philosopher, Artemidorus.* London, 1690.

———. *The interpretation of dreams: by the most celebrated philosopher Artimedorus, and other authors.* London, 1755.

———. *The interpretation of dreams, by that most celebrated philosopher Artimedorus.* London, 1786.

———. *The interpretation of dreams: Oneirocritica.* Translated by Robert J. White. Park Ridge, NJ: Noyes Classical Studies, 1975.

———. *The judgement, or exposition of dreames, written by Artimodorus, an auntient and famous author, first in Greeke, then translated into Latin, after into French, and now into English.* London, 1606.

Ashmole, Elias. *Elias Ashmole, His Autobiographical and Historical Notes, His Correspondences, and Other Contemporary Sources Relating to His Life and Work.* Vol. 2. Edited by C.H. Josten. Oxford: Clarendon Press, 1966.

Aubrey, John. *Miscellanies upon the following subjects collected by J. Aubrey, Esq.* London, 1696.

Austen, Katherine. *Katherine Austen's* Book M *British Library, Additional Manuscript 4454.* Edited by Sarah C. E. Ross. Tempe, AZ: ACMRS, 2011.

Bacon, Francis. *Of the advancement and proficience of learning.* Oxford, 1640.

———. *Sylva sylvarum: or A naturall historie in ten centuries.* London, 1627.

Barrough, Philip. *The methode of phisicke conteyning the causes, signes, and cures of inward diseases in mans body from the head to the foote.* London, 1583.

Baxter, Andrew. *An enquiry into the nature of the human soul.* London, 1733.

Bayfield, Robert. *Tes iatrikes kartos, or, A treatise de morborum capitis essentiis & pronosticis adorned with above three hundred choice and rare observations.* London, 1663.

Beattie, James. *Dissertations moral and critical.* London, 1783.

Blackmore, Richard. *A treatise of the spleen and vapours: or, hypocondriacal and hysterical affections.* London, 1725.

Blacksmith. *A defence of Christianity against the power of enthusiasm.* Bristol, 1764.

Blankaart, Steven. *The physical dictionary.* London, 1702.

Bond, John. *Dissertatio medica inauguralis, de incubo: quam … pro gradu doctoratus … eruditorum examini subjicit Joannes Bond.* London, 1751.

———. *An essay on the incubus, or night-mare.* London, 1753.

176   *Bibliography*

Booker, John. *The Dutch fortune-teller.* London, 1650.

———. *The history of dreams. Or dreams interpreted, &c.* Edinburgh, 1800.

———. *Six penny-worth of wit for a penny. Or, dreams interpreted.* London, 1690.

Boorde, Andrew. *The breviarie of health wherin doth folow, remedies, for all maner of sicknesses & diseases, the which may be in man or woman.* London, 1587.

Branch, Thomas. *Thoughts on dreaming.* London, 1738.

Brinley, John. *A discovery of the impostures of witches and astrologers.* London, 1680.

Browne, Thomas. *The Major Works.* Vol. 1. Edited by Geoffrey Keynes. London: Faber & Faber, 1964.

———. *The Religio Medici and Other Writings.* London: J.M. Dent, 1962.

Bruele, Gualtherus. *Praxis medicinae, or, the physicians practice wherein are contained inward diseases from the head to the foote.* London, 1632.

Buchan, William. *Domestic medicine: or, a treatise on the prevention and cure of diseases by regimen and simple medicines.* London, 1772.

Burton, Robert. *The anatomy of melancholy.* Oxford, 1621.

———. *The Anatomy of Melancholy.* Edited by Holbrook Jackson. New York: NYRB Press, 2001.

Calamy, Edmund and Samuel Palmer. *The Nonconformists Memorial; Being an Account of the Lives and Sufferings and Printed Works of the Two Thousand Ministers Ejected from the Church of England.* Vol. II, 2nd ed. London, 1802.

Calvin, John. *Commentaries on the prophet Daniel, Vol. 1.* Translated by Thomas Myers. Edinburgh: Calvin Translation Society, 1852.

Casaubon, Meric. *A treatise concerning enthusiasme.* London, 1654.

Chambers, Ephaim. *Cyclopædia: or, an universal dictionary of arts and sciences.* Vol. 2. London, 1728.

Channel, Elinor. *A message from God, by a dumb woman to his Highness the Lord Protector.* London, 1653.

Chauncy, Charles. *Enthusiasm describ'd and caution'd against: a sermon.* Boston, 1742.

Cheesman, Thomas. *Death compared to sleep in a sermon preacht upon the occasion of the funeral of Mrs. Mary Allen, who died Feb. 18, anno Dom. 1695.* London, 1695.

Chubb, Thomas. *A discourse concerning reason, with regard to religion and divine revelation.* London, 1731.

Cogan, Thomas. *The haven of health.* London, 1584.

———. *The haven of health.* London, 1636.

Conover, Samuel Forman. *An inaugural dissertation on sleep and dreams; their effects on the faculties of the mind, and the causes of dreams.* Philadelphia, 1791.

Cotta, John. *The infallible true and assured witch, or, the second edition of the tryall of witch-craft.* London, 1625.

Crawford, Patricia, and Laura Gowing, eds. *Women's Worlds in Seventeenth-Century England.* London and New York: Routledge, 1999.

Crooke, Helkiah. *Mikrokosmographia a description of the body of man.* London, 1615.

Culpeper, Nicholas. *Culpeper's school of physick.* London, 1659.

———. *The English physitian.* London, 1652.

Day, Richard. *A booke of Christian prayers.* London, 1578.

Dee, John. *The Private Diary of Dr. John Dee, and the Catalogue of His Library of Manuscripts.* Edited by J. O. Halliwell. London: Camden Society, 1842.

Elyot, Thomas. *The castle of healthe.* London, 1539.

Bibliography 177

———. *The castle of health*. London, 1610.

Evans, Arise. *The bloudy vision of John Farly, interpreted by Arise Evans*. London, 1653.

———. *An eccho to the book called A voyce from heaven*. London, 1653.

———. *Mr. Evans and Mr. Penningtons prophesie: concerning seven yeers of plenty, and seven yeers of famine and pestilence*. London, 1655.

———. *The voice of Michael the archangel, to his Highness the Lord Protector: for the salvation of himself and the three nations*. London, 1653.

Evans, Theophilus. *The history of modern enthusiasm, from the Reformation to the present times*. London, 1752.

Eyre, Joseph. *A dispassionate inquiry into the probably causes and consequences of enthusiasm: a sermon, preached July 30, 1798, in the parish church of St. Mary's, Reading*. Reading, London and Oxford, 1798.

Felltham, Owen. *Resolves divine, moral, political*. London, 1677.

Ferrand, James. *Erotomania or A treatise discoursing of the essence, causes, symptomes, prognosticks, and cure of love, or erotique melancholy*. Oxford, 1640.

Fischer, Steven R. ed., *The Complete Medieval Dreambook*. Bern und Frankfurt am Main: Peter Lang, 1982.

Galen. "Galen: On Diagnosis in Dreams." *Medicina Antiqua*, 2008. Translated by Lee Pearcy. Accessed 20 May 2009. http://www.ucl.ac.uk/~ucgajpd/medicina%20 antiqua/tr_GalDreams.html.

Gardiner, Edmund. *Phisicall and approved medicines, aswell in meere simples, as compound observations*. London, 1611.

Gaule, John. *Pus-mantia the mag-astro-mancer, or, The magicall-astrologicall-diviner posed, and puzzled*. London, 1652.

Gibson, Bishop. *The Bishop of London's pastoral letter to the people of his diocese; … by Way of Caution, Against lukewarmness on one hand, and enthusiasm on the other*. London, 1739.

Goodwin, Philip. *Dies Dominicus redivivus; or, The Lords Day enlivened*. London, 1654.

———. *The evangelicall communicant in the eucharisticall sacrament*. London, 1649.

———. *The mystery of dreames, historically discoursed*. London, 1658.

———. *Religio domestica rediviva: or, Family-religion revived*. London, 1655.

Hall, Joseph. *The contemplations upon the history of the New Testament, now complete: together with divers treatises reduced to the greater volume*. London, 1661.

Hartley, David. *Observations on man, his frame, his duty, and his expectations. In two parts*. London, 1749.

Harwood, Edward. *A View of the Various Editions of the Greek and Roman Classics, with Remarks*. London, 1790.

Hill, Thomas. *A brief and most pleasau[n]t epitomye of the whole art of phisiognomie*. London, 1556.

———. *The contemplation of mankinde*. London, 1571.

———. *A contemplation of mysteries*. London, 1574.

———. *A joyfull jewell contayning aswell such excellent orders, preservatives and precious practises for the plague*. London, 1579.

———. *A little treatise of the interpretation of dreams, fathered on Joseph*. London, 1567.

———. *A most briefe and pleasant treatise of the interpretation of sundrie dreames intituled to be Josephs*. London, 1601.

———. *A most briefe and pleasant treatise of the interpretation of sundry dreames intituled to be Josephs*. London, 1626.

178   *Bibliography*

———. *The most pleasaunt arte of the interpretation of dreames.* London, 1571.

———. *The moste pleasuante arte of the interpretacion of dreames.* London, 1576.

———. *The newe jewell of health wherein is contayned the most excellent secretes of phisicke and philosophie, devided into fower bookes.* London, 1576.

Hobbes, Thomas. *Leviathan.* London: Penguin, 1985.

———. *Philosophicall rudiments concerning government and society.* London, 1651.

Howard, Henry. *A defensative against the poyson of supposed prophecies.* London, 1583.

Hume, David. *An Enquiry Concerning Human Understanding.* Edited by Eric Steinberg. Indianapolis: Hackett Pub. Co., 1977.

Hunter, M. and E.A. Gregory eds. *An astrological diary of the seventeenth century, Samuel Jeake of Rye.* Oxford: Oxford University Press, 1988.

Jessey, Henry. *The exceeding riches of grace advanced by the spirit of grace.* London, 1647.

Josselin, Ralph. *The Diary of Ralph Josselin 1616 - 1683.* Edited by Alan Macfarlane. London: Oxford University Press, 1976.

L., G. *The amorous gallant's tongue tipp'd with golden expressions: or, The art of courtship refined, being the best and newest academy.* London, 1741.

Laud, William. *The Works of the Most Reverend Father in God, William Laud, D.D.* Edited by James Bliss. Vol. 3. Oxford: John Henry Parker, 1975.

Lemnie, Levine. *The touchstone of complexions expedient and profitable for all such as bee desirous and carefull of their bodily health.* London, 1633.

Lilly, William. *The Book of Knowledge: Treating of the Wisdom of the Ancients ... Made English by W. Lilly.* London, 1720.

———. *The Book of Knowledge; Treating of the Wisdom of the Ancients. In Four Parts.* London, 1753.

———. *The Book of Knowledge, Treating of the Wisdom of the Ancients, in Four Parts.* Glasgow, 1780.

———. *A groats worth of wit for a penny, or, The interpretation of dreams.* London, 1670.

———. *A groatsworth of wit for a penny, or the Interpretation of Dreams.* London, 1750.

———. *The Life of William Lilly: Student of Astrology.* London: The Folklore Society, 1974.

Locke, John. *An Essay on Human Understanding.* Oxford: Oxford University Press, 1964.

Luther, Martin. *Luther's Works, Volume 3, Lectures on Genesis Chapters 15–20.* Edited by Jaroslav Pelikan. Saint Louis: Concordia, 1961.

———. *Luther's Works, Volume 5, Lectures on Genesis, Chapters 26–30.* Edited by Jaroslav Pelikan. Saint Louis: Concordia, 1968.

———. *Luther's Works, Volume 6, Lectures on Genesis, Chapters 31–37.* Edited by Jaroslav Pelikan and Hilton C. Oswald. Saint Louis: Concordia, 1970.

———. *Luther's Works, Volume 7, Lectures on Genesis, Chapters 38–44.* Edited by Jaroslav Pelikan and Walter A. Hansen. Saint Louis: Concordia, 1965.

Magomastix, Hieronymus. *The strange witch at Greenwich.* London, 1650.

Mather, Cotton. *Awakening thoughts on the sleep of death.* Boston, 1712.

Melton, John. *The Astrologaster, or, The figure-caster.* London, 1620.

More, Henry. *Enthusiasmus triumphatus, or, A discourse of the nature, causes, kinds, and cure, of enthusiasme.* London, 1656.

Bibliography 179

Mortimer, Thomas. *Die and be damned. Or an antidote against every species of Methodism and enthusiasm.* London, 1758.

Nashe, Thomas. *The terrors of the night or, A discourse of apparitions.* London, 1594.

Oberhelman, Steven M. "Galen, *On Diagnosis from Dreams.*" *Journal of the History of Medicine and Allied Sciences* 38 (1983): 36–47.

Pater, Erra. *The pronostycacyon for ever of Erra Pater: a Jewe borne in Jewery, a doctour in astronomye, and physycke profytable to kepe the bodye in helth.* London, 1540.

Pepys, Samuel. *The Diary of Samuel Pepys: A New and Complete Transcription.* Edited by Robert Latham and William Matthews. 11 vols. Berkeley: University of California Press, 1970–1983.

Perkins, William. *A discourse of the damned art of witchcraft.* Cambridge, 1608.

Plato. *Complete Works.* Edited by John M. Cooper. Indianapolis: Hacket Pub. Co., 1997.

Poole, Elizabeth. *An alarum of war, given to the army, and to their high court of justice.* London, 1649.

———. *A vision: wherein is manifested the disease and cure of the kingdome.* London, 1649.

Powell, Vavasor. *Spirituall experiences, of sundry beleevers.* London, 1653.

Pryme, Abraham de la. *The Diary of Abraham de la Pryme, the Yorkshire Antiquary.* Durham: Andrews and Company, 1870.

Radcliffe, John. *Pharmacopoeia Radcliffeana: or, Dr. Radcliffe's prescriptions, faithfully gather'd from his original recipe's. To which are annex'd, useful observations upon each prescription.* 3rd ed. London, 1718.

Roberts, Julian and Andrew G., Watson, eds. *John Dee's Library Catalogue.* London: The Bibliographical Society, 1990.

Rogers, John. *Ohel or Beth-shemesh A tabernacle for the sun.* London, 1653.

S., J. *The true fortune-teller, or, Guide to knowledge Discovering the whole art of chiromancy, physiognomy, metoposcopy, and astrology.* London, 1698.

Saunders, Richard. *Physiognomie and chiromancie, metoposcopie.* London, 1653.

———. *Saunders Physiognomie, and chiromancie, metoposcopie.* London, 1671.

———. *Two groatsworth of wit for a penny. Or the English fortune-teller.* London, 1675.

Scot, Reginald. *The discoverie of witchcraft.* London, 1584.

Scribonius, Wilhelm. *Naturall philosophy, or, A description of the world.* Translated by Daniel Widdowes. London, 1621.

Shaftesbury, Anthony Ashley Cooper. *A letter concerning enthusiasm, to My Lord *****.* London, 1708.

Shipton, Mother (Ursula). *Mother Shipton's legacy. Or, a favorite fortune-book in which is given a pleasing interpretation of dreams.* York, 1797.

Smith, Nicholas. *A warning to the world, being sundry strange prophecies revealed to Nicholas Smith.* London, 1653.

The Spectator. Edited by Donald F. Bond. Vol. 5. No. 585–635. Oxford: Clarendon Press, 1965.

Spencer, John. *A discourse concerning vulgar prophecies.* London, 1665.

Strangehopes, Samuel. *A book of knowledge. In four parts.* London, 1679.

Thornton, Alice. *The Autobiography of Mrs Alice Thornton of East Newton, Co. York.* Vol. 62. Surtees Society Durham Publications. Durham: Andrews and Co., 1875.

Trapnel, Anna. *Strange and wonderful newes from White-Hall.* London, 1654.

180   *Bibliography*

Trenchard, John. *The natural history of superstition.* London, 1709.

Tryon, Thomas. *The good house-wife made a doctor.* London, 1692.

———. *Healths grand preservative: or The womens best doctor.* London, 1682.

———. *Miscellania: or, A collection of necessary, useful, and profitable tracts on variety of subjects which for their excellency, and benefit of mankind, are compiled in one volume.* London, 1696.

———. *Pythagoras his mystick philosophy reviv'd, or, The mystery of dreams unfolded wherein the causes, natures, and uses of nocturnal representations … are theosophically unfolded.* London, 1691.

———. *Some memoirs of the life of Mr. Tho. Tryon, late of London, merchant.* London, 1705.

———. *A treatise of cleanness in meats and drinks of the preparation of food, the excellency of good airs and the benefits of clean sweet beds also of the generation of bugs and their cure.* London, 1682.

———. *A treatise of dreams & visions.* London, 1689.

———. *A treatise of dreams & visions.* London, 1695.

———. *A treatise of dreams & visions.* London, 1700.

Valangin, Francis de. *A treatise on diet, or the management of human life; by physicians called the six non-naturals.* London, 1768.

Van Diemerbroeck, Isbrand. *The anatomy of human bodies comprehending the most modern discoveries and curiosities in that art … translated from the last and most correct and full edition of the same by William Salmon.* London, 1694.

Vaughan, William. *Approved directions for health, both naturall and artificiall derived from the best physitians as well moderne as auncient.* London, 1612.

Walkington, Thomas. *The optick glasse of humors.* London, 1607.

Wallington, Nehemiah. *The Notebooks of Nehemiah Wallington, 1618–1654: A Selection.* Edited by David Booy. Aldershot: Ashgate, 2007.

Walton, Izaak. *The lives of Dr. John Donne, Sir Henry Wotton, Mr. Richard Hooker, Mr. George Herbert written by Izaak Walton.* London, 1670.

Whytt, Robert. *Observations on the nature, causes, and cure of those disorders which have been commonly called nervous hypochondriac, or hysteric.* Edinburgh, 1765.

Willis, Thomas. *Dr. Willis's practice of physick.* London, 1684.

———. *Two discourses concerning the soul of brutes which is that of the vital and sensitive of man.* London, 1683.

Woodman, Philip. *Medicus novissimus; or, the modern physician.* 2nd ed. London, 1722.

Wright, Thomas. *The passions of the minde in generall. Corrected, enlarged, and with sundry new discourses augmented.* London, 1604.

Secondary sources

Barbour, Reid. "Liturgy and Dreams in Seventeenth-Century England." *Modern Philology* 88, no. 3 (1991): 227–42.

Blécourt, Willem de. "Bedding the Nightmare: Somatic Experience and Narrative Meaning in Dutch and Flemish Legend Texts." *Folklore* 114, no. 2 (2003): 227–45.

Bremmer, Jan N. "Prophets, Seers, and Politics in Greece, Israel, and Early Modern Europe." *Numen* 40, no. 2 (1993): 150–83.

Brown, Peter, ed. *Reading Dreams: The Interpretation of Dreams from Chaucer to Shakespeare.* Oxford: Oxford University Press, 1999.

Bibliography   181

Bulkeley, Kelly. "Reflections on the Dream Traditions of Islam." *Sleep and Hypnosis* 4 (2002): 1–11.

Bulman, William J. and Robert G. Ingram, eds., *God in the Enlightenment.* New York, NY: Oxford University Press, 2016.

Burke, Peter. *Varieties of Cultural History.* Cambridge: Polity Press, 1997.

Burson, Jeffrey D. *The Rise and Fall of Theological Enlightenment: Jean-Martin de Prades and Ideology in Eighteenth-Century France.* Notre Dame, IN: University of Notre Dame Press, 2010.

Caciola, Nancy. *Discerning Spirits: Divine and Demonic Possession in the Middle Ages.* Ithaca: Cornell University Press, 2003.

Caciola, Nancy and Moshe Sluhovsky. "Spiritual Physiologies: The Discernment of Spirits in Medieval and Early Modern Europe." *Preternature: Critical and Historical Studies on the Preternatural* 1, no. 1 (2012): 1–48.

Capp, Bernard. *English Almanacs 1500–1800.* Ithaca, NY: Cornell University Press, 1979.

———. *The Fifth Monarchy Men: A Study in Seventeenth-Century English Millenarianism.* Totowa: Rowman and Littlefield, 1972.

Carlton, Charles. "The Dream Life of Archbishop Laud." *History Today* 36, no. 12 (1986): 9–14.

Chambers, Andrew and Michelle Wolfe. "Reading Family Religion and Evangelical Identity in Late Stuart England." *The Historical Journal* 47, no. 4 (2004): 875–96.

Cheyne, J.A. "The Ominous Numinous: Sensed Presence and "Other" Hallucinations." *Journal of Consciousness Studies* 8, no. 5 (2001): 1–18.

Christian, William. *Apparitions in Late and Medieval Spain.* Princeton: Princeton University Press, 1981.

———. "Six Hundred Years of Visionaries in Spain: Those Believed and Those Ignored." In *Challenging Authority: The Historical Study of Contentious Politics.* Edited by Michael Hanagan, 107–19. Minneapolis: University of Minnesota Press, 1998.

Clark, Stuart. *Vanities of the Eye: Vision in Early Modern European Culture.* New York; Oxford: Oxford University Press, 2009.

Coffey, John and Paul C.H. Lim, eds. *The Cambridge Companion to Puritanism.* Cambridge: Cambridge University Press, 2008.

Considine, John. "Hill, Thomas (c.1528–c.1574)." In *Oxford Dictionary of National Biography*, online edn. Edited by Lawrence Goldman. Oxford: OUP, 2004. Accessed 6 June 2010. http://www.oxforddnb.com/view/article/13303.

Crawford, Patricia. "Women's Dreams in Early Modern England." *History Workshop Journal* 49 (2000): 129–41.

Curry, Patrick. "Culpeper, Nicholas (1616–1654)." In *Oxford Dictionary of National Biography*, online edn. Edited by Lawrence Goldman. Oxford: OUP, 2004. Accessed 15 November 2010. http://www.oxforddnb.com/view/article/6882.

———. "Lilly, William (1602–1681)." In *Oxford Dictionary of National Biography*, online edn. Edited by Lawrence Goldman. Oxford: OUP, 2004. Accessed 12 May 2011. http://www.oxforddnb.com/view/article/16661.

Dacome, Lucia. "'To What Purpose Does It Think': Dreams, Sick Bodies and Confused Minds in the Age of Reason." *History of Psychiatry* 15, no. 4 (2004): 395–416.

Dannenfeldt, Karl H. "Sleep: Theory and Practice in the Late Renaissance." *Journal of the History of Medicine and Allied Sciences* 41, no. 4 (1986): 415–41.

182 *Bibliography*

Davies, Ceri. "Vaughan, Sir William (*c*.1575–1641)." In *Oxford Dictionary of National Biography*, online edn. Edited by Lawrence Goldman. Oxford: OUP, 2004. Accessed 1 December 2010. http://www.oxforddnb.com.myaccess.library.utoronto.ca/view/article/28151.

Davies, Owen. "Hag-riding in Nineteenth-century West Country England and Modern Newfoundland: An Examination of an Experience-centred Witchcraft Tradition." *Folk-Life* 35, no. 1 (1997): 36–53.

———. *The Haunted: A Social History of Ghosts.* Houndsmills: Palgrave, 2007.

———. "The Nightmare Experience, Sleep Paralysis, and Witchcraft Accusations." *Folklore* 114, no. 2 (2003): 181–203.

———. *Witchcraft, Magic and Culture 1736–1951.* Manchester: Manchester University Press, 1999.

Davies, Owen and Willem de Blécourt, eds. *Witchcraft Continued: Popular Magic in Modern Europe.* Manchester; New York: Manchester University Press, 2004.

Davies, Stevie. "Trapnel, Anna (*fl.* 1642–1660)." In *Oxford Dictionary of National Biography*, online edn. Edited by Lawrence Goldman. Oxford: OUP, 2004. Accessed 6 June 2008. http://www.oxforddnb.com.myaccess.library.utoronto.ca/view/article/38075.

Diószegi, Vilmos and Mihály Hoppál, eds. *Shamanism in Siberia.* Budapest: Akadémiai, 1978.

Durston, Christopher and Jacqueline Eales, eds. *The Culture of English Puritanism, 1560–1700.* Houndsmills: St. Martin's Press, 1996.

Ekirch, A. Roger. *At Day's Close: Night in Times Past.* New York; London: W.W. Norton & Co., 2005.

———. "Sleep We Have Lost: Pre-Industrial Slumber in the British Isles." *The American Historical Review* 106, no. 2 (2001): 343–86.

Eliade, Mircea. *Le chamanisme et les techniques archaïques de l'extase.* Paris: PUF, 1951.

Elliott, Dyan. "Seeing Double: John Gerson, the Discernment of Spirits, and Joan of Arc." *The American Historical Review* 107, no. 1 (2002): 26–54.

Finn, Nathan A. "Curb Your Enthusiasm: Martin Luther's Critique of Anabaptism." *Southwestern Journal of Theology* 56, no. 2 (Spring 2014): 163–82.

Fissell, M.E. "Readers, Texts and Contexts: Vernacular Medical Works in Early Modern England." In *The Popularization of Medicine 1650–1850.* Edited by Roy Porter, 72–96. London: Routledge, 1992.

Freeman, Curtis W. "Visionary Women among Early Baptists." *Baptist Quarterly* 43 (2010): 260–83.

French, H. R. "Goodwin, Philip (*d.* 1667)." In *Oxford Dictionary of National Biography*, online edn. Edited by Lawrence Goldman. Oxford: OUP, 2004. Accessed 6 June 2010. http://www.oxforddnb.com.myaccess.library.utoronto.ca/view/article/10995.

Gantet, Claire. "Dreams, Standards of Knowledge and Orthodoxy in Germany in the Sixteenth Century." In *Orthodoxies and Heterodoxies in Early Modern German Culture Order and Creativity, 1500–1750.* Edited by Randolph Head and Daniel Eric Christensen, 69–90. Leiden: Brill, 2007.

Gay, Peter. *The Enlightenment: An Interpretation*, Vol. 1, *The Rise of Modern Paganism.* New York: Alfred E. Knopf, 1966.

Ginzburg, Carlo. *Ecstasies: Deciphering the Witches' Sabbath.* New York: Pantheon Books, 1991.

Bibliography 183

————. *The Night Battles: Witchcraft & Agrarian Cults in the Sixteenth & Seventeenth Centuries.* London: Routledge, 1983.

Goodwin, Gordon. "Goodwin, Philip (d. 1699), divine." In *Dictionary of National Biography.* Oxford: Oxford University Press, 1890. Accessed 12 June 2013. http://www.oxforddnb.com.myaccess.library.utoronto.ca/view/olddnb/10995.

Hadfield, Andrew. *Literature and Censorship in Renaissance England.* Houndmills, Basingstoke, Hampshire; New York: Palgrave, 2001.

Handley, Sasha. "From the Sacral to the Moral: Sleeping Practices, Household Worship and Confessional Cultures in Late Seventeenth-Century England." *Cultural and Social History* 9, no. 1 (2012): 27–46.

————. *Sleep in early modern England.* London; New Haven: Yale University Press, 2016.

————. "Sleepwalking, Subjectivity and the Nervous Body in Eighteenth-Century Britain." *Journal for Eighteenth-Century Studies* 35, no. 3 (September 2012): 305–23.

————. "Sociable Sleeping in Early Modern England, 1660–1760." *History* 98, no. 329 (January 2013): 79–104.

Hanegraaff, Wouter J. "How Magic Survived the Disenchantment of the World." *Religion* 33 (2003): 357–80.

Haugen, Kristine Louise. "Aristotle My Beloved: Poetry, Diagnosis, and the Dreams of Julius Caesar Scaliger," *Renaissance Quarterly* 60, no. 3 (2007): 819–51.

Hirshkowitz, Max et al. "National Sleep Foundation's Sleep Time Duration Recommendations: Methodology and Results Summary." *Sleep Health: Journal of the National Sleep Foundation* 1, no. 1 (March 1, 2015): 40–43.

Hodgkin, Katherine. "Dreaming Meanings: Some Early Modern Dream Thoughts." In *Reading the Early Modern Dream: The Terrors of the Night,* edited by Katherine Hodgkin et al., 109–24. London: Routledge, 2008.

Hodgkin, Katherine, Michelle O' Callaghan and S.J. Wiseman, eds. *Reading the Early Modern Dream: The Terrors of the Night.* London: Routledge, 2008.

Holland, Peter. "'The Interpretation of Dreams' in the Renaissance." In *Reading Dreams: The Interpretation of Dreams from Chaucer to Shakespeare.* Edited by Peter Brown, 125–46. Oxford: Oxford University Press, 1999.

Holowchak, M. Andrew. *Ancient Science and Dreams: Oneirology in Greco-Roman Antiquity.* New York, Oxford: University Press of America, 2002.

Holstun, James. *Ehud's dagger: Class struggle in the English Revolution.* London; New York: Verso, 2002.

Honko, Lauri. "Role-taking of the Shaman," *Temenos* 4 (1969): 26–55.

Hughes, J. Donald. "Dream Interpretation in Ancient Civilizations." *Dreaming* 10, no. 1 (2000): 7–18.

Hultkrantz, Åke. "A Definition of Shamanism." *Temenos* 9 (1973): 25–37.

————. *The Religion of the American Indians.* Translated by Monica Setterwell. Berkeley and Los Angeles: University of California Press, 1979.

Hunter, Michael. *The occult laboratory: magic, science and second sight in late seventeenth-century Scotland.* Woodbridge: Boydell Press, 2001.

Johnson, Francis R. *Astronomical Thought in Renaissance England: A Study of the English Scientific Writings from 1500 to 1645.* Baltimore: The Johns Hopkins Press, 1937.

————. "Thomas Hill: An Elizabethan Huxley." *Huntington Library Quarterly* 7, no. 4 (1944): 329–51.

184 *Bibliography*

Juster, Susan. "Mystical Pregnancy and Holy Bleeding: Visionary Experience in Early Modern Britain and America." *The William and Mary Quarterly* 57, no. 2 (2000): 249–88.

Kagan, Richard L. *Lucretia's Dreams: Politics and Prophecy in Sixteenth-Century Spain*. London: University of California Press, 1990.

Kassell, Lauren. "Casebooks in Early Modern England: Medicine, Astrology, and Written Records." *Bulletin of the History of Medicine* 88, no. 4 (2014): 595–625.

Kassell, Lauren et al. ed., "Welcome | Casebooks Project." *Casebooks Project.* Accessed 29 June 2015. http://www.magicandmedicine.hps.cam.ac.uk.

Kirchhoff, Karl-Heinz and Hans J. Hillerbrand. "Münster." In *The Oxford Encyclopedia of the Reformation*. Oxford University Press, 1996. Accessed 25 June 2016. http://www.oxfordreference.com.myaccess.library.utoronto.ca/view/10.1093/acref/9780195064933.001.0001/acref-9780195064933-e-0969.

Klaniczay, Gábor. "The Process of Trance: Heavenly and Diabolic Apparitions in Johannes Nider's 'Formicarius.'" In *Procession, Performance, Liturgy and Ritual: Essays in Honor of Bryan R. Gillingham*. Edited by Nancy Van Deusen, 203–58. Ottawa: The Institute of Medieval Music, 2007.

———. "Shamanism and Witchcraft." *Magic, Ritual, and Witchcraft* 1, no. 2 (2006): 214–21.

Klaniczay, Gábor and Éva Pócs, eds. *Communicating with the Spirits*. Budapest: CEU Press, 2005.

Koslofsky, Craig. *Evening's Empire: A History of the Night in Early Modern Europe*. Cambridge: Cambridge University Press, 2011.

Krajnik, Filip. "In the Shadow of Night: Sleeping and Dreaming and Their Technical Roles in Shakespearian Drama." (PhD, Durham University, 2013). Accessed 18 April 2016. http://etheses.dur.ac.uk/7764/.

Kruger, S.F. *Dreaming in the Middle Ages*. Cambridge: Cambridge University Press, 1992.

Landfester, Manfred. "Artemidorus of Daldis (Lydia)/Artemidorus of Ephesus." *Brill's New Pauly Supplements I - Volume 2: Dictionary of Greek and Latin Authors and Texts*. Edited by Manfred Landfester and Brigitte Egger. Brill Online, 2015. Accessed 8 October 2015. <http://referenceworks.brillonline.com/entries/brill-s-new-pauly-supplements-i-2/artemidorus-of-daldis-lydiaartemidorus-of-ephesus-COM_0036>.

Lehmberg, Stanford. "Elyot, Sir Thomas (*c.*1490–1546)." In *Oxford Dictionary of National Biography* online edn. Edited by Lawrence Goldman. Oxford: OUP, 2004. Accessed 30 November 2010. http://www.oxforddnb.com/view/article/8782.

Lehner, Ulrich L. *The Catholic Enlightenment: The Forgotten History of a Global Movement*. New York, NY: Oxford University Press, 2016.

———. *Enlightened Monks: The German Benedictines, 1740–1803*. Oxford: Oxford University Press, 2011.

Leong, Elaine. "Collecting Knowledge for the Family: Recipes, Gender and Practical Knowledge in the Early Modern English Household." *Centaurus; International Magazine of the History of Science and Medicine* 55, no. 2 (May 2013): 81–103.

———. "Making Medicines in the Early Modern Household." *Bulletin of the History of Medicine* 82, no. 1 (2008): 145–68.

Levin, Carole. *Dreaming in the English Renaissance: Politics and Desire in Court and Culture*. New York: Palgrave Macmillan, 2008.

Bibliography   185

Lewis, M. *Ecstatic Religion: An Anthropological Study of Spirit Possession and Shamanism.* Harmondsworth: Penguin, 1971.

Lindemann, Mary. *Medicine and Society in Early Modern Europe.* Cambridge: Cambridge University Press, 1999.

MacDonald, Michael. *Mystical Bedlam: Madness, Anxiety and Healing in Seventeenth-Century England.* Cambridge: Cambridge University Press, 1985.

Mack, Phyllis. *Visionary Women: Ecstatic Prophecy in Seventeenth-Century England.* Berkeley: University of California Press, 1992.

Mageo, Jeanette Marie. *Dreaming and the Self: New Perspectives on Subjectivity, Identity and Emotion.* New York: State University of New York Press, 2003.

———. "Women as Prophets during the English Civil War." *Feminist Studies* 8, no. 1 (1982): 19–45.

Marshall, Peter. "'The Map of God's Word': Geographies of the Afterlife in Tudor and Early Stuart England." In *The Place of the Dead: Death and Remembrance in Late Medieval and Early Modern Europe.* Edited by Peter Marshall and Bruce Gordon, 110–30. Cambridge: Cambridge University Press, 2000.

———. *Reformation England 1480–1642.* London: Hodder Arnold, 2003.

Martin, Lawrence T. "The Earliest Versions of the Latin 'Somniale Danielis.'" *Manuscripta* 23, no. 3 (1979): 131–41.

Martin, Luther H. "Artemidorus: Dream Theory in Late Antiquity." *The Second Century: A Journal of Early Christian Studies* 8, no. 2 (Summer 1991): 97–108.

McGregor, J.F. "The Baptists: Fount of All Heresy." In *Radical Religion in the English Revolution.* Edited by J.F. McGregor and B. Reay, 23–64. Oxford: Oxford University Press, 1984.

McGregor, J.F., and Barry Reay, eds. *Radical Religion in the English Revolution.* Oxford: Oxford University Press, 1984.

Mittermaier, Amira. *Dreams That Matter: Egyptian Landscapes of the Imagination.* Berkeley: University of California Press, 2011.

Newman, Barbara. "Possessed by the Spirit: Devout Women, Demoniacs, and the Apostolic Life in the Thirteenth Century." *Speculum* 73, no. 3 (1998): 733–70.

Oberhelman, Steven M. *The Oneirocriticon of Achmet: A Medieval Greek and Arabic Treatise on the Interpretation of Dreams.* Lubbock, TX, USA: Texas Tech University Press, 1991.

Oldridge, Darren. *The Supernatural in Tudor and Stuart England.* Reprint edition. London: Routledge, 2016.

O'Nell, C.W. *Dreams, Culture and the Individual.* San Francisco: Chandler and Sharp, 1976.

Owen, Alex. *The Place of Enchantment: British Occultism and the Culture of the Modern.* Chicago: Chicago University Press, 2004.

Neuburg, Victor. *Popular Literature: a history and guide.* Middlesex: Penguin, 1977.

Pack, Roger A. "On Artemidorus and His Arabic Translator." *Transactions and Proceedings of the American Philological Association* 98 (January 1, 1967): 139–44.

Parman, Susan. *Dream and Culture: An Anthropological Study of the Western Intellectual Tradition.* New York: Praeger, 1991.

Perkins, Maureen. "The Meaning of Dream Books." *History Workshop Journal* 48 (1999): 103–14.

Plane, Ann Marie. *Dreams and the Invisible World in Colonial New England: Indians, Colonists, and the Seventeenth Century.* Philadelphia, PA: University of Pennsylvania Press, 2014.

186 Bibliography

Plane, Ann Marie and Leslie Tuttle, eds. *Dreams, Dreamers, and Visions: The Early Modern Atlantic World*. Philadelphia: University of Pennsylvania Press, 2013.

Pócs, Éva. *Between the Living and the Dead*. Budapest: CEU Press, 1999.

Porter, M.H. "Saunders, Richard (1613–1675)." In *Oxford Dictionary of National Biography*, online edn. Edited by Lawrence Goldman. Oxford: OUP, 2004. Accessed 2 February 2013. http://www.oxforddnb.com.myaccess.library.utoronto.ca/view/article/24702.

Porter, Roy. *The Popularization of Medicine*. London: Routledge, 2013.

Price, S.R.F. "The Future of Dreams: From Freud to Artemidorus." *Past and Present* 113 (1986): 3–37.

Purkiss, Diane. *Literature, Gender and Politics during the English Civil War*. Cambridge: Cambridge University Press, 2005.

Reay, Barry. "Popular Literature in Seventeenth-century England." *Journal of Peasant Studies* 10, no. 4 (1983): 243–49.

Redwood, John. *Reason, Ridicule and Religion*. London: Thames & Hudson, 1976.

Roper, Lyndal, and Daniel Pick, eds. *Dreams and History: The Interpretation of Dreams from Ancient Greece to Modern Psychoanalysis*. London: Routledge, 2004.

Rosenthal, Franz. "From Arabic Books and Manuscripts XII: The Arabic Translation of Artemidorus." *Journal of the American Oriental Society* 85, no. 2 (April 1, 1965): 139–44.

Scarlett, E.P. 'Richard Haydock: Being the Account of a Jacobean Physician Who is Also Known to History as "The Sleeping Clergyman."' *Canadian Medical Association Journal* 60, no. 2 (1949): 177–82.

Schmidt, Roger. "Caffeine and the Coming of the Enlightenment." *Raritan* 23, no. 1 (Summer 2003): 129–49.

Scott, J.M. "Branch, Thomas (*fl.* 1738–1753)." Rev. Robert Brown. In *Oxford Dictionary of National Biography*, online ed., edited by Lawrence Goldman. Oxford: OUP, 2004. Accessed 1 December 2010. http://www.oxforddnb.com/view/article/3247.

Scott, Richard. "Dreams and the Passions in Revolutionary England." PhD, University of Sheffield, 2014. Accessed 18 June 2014. http://etheses.whiterose.ac.uk/5917/.

Scribner, Robert. "The Reformation, Popular Magic, and the 'Disenchantment of the World.'" *Journal of Interdisciplinary Studies* 23, no. 3 (Winter 1993): 475–94.

Seaver, Paul S. *The Puritan Lectureships: The Politics of Religious Dissent 1560–1662*. Stanford, CA: Stanford University Press, 1970.

———. *Wallington's World: A Puritan Artisan in Seventeenth-Century London*. Stanford, CA: Stanford University Press, 1985.

Shaw, Jane. *Miracles in Enlightenment England*. Cambridge: Cambridge University Press, 2008.

Sheehan, Jonathan. *The Enlightenment Bible: translation, scholarship, culture*. Princeton, NJ: Princeton University Press, 2005.

Siikala, Anna-Lena. *The Rite Technique of the Siberian Shaman*, FF Communications 220. Helsinki: Academia Scientiarum Fennica, 1978.

Sluhovsky, Moshe. *Believe Not Every Spirit: Possession, Mysticism, & Discernment in Early Modern Catholicism*. Chicago; London: University of Chicago Press, 2007.

———. "The Devil in the Convent." *The American Historical Review* 107, no. 5 (2002): 1379–1411.

Bibliography 187

Smith, Nigel. *Perfection Proclaimed: Language and Literature in English Radical Religion 1640–1660*. Oxford: Clarendon Press, 1989.

Sorkin, David. *The Religious Enlightenment: Protestants, Jews, and Catholics from London to Vienna*. Princeton: Princeton University Press, 2011.

Spurr, John. *English Puritanism 1603–1689*. New York: St. Martin's Press, 1998.

———. "'Rational Religion' in Restoration England." *Journal of the History of Ideas* 49, no. 4 (1988): 563–85.

Stearnes, Peter, Perrin Rowland and Lori Giarnella. "Children's Sleep: Sketching Historical Change." *Journal of Social History* 30, no. 2 (1996): 345–66.

Stroumsa, Guy G. "Dreams and Visions in Early Christian Discourse." In *Dream Cultures: Explorations in the Comparative History of Dreaming*. Edited by David Shulman and Guy G. Stroumsa, 189–212. New York; Oxford: Oxford University Press, 1999.

Sullivan, Garrett A. *Sleep, Romance and Human Embodiment: Vitality from Spenser to Milton*. Cambridge: Cambridge University Press, 2012.

Tedlock, Barbara. *Dreaming: An Anthropological and Psychological Interpretation*. Cambridge: Cambridge University Press, 1987.

Thomas, Keith. *Religion and the Decline of Magic*. London: Penguin, 1991.

Todd, Barbara J. "Property and a Woman's Place in Restoration London." *Women's History Review* 19, no. 2 (2010): 181–200.

Voaden, Rosalynn. *God's Words, Women's Voices: The Discernment of Spirits in the Writing of Late-Medieval Women Visionaries*. Rochester: York Medieval Press, 1999.

Walsham, Alexandra. "'Frantick Hacket:' Prophecy, Sorcery, Insanity, and the Elizabethan Puritan Movement." *The Historical Journal* 41, no. 1 (1998): 27–66.

———. "The Reformation and 'the Disenchantment of the World' Reassessed." *The Historical Journal* 51, no. 2 (2008): 497–528.

Watt, Diane. *Secretaries of God: Women Prophets in Late Medieval and Early Modern England*. Woodbridge: D.S. Brewer, 1997.

Weber, Alison. "Spiritual Administration: Gender and Discernment in the Carmelite Reform." *Sixteenth Century Journal* 31, no. 1 (2000): 123–46.

Williams, Simon J. *Sleep and Society: Sociological Ventures into the (Un)known*. London; New York: Routledge, 2005.

Index

abrupt waking 142
Adam being the first to dream 22
Addison, Joseph 38, 42
Ady, Thomas 103–4, 106, 107, 125
Agrippa, Cornelius 71
air impacting dreams and sleep 19, 21,
   39–41
alien dreams 55
allegorical dreams 55
Almanacs 2, 5, 50–51, 53–54, 56, 58–61,
   66, 77
Ambrose, Isaac 30
Amyraut, Moses 33, 37, 111
Anabaptists 9, 90, 93, 97, 101, 115
anti-astrological treatises 104–5
Aquinas, Thomas 94
Aristotle 9, 18, 19, 25, 32, 34, 36, 63, 66,
   94, 102, 166
*Aristotle's legacy: or his golden cabinet of
   secrets opened* 60, 66, 74, 78
Armourer, Nicholas 42
Artemidorus 2, 9, 11, 37, 44, 50–51,
   54–56, 63–65, 67, 77, 78, 81, 91, 94, 99
*art of courtship or school of delight,
   The* 61
Ashmole, Elias 52, 59, 69, 70, 78, 142
*astrologaster-or figure-caster,
   The* (Melton) 104, 105
astrology 51, 59, 62, 70–72, 104–6;
   dream interpretation 70–72; impacting
   dreams 41–42
atheism 33, 109, 125
Aubrey, John 80
Augustine, St. 94
Austen, Katherine 28, 51, 52, 75–76, 168
Averroes 63

Bacon, Francis 155
Barrough, Philip 151, 155–6
Barton, Elizabeth 90, 96
Baxter, Andrew 34–35, 156

Bayfield, Robert 155
Beale, John 5, 9, 10, 22, 68, 81, 99, 101,
   109, 126, 166, 168; advocating dreams
   119–24
Beattie, James 39, 42–43, 142
bed bugs 41
bedroom topography impacting dreams
   and sleep 40–41
Bell, Andrew 21
Bible: conflicting message about visions
   and dreams 7, 53, 91, 95, 106; dream
   interpretation and 10, 11, 102, 111;
   predictive dreams 76
biphasic sleep 6, 18
birth dream motif 74
Blankaart, Steven 152
body: being porous and sensitive to the
   humours 21–24; having moving spirits
   22–23; position impacting dreams 43
body parts as dream symbols 77
Bohemian Protestants 121
Bonatus, Guido 70
Bond, John 8, 148, 149, 156–9
Booker, John 2, 60, 62
Boorde, Andrew 21, 140, 142, 151
Booy, David 116
Boyle, Robert 120
Braddock, R. 56
brain remoistening to cure sleep
   disorders 139–40
Branch, Thomas 34, 35, 156
breviarie of health, The (Boorde) 21
Bridget of Sweden 90, 94
Brinley, John 106
Brown, Peter 5
Browne, Thomas 38, 145
Buchan, William 146
Burke, Peter 4
Burton, Robert 29, 32, 89, 108, 139,
   144, 146
Byron, John 38

190 *Index*

Caciola, Nancy 136
Calvin, John 101–3
candlie in the dark, A (Ady) 103–4
Capp, Bernard 59
Cardano, Girolamo 71
Carlton, Charles 4
Casaubon, Meric 36, 89
castle of health, The (Elyot) 20, 21, 24
Catherine of Siena 90, 94
Causabon, Meric 108, 125
Chambers, Ephraim 152
Chandeler, Williame 75
charismatic visionaries 89–91, 93–97,
    103, 108–9, 111, 115–16, 122,
    125, 166
Cheesman, Thomas 29
chiromancy 71
choleric person and their dreams 27–28
Christian, William A., Jr. 5
Christian astrology (Lilly) 70
Christianity: enhancing association
    between sleep and death 30; visions as
    revealed religion 7, 22, 34, 53, 69–70,
    90, 95, 99, 106, 109–26
Christmas day dreams 69
Cicero 94, 102
circulatory system disorders causing
    nightmares 149, 156–7
Clark, Stuart 5
Cogan, Thomas 20, 29, 146
Collins, Samuel 154, 155
Comenius, John Amos 121
Commentaries on Genesis (Luther) 10
common sense 32
compleat book of knowledge, The 58,
    60, 78
complexions affecting dreams 27–28
concoction. *See* digestion
Conover, Samuel Forman 39
consumption, excess revealed by dreams
    3, 155
Continental influences on ideas about
    dreams 9–12
Cornarius, Janus 9, 55
cosmic dreams 55
Cotta, John 103, 107
courtesy books 61
courtship manuals 54, 61, 66
Cowper, Sarah 17, 28, 31, 42, 141–2, 145
Crawford, Patricia 4, 74, 76
Culpeper, Nicholas 20, 140, 155
culture influencing dreams 4, 27,
    64–65
Curry, Patrick 70

Dacome, Lucia 36, 146, 158
Daniels dreams 58, 73, 78
Dannenfeldt, Karl H. 24
Davies, Owen 8, 136, 149–50, 152
Day, Richard 144
death: in dreams 50, 52, 79–80, 142–4;
    as sleep 29–32
de Blécourt, Willem 8, 136, 152
Dee, John 9, 50, 55–56, 59, 70, 143–4
demonic dreams 3, 91, 92, 94, 107,
    110–14, 125, 136, 144–5, 167
demons suffocating dreamer in
    nightmares 148–53
De Valangin, Francis 25, 29
Devil: associated with the night 6;
    attacking in dreams 158; sending
    dreams 7, 11, 92, 98, 100, 107, 111–14,
    134–6, 144–5
*Dies dominicus redivivus, or, The Lords
    Day enlivened* (Goodwin) 110
digestion aided by sleeping 24–25
discernment of dreams 9–10, 90–126, 166
discoverie of witchcraft, The (Scot) 67
discretio spirituum 90
disenchantment of the world 8, 12, 59, 133
divination. *See* dream divination
divine dreams 3, 6, 7, 10, 11, 17, 89–126,
    168; ceasing with the New Testament
    99, 103, 107, 166; John Calvin on
    101–3; Martin Luther on 96–101
Donne, John 30
dream body in relation to the social
    body 77–78
dreambooks 2, 5, 11, 44, 54, 61–62, 167,
    168; adapted to changing readership
    65; dreamer being a male 72–73;
    Oneirocritica (Artemidorus) 54–56;
    Somniale Danielis 56–58, 60, 61
dream divination 2–3, 5, 11, 52–81; as
    diabolical 103–5; techniques of 64–66
dreamer: gender of 72–76; vulnerable to
    internal and external forces 7, 111, 167
dreaming: as form of possession 35;
    as litigation of the senses 29–39; of
    treasure 72
dream interpretation 11, 55–81;
    astrological 70–72; gendering 72–76;
    techniques of 64–66
dream interpreters 54, 65–66, 101
dream narratives 3–4, 7, 18, 27–28,
    50–52, 116–19, 165
dreams: advocated by John Beale
    119–24; affected by complexions
    27–28; alien 55; allegorical 55;

ascribing meaning to 17; as catalysts of disorder 36; categories of 55, 98–99, 113–14; caused by daily preoccupations 36; caused by psychological processes 18; as chimeras of the mind 33; on Christmas day 69; as clues to future health, wealth and relationships 2; codification of 10; cosmic 55; of death 50, 52; decoding 50–81; demonic 3, 91, 92, 94, 107, 110–14, 125, 136, 144–5, 167; diabolic 98; discerning between natural and supernatural dreams 89–94, 113, 126, 166; discernment of 9–10, 90–126, 166; divine 3, 6, 7, 10, 11, 17, 89–126, 166, 168; false and deluding 113–15; on feast days 69; filthy and defiling 114; as food for the soul 111; health and 7, 10, 11, 18–44, 66, 169; histories of 3–5; ideas about impacted by Protestant Reformation 9–10, 91, 93–97, 99, 126, 166; impacted by astrology 41–42; impacted by body's position 43; impacted by environmental factors 39–43; impacted by noises 42; impacted by planets 41–42; impacted by the season 69; insight into secret inclinations 38; interpretation of 2, 5; latent content of 64; manifest content of 64–65; morning 68–69; natural 3, 8, 11, 17–44, 91, 125, 167; pathologization of 107–9, 157; personal 55; physical 99; predictive 7, 10, 11, 50, 55, 74–76, 80, 89, 123–4, 168; preternatural 3, 92, 134, 167; produced by fears 38–39; produced by imagination 29–39; as product of culture and psyche 4; profitable and instructing 114, 119; as prognostic tools to body's health 19, 28; public 55; reflecting balance of humours in body 3, 8, 18, 19, 26–28, 165–6; reflecting one's profession 37; of sex 70; sexual 78; significant 55; as source of terror and anxiety 8, 11, 18, 32, 37–38, 116, 118, 133–59; spiritual 109–16; supernatural 3, 11, 17, 21, 90, 167; symbiotic relationship with sleep 25–26; temporality of 68–69; theoremetic 55; troublesome and affrighting 114, 117, 134; understood as different things 1–2; vain and idle 114, 118

Dreams and Moles 74
dream symbols 2, 52, 54, 58, 60, 64; body parts as 77; death and the dead 79–80; teeth falling out 77
Dr Flamstead's and Mr Partridge's new Fortune Book 58, 73
Drinker, Elizabeth 42
Dugdale, Richard 153
Dury, John 122
Dutch Fortune-teller, The (Booker) 60

Ekirch, A. Roger 6, 18, 42, 146
Elizabeth I, queen of England 95
Elyot, Thomas 20, 21, 24, 27, 43
emotions and dreams 20–21, 27, 50, 100, 144, 165; emotions and history 27, 50, 64–65
emotions of a dream reflecting the dominant humour 27
English physitian, The (Culpeper) 20
enhypnion 55
Enlightenment 8, 18, 36, 125–6
Enquiry into the Nature of the Human Soul, An (Baxter) 34
entertaining fortune book, The 60
enthusiasm, religious 33, 35–36, 89–90, 107–9
Enthusiasmus triumphatus (More) 108
environmental factors effecting sleep 39–43
ephialtes 150–2
Erra Pater: The book of knowledge 59–60, 66, 74, 78
essay on the incubus, or night-mare, An (Bond) 147, 157
evangelicall communicant in the eucharisticall sacrament, or, a treatise declaring who are to receive the supper of the Lord, The (Goodwin) 109
Evans, Arise 91
Evelyn, John 120

Fairfax, Edward 152
Fairfax, Helen 152
fancy. *See* imagination
fearful dreams. *See* nightmares
fears producing dreams 38–39
feast days impacting dreams 69
Felltham, Owen 19, 38
Fenwick, Elizabeth 152
Fifth Monarchists 9, 90
Firth, John 30
Fludd, Robert 71
Foreman, Simon 71–72, 137–8

192 Index

Forman, Simon 51, 136
fortune-telling books 2–3, 5, 51, 54, 59, 60, 66, 168
Fox, Adam 53
Froben, Hieronymus 55
future told in dreams. *See* predictive dreams

Galen 3, 19, 21, 34, 66, 91
Gardiner, Edmund 153
Gaule, John 104–6, 111, 125
Gay, Peter 8
gender of the dreamer 72–76
gluttony causing nightmares 3, 155
God: dreams as a sign of God's care 52; giving sleep as a gift to alleviate punishment of sin 22; sending dreams 3, 7, 11, 76, 90, 101, 102, 109–16, 122–5, 134
Goodwin, Philip 5, 7, 10, 33–34, 81, 90, 92, 99, 101, 124, 126, 134, 144, 166, 168, 169; as advocate of dreams 109–16; *Dies dominicus redivivus, or, The Lords Day enlivened* (Goodwin) 110; *The evangelicall communicant in the eucharisticall sacrament, or, a treatise declaring who are to receive the supper of the Lord* 109; *The mystery of dreames, historically discoursed* 3, 9, 54, 97, 110–16; *Religio domestica rediviva: or, Family-religion revived* 110
graves in dreams 79
Greeks, ancient on dreams 19, 53, 94, 150–1, 166
groatsworth of wit for a penny, or the interpretation of dreames, A (Lilly) 62

Hackete, William 95, 96
"hag-riding" tradition 148, 149, 151, 152
Hall, Joseph 34
Hamlet 29–30
Handley, Sasha 5, 6, 18–19, 135, 145–6
Hartley, David 35
Hartlib, Samuel 120–2, 122
Harvey, William 149
haven of health, The (Cogan) 20
Haydock, Richard 20, 22, 25, 26, 28, 34, 153–4
health: and dreams 7, 10, 11, 18–44, 66, 169; and sleeping 39
Hendrick van Hove, Frederick 62
Henry VIII, king of England 96

High Dutch Fortune-teller, The 60, 61, 73–74
Hildegard von Bingham 94
Hill, Thomas 2, 5, 10, 11, 20, 25, 26, 41, 52, 53, 55, 62–68, 72, 77, 78, 79, 110
history of dreams, interpreted, The (Booker) 62
Hobbes, Thomas 33, 36, 90, 116, 154–5
Hodgkin, Katherine 4, 5
Holland, Peter 63
Homer 30
Hume, David 36, 39
humours: imbalance of 26, 139–40, 148, 153–4, 165–6; models of system 21–28; reflected by dreams 3, 8, 18, 19, 26–28
Hypnos (god) 30
hysteria causing nightmares 149

Iliad (Homer) 30
illness as theme in nightmares 142–4, 146
imagination producing dreams 32–39
incubus 8, 12, 43, 133, 147–59, 167
inner senses producing dreams 32
insomnia 27, 135–142; remedies for 140–142
insomnium 124
Isham, Elizabeth 32

Jackson, Dorothy 152
Jacob, Elizabeth 140–1
Jeake of Rye, Samuel 59, 70
Jeanne d'Arc 90
Jones, Katherine 123
Josselin, Ralph 28, 50, 52, 69, 80, 168
judgement, or exposition of dreames, The 56

Kagan, Richard 5
Kassell, Lauren 136
Kempe, Margery 90
Koslofsky, Craig 6, 32, 135, 136
Krajnik, Filip 30
Kruger, Steven 57, 68, 70

Laud, William 51, 59, 69
"law of contraries" in dream divination 52, 64, 66–68
"law of similitudes" in dream divination 52, 64, 66–68, 76, 77
Leiden, Jan van 97, 166
Lemnie, Levine 24, 140, 142
Leong, Elaine 137

Index 193

Levin, Carole 5
Lilly, William 2, 53, 59, 60, 70, 71;
   *A groatsworth of wit for a penny, or the
   interpretation of dreames* 62
*little treatise of the interpretation of
   dreams, A* (Hill) 2, 63, 72, 79
Locke, John 35
Lucia de Leon 96
Luther, Martin 10, 30, 96, 135, 166;
   writings on dreams 96–101

MacDonald, Michael 137
Mack, Phyllis 5, 7
Macrobius 9, 91, 94, 99, 102, 124
Mageo, Janette 4
Marshall, Peter 96
Martin, Lawrence T. 57
Mather, Cotton 29
Matthijs, Jan 97
Maximus, Cassius 54
McGregor, J. F. 115
melancholic person and their dreams
   27–28
melancholy: causing nightmares 144, 153;
   and pathologization of dreams 107–9
Melanchthon, Philip 99
Melton, John 104, 105, 107, 108
memory 32
men's dreams 72–74
metoposcopy 71
Milton, John 30
moleoscopy 2, 54, 59, 71
More, Henry 33, 34, 36, 89, 108, 116, 125
morning dreams 68–69
*moste pleasaunte arte of the
   interpretacion of dreames, The* (Hill)
   10, 20, 41, 55, 63–64, 65, 72, 110
Münster Rebellion 10, 97, 115, 166
*mystery of dreames, historically
   discoursed, The* (Goodwin) 3, 9, 54,
   97, 110–16

Napier, Richard 71–72, 136, 137–8
Nashe, Thomas 26, 28, 33, 42, 67, 103,
   107, 144
natural dreams 3, 8, 11, 17–44, 91,
   125, 167
Naturalis philosophia parse tertia
   (Ponzetti) 9
nervous system disorders causing
   nightmares 149, 156–7
night: change in cultural views of 6,
   135; death and sleep 30; as province

of the otherworld 135–6; as time of
   fear 7–8, 144, 146; as vulnerable time
   116–17, 167
"Nightmare, The" (Fuseli) 148
nightmares 3, 8, 11–12, 43, 133–59, 167;
   caused by circulatory and nervous
   systems' disorders 149, 156–7; caused
   by gluttony 3, 155; caused by hysteria
   149; caused by melancholy 144, 153;
   caused by supine position 149, 154;
   causes of 134; as a disease of the body
   148–52; etymology of word 149–51;
   prophylactic treatments for 155–6;
   supernatural theory of 149–53
night terrors 42
nocturnalization 6, 11, 32, 133, 135
Nocturnal revels (Tryon) 21
noises of the environment impacting
   dreams 42
Norris, T. 60
North, Roger 37
Nun of Kent. *See* Barton, Elizabeth
Nyx (goddess) 30

Oldridge, Darren 167
Oneirocritica (Artemidorus) 2, 9, 44, 50,
   54–56, 61, 63, 65, 67, 77, 78
Oneirologia (Haydock) 20
oneiromancy 2–3, 5, 7, 9, 11, 37, 44,
   50, 52, 55, 66, 70–74, 77, 79, 89,
   104; in almanacs 59–63; defended as
   supported by Scriptures 53
oneiros 55
Oniropolus 2, 62, 66, 73
Owen, Alex 8

palmistry 71
Paracelsus 71
Pater, Erra 59
pathologization of dreams 157
Pepys, Samuel 51, 78, 80, 133, 143
Perkins, William 103, 104, 105, 106, 107
personal dreams 55
Peucer, Caspar 99
phantasy 32, 34
phlegmatic person and their dreams
   27–28
phlegm causing nightmares 155
physical dreams 99
*Physiognomie and chiromancie,
   metoposcopie* (Saunders) 71
Pick, Daniel 4, 5, 64
Plane, Ann Marie 4, 5, 27

194 *Index*

planets impacting dreams 41–42
Plato 9, 18, 19, 32, 36, 37, 94, 166
Poniatowska, Christina 121–2
Ponzetti, Ferdinand 9
Poole, Elizabeth 91
Porta, Giambattista Della 71
prayer to prevent nightmares 144
predictive dreams 7, 10, 11, 50, 55, 74–76, 80, 89, 123–4, 168
preternatural explanation of dreams 3, 92, 134, 167
profession giving rise to dreams 37
prognostic dreams. *See* predictive dreams
pronostycacyon for ever of Erra Pater: A Jewe borne in Jewery, a Doctour in Astronomye,and Physycke Profytable to kepe the bodye in helth, The 59
Protestant Reformation influencing ideas on dreams 9–10, 91, 93–97, 99, 126, 136, 166
Providentialism and dreams 10, 52–53, 76, 99, 105–106, 116, 121, 123, 126
psyche influencing dreams 4, 64
psychoanalysis 4
public dreams 55
public lighting changing sleep habits 18
Puritans and dreams 112–19
Pus-mantia: the mag-astro-mancer (Gaule) 104

Quakers 9, 90

Ranalagh, Katherine 120
Raynes, Nicolas 152
recipe books with cures for sleep disorders 137, 140–1
Religio domestica rediviva: or, Family-religion revived (Goodwin) 110
religion. *See also* Bible; Christianity; specific types of religion: and dreams 7, 90, 109–10; and the Enlightenment 8, 125–6
religious enthusiasm 33, 35–36, 89–90, 107–9
religious melancholy 89, 107–9
religious radicalism 90–91
Rogers, John 145
Roper, Lyndal 4, 5, 64

sacralization of household piety 145
sadducism 109, 125
Saint John, Joanna 141

sanguine person and their dreams 27
Saunders, Richard 41–42, 53, 71
Schmidt, Roger 18, 135
Scot, Michael 71
Scot, Reginald 67, 68, 103, 106, 111, 125
Scribonius, Wilhelm 23, 25
season impacting dreams 69
Seaver, Paul 116
segmented sleep 18
senses 29, 32–43, 125, 148, 154, 158
sexual dreams 70, 78
Shakespeare, William 29–30
Shaw, Jane 8
significant dreams 55
sleep: aiding digestions 24–25; biphasic 6, 18; and fear and anxiety 18; as God's gift to alleviate punishment of sin 22; history of 5–6; impacted by environmental factors 39–43; as a metaphor for death 29–32; physiology of 20–44; recommended length of 146–7; segmented 18; symbiotic relationship with dreams 25–26; time of 147; as a vulnerable state 7, 32, 167
sleep disorders 5, 8, 11, 133–59, 167; causes and remedies 137–42
sleeping, sociable 18
sleep paralysis 43, 133, 148–59
sleep-piety 145–6
Sluhovsky, Moshe 136
social body in relation to the dream body 77–78
social sleeping 18
Somniale Danielis 50–51, 54, 56–58, 60, 61, 64, 67, 73
somnium 124
soul: and its role in sleep 33–35; reflected in dreams 38
soul-sleep 30
Southwell, Robert 30
Spencer, John 89, 125
spirits: injecting dreams into the sleeping mind 35; moving through the body 22–23
spiritual dreams 7, 10, 11, 89–126; advocates of 109–16
Stearnes, Peter 147
succubus 150–1
supernatural dreams 3, 11, 17, 21, 90, 167
superstition 36
supine position causing nightmares 149, 154

teeth feeling out as dream symbols 3, 58, 64, 77
temperature impacting dreams and sleep 39
terrors of the night, The (Nashe) 67, 103
Thanatos (god) 30
theorematic dreams 55
Theus, Homme 122
Thomas, Keith 59
Thornton, Alice 51, 52, 74, 143, 168
Thoughts on dreaming (Branch) 35
tombs in dreams 79
Trapnel, Anna 89, 91
treatise of dreams and visions, A (Tryon) 21, 26, 54, 110, 153
Treatise on the Art of Interpreting Dreams, A (Beale) 22, 124
Trenchard, John 36
true fortune-teller, The 2, 60, 61
Tryon, Thomas 1, 12, 20–21, 26, 27, 38, 40–41, 54, 81, 92, 110, 153, 155, 168
two sleeps 6
Tyndale, William 30

unconscious: early modern ideas of 19, 35–39, 42, 53, 64, 166
unconscious impacting dreams 37–38

Valangin, Francis de 147
Vaughan, Thomas 80, 142–3, 165
Vaughan, William 24, 144

vigilance. *See* insomnia
visionaries 89–91, 93–97, 103, 111, 115–16, 122, 125, 166; caused by melancholy 108–9

waking abruptly 142
Wallington, Nehemiah 51, 126, 136, 142, 168; dreams of 116–19
Walsham, Alexandra 8, 136, 151
Walton, Izaak 36
Wars of Religion 93
Wharton, George 71
White, Robert J. 55
Whytt, Robert 157
Williams, Simon J. 5
Willis, Thomas 153
witchcraft: causing nightmares 152–3; linked to dream divination 103–5, 107; resulting in insomnia 138
Wit's cabinet 61, 66, 73
women: dreams of 72–74; as visionaries increased their role in the Church 94–95
Wood, Robert 56
Worsley, Benjamin 121–2
Worthington, John 122
Wotton, Nicholas 36
Wright, Thomas 28, 39
Wyer, Robert 59

Zwickau Prophets 93